My Reign in Spain

A Short Life in Spain

January – July 1974

Michael Giddings

2QT Limited (Publishing)

First Edition published 2018 by
2QT Limited (Publishing)
Settle, North Yorkshire BD24 9RH United Kingdom

Copyright © Michael Giddings 2018

The right of Michael Giddings to be identified as the author of this work has been asserted by him in accordance with the Copyright, Designs and Patents Act 1988

All rights reserved. This book is sold subject to the condition that no part of this book is to be reproduced, in any shape or form. Or by way of trade, stored in a retrieval system or transmitted in any form or by any means, electronic, mechanical, photocopying, recording, be lent, re-sold, hired out or otherwise circulated in any form of binding or cover other than that in which it is published and without a similar condition, including this condition being imposed on the subsequent purchaser, without prior permission of the copyright holder.

This is a work of fiction and any resemblance to any person living or dead is purely coincidental. The place names mentioned are real but have no connection with the events in this book.

Cover Design by Charlotte Mouncey
Printed in Great Britain by IngramSpark UK

A CIP catalogue record for this book is available
from the British Library
ISBN 978-1-912014-XX-X

For Carolyn, Philip, Alex and Eleanor

I

'I don't think this number exists,' croaked the old crone. In fact, because this was Spain, what she actually said was,

'*Creo que este numero no existe.*'

I looked at her with alarm. It was all I had – just a seven-figure phone number on a slip of paper. I already knew that it had the correct number of digits. All phone numbers in Madrid were like that, but she seemed to be saying that it was wrong.

She was, as all Spanish women of a certain age and class were in those days, dressed in black, with a headscarf tied tightly under her chin and a jumper that exuded a smell of sweaty wool. Not the average professional, but she was in charge of the tokens that you had to buy to use the phones, so perhaps she knew what she was talking about.

So here I was in front of the bank of phones, newly arrived at Chamartín station in Madrid and getting more nervous by the second. I had already tried the number several times and I kept getting a tone that I did not recognise. My token was returned every time I hung up. What with the three-day week at home, the trip across Paris to change stations, no through ticket to begin with and no sleep in a train compartment full of snoring Spanish returnees, I was ready to turn round and get back on a train home.

But it wasn't as easy as that. I would need another ticket, and anyway I knew that going straight back would be cowardly and very hard to explain. This was the start of my real life. I'd travelled eight hundred miles to get here and I wasn't going to give it up just yet. So, somehow, I summoned up what little courage I had, took the slip of paper from her, went back over to the bank of phones and tried again.

It had been a harrowing journey to get this far. Because of the three-day week, the trade unions' ultimately successful attempt to bend Ted Heath's government to their will, the power had kept going off. Everything was plunged into gloom and cold, enhancing the post-Christmas air of anticlimax and the unsettling feeling of excitement mixed with foreboding that I was experiencing more and more every day.

Then, just before Christmas, ETA blew up Admiral Carrero Blanco, the right-hand man of Spain's aged dictator, General Franco. The atmosphere was edgy and uncertain when, a few days before I was due to leave, ETA terrorists got the admiral.

His assassination was quite a coup for them. Mum, Dad and I had seen it on the news and they had gone very silent. They were worried but did not want to spoil my great post-school (and pre-university) adventure. We were relieved when a telegram arrived from Peter Garrett to say that the situation was normal in Madrid and there was no reason to worry. I was to call the seven-digit number when I arrived and he would pick me up.

I'd never received a telegram until that December in 1973. Then I received two in the space of a fortnight: one from The Queen's College in Oxford, congratulating me on my place there to read French and Spanish the following October, and this one from Peter Garrett, confirming that all was well in Madrid and that I should come out at the beginning of January as agreed to start teaching at his language institute.

I had never been to Spain before so it had seemed almost pre-determined that I should spend the free months between passing the Oxford entrance exam and the following summer experiencing the country whose language and literature I was so keen to study. Teaching English as a foreign language was an obvious way of getting a job to support myself. I was clearly a native speaker and my level of education seemed to indicate that I would be able to talk and instruct with some degree of proficiency. Peter Garrett thought so. He answered the letter that I wrote to him promptly, inviting me to join his teaching staff from January to July.

So it looked as if I was really going. Nationwide power cuts and Spanish separatists did not appear able to stop me. But March's only travel agent very nearly did.

March, where I had lived with Mum and Dad for almost all my life, is a small Fenland town. In those days it only had one travel agent called, appropriately, the Fenland Travel Agency. Mum and I went there the day after I received Peter Garret's telegram to book a through ticket to Madrid. I planned to get to Spain a few days before he wanted me to start on 7 January.

As we entered the agency a bell above the door gave a reassuring little tinkling sound. We waited a couple of moments until a middle-aged man with a ruddy complexion and a pair of enormous black-rimmed glasses pushed aside a curtain at the back and stepped over to us.

'We'd like to book a ticket to Madrid,' said Mum. 'My son's got a job out there,' she added for clarification.

I shifted my weight as he stared at me through the large glasses. I was both touched and embarrassed by the extra information Mum was supplying.

'I see,' he said. 'That's no problem at all. Will you be flying or going by train?'

'Well...' Mum seemed undecided. Frankly, we had never considered going by plane. We'd only ever been on one flight, several years before. It had been a holiday to the Netherlands in an ancient propeller-driven aircraft that had put us all off flying for life.

A quick comparison of prices made the decision for us. It would be a train to Dover, then the hovercraft across the Channel, another train to Paris and then an overnight sleeper all the way from Paris to Madrid.

'Righto,' the man said jovially, and got a large pad of printed forms from one of the drawers in a battered desk by the wall. He proceeded to fill out the form with dates, stations and ports all entered on to it. He finished off by printing the word 'Madrid' in a box near the bottom. We couldn't actually see what he was writing but he spelt out the word as he wrote.

'M-A-D-R-I-D. That's Madrid in Spain,' he confirmed and intoned, as he wrote, 'S-P-A-I-N.' I wasn't aware of any other Madrids, but I was sure he knew best.

He signed the form with a flourish and handed it to Mum, whom he clearly considered was the person in charge on our side.

'We'll set the wheels in motion,' he told us confidently, and as we left the shop I felt that I really was inching further towards an exciting future.

On reflection I suppose back then it was quite an unusual request for a small-town travel agent. Week-long package trips to the Costa Wherever were as demanding as it ever got. So, despite constant reassurances from the man in the black-rimmed glasses that the tickets were on their way, the day before I was due to leave they admitted that they had managed to book me only as far as the French–Spanish border. After that I would be on my own.

(As if to presage further difficulties Mum discovered that she had dropped one of her new top-of-the-range sheepskin gloves on our last trip to Fenland Travel and, scour the streets as we might, we couldn't find it.)

The day for me to leave March and my childhood soon arrived, and Mum and I went up to London. We were staying at my grandmother's flat in the East End for the night and I was then leaving from Charing Cross the following morning. On the recommendation of Fenland Travel we first visited the offices of the French railways in Piccadilly to see if anything could be done to get me a ticket over the border and into Spain.

The offices of the French railways, or the SNCF, as it proclaimed over the door, were about halfway along Piccadilly. Fenland Travel could have fitted inside about ten times over. As we went in and I gazed around I felt confident that they would succeed where the local travel agent had failed, and I would walk out with a ticket for the entire journey. All over the walls were colourful posters showing various attractive scenes – the mountains, cities and coastlines of France – with a train of some sort featuring prominently. Although they were not on my itinerary I still felt a surge of excitement as I imagined myself gazing at strange, enchanted landscapes from a train window.

We came to the head of the queue. Behind the polished wooden counter was a young woman, also wearing large black-rimmed glasses. I wondered briefly if this was perhaps some official requirement for selling tickets for international travel. As she leant forward slightly across the counter I caught a whiff of a heady, sweet-smelling scent and I forgot instantly about this possible travel agent dress code and concentrated instead on her eyes as she looked over her glasses at us.

'How can I help you?' she asked in a captivating French accent.

I drew myself up slightly and opened my mouth to speak. As the atmosphere here was much more international I decided that I should take the lead.

'I'd like to buy a ticket to—'

This was as far as I got. The lights went out as the power

was cut yet again and the entire building was plunged into darkness. A groan went up from the queue behind us. They all knew that any further business transactions were now impossible.

'Oh, I am so sorry,' said the young lady, drawing back again behind the counter. 'We cannot sell any tickets now. We cannot help you in the dark.'

A further very brief conversation, which now included Mum, led to the recommendation that I should travel to the French–Spanish border as planned and buy an onward ticket there. Once again I felt my anxiety levels rise. But there was a curious feeling of bravado underneath somewhere as well, trying to surface but not quite making it. I really was off into the unknown. With or without a ticket, I felt more than ever resolved to get there and exploit every opportunity that the world outside could offer.

So next day, after a brave farewell to my grandmother, I set out with Mum for Charing Cross and the start of the rest of my sparkling new life. We got there far too early but, laden with two suitcases and a rucksack, I just wanted to get on the train. We walked along the platform. I flung my arms round Mum's neck, and said,

'I want you to go now,' and swallowed hard as I felt a sob rise in my throat. I got on the train as she gave me a last look and walked back down the platform. (She later told me that she sat and waited for twenty minutes until the train pulled out and then went back to my grandmother's flat, where they both burst into tears.)

I left England and crossed the Channel to France feeling less and less like a conqueror and more like a timid refugee, excited to escape one life but wary about the new one.

The hovercraft crossing was particularly unpleasant. It was early January and the sea was rough. I spent fifty minutes strapped in my seat being shaken to the edge of unconsciousness while next to me a similarly afflicted lady lolled forward, restrained only by the seat belt round her middle, and threw up her breakfast into a specially provided paper bag.

The train journey to Paris was uneventful, but then I had to cross the city from the Gare du Nord to the Gare d'Austerlitz.

I studied the route map before going down the steps into the *Métro* station. I didn't want to go the wrong way. Even though I had plenty of time my arms ached already with the effort of lugging my two suitcases along, and even the rucksack was starting to drag on my shoulders.

I bought a ticket and set out. The *Métro* platforms seemed to be a long way from the ticket office and I had to stop about halfway along the crowded tunnel. My hands and fingers hurt even more than my arms and I suddenly felt very weary. I gave a big sigh and reached down to pick up the suitcases. As I did so a young man and woman came swiftly up to me. Their appearance was slightly dishevelled – exactly what one would expect from students, which they clearly were.

'Would you like to buy a postcard?' asked the young woman, smiling sweetly at me. 'I think you are probably a stranger here, aren't you?'

'Yes, I am,' I said naively. 'I'm on my way to Madrid.'

'Well, a nice postcard will give you happy memories of Paris.' She thrust a grimy, rumpled card into my hand. 'Just give us a few francs to help us with our studies.'

'Well…' Slowly I took out my wallet and started to extract a ten franc note.

'Yes. That'll do,' she said, snatching it from me.

I suddenly realised that this was quite a lot of money and I didn't want a grubby souvenir of Paris. I grabbed the ten franc note back again with one hand and gave her back the postcard with the other. Butterflies were fluttering and churning in my stomach. I felt nervous and very alone.

'I don't want it,' I mumbled in my hesitant French, took firm hold of both suitcases and scuttled as quickly as I could along the crowded tunnel, dodging past the streams of people travelling in both directions. I heard the woman shout after me – something extremely uncomplimentary, I think. Embarrassment and anger made me blush. I was sure everyone was looking at me. I hadn't realised that I would have to be this brave in my new life.

I reached the Gare d'Austerlitz without further incident and found the train that was going to the Spanish border. It left after a couple of hours and I spent the night in a couchette compartment with five other travellers heading from Paris to Spain. I slept fitfully on my wallet and passport, checking my luggage every twenty minutes as everyone else snored.

Finally there was a growing tension in the early light as we got ever nearer to Hendaye on the French–Spanish border, and I headed into the unknown without a ticket.

In fact it was very easy at the border in the end. I got off the train and walked to the end of the platform and through an archway into the customs hall that marked the frontier. I was waved straight through into a ticket office with almost no queue, where I bought a ticket for a Talgo express train to Madrid. I began to feel that it all might just work out.

Then I got to Madrid and began my half-hour of phoning a number that the phone token crone told me didn't exist.

*

With a rising sense of panic I tried the number one last time. It rang with a different tone and eventually there was a click and a voice.

'*Dígame*,' it said. Wow. So they really did say that when they answered the phone. I'd heard it enough times in Spanish A level classes but I was still momentarily disconcerted. I had heard all about it in theory, but now I was hearing it for real. I hesitantly trotted out the phrase that I had rehearsed when we were gliding into the station forty minutes earlier.

'*Quiero hablar con el Señor Garrett, por favor,*' I said.

'Oh, he's not here at the moment. Are you the chap who's arriving by train?' returned the voice in perfect English.

I was taken aback that my Spanish had fooled nobody. Nevertheless relief flooded over me. This English speaker obviously expected me and sounded very friendly. After nearly thirty-six hours on trains and a hovercraft I had made contact as agreed. Maybe I really would get to stay in Madrid.

'Err, yes. My name's Michael Giddings,' I explained. 'Mr Garrett told me to ring this number when I arrived.'

'He's expecting you but he's not here at the moment. I'm his son, Michael. I'll come and pick you up. Are you at Chamartín?'

'Yes,' I replied. I was rather put out that Peter Garrett himself wasn't coming to meet me. I was also confused. Was the Michael addressed to me or was his son called Michael as well?

'Yes, I'm just at the phones near the entrance.'

'Stay there and I'll come and get you. I'll be about ten minutes.'

I thanked him and hung up. Weighed down with two suitcases and a rucksack, I wasn't about to skip off. Anyway the sights and smells of this main Madrid railway station already seemed rather exotic to me and I had no wish to stray anywhere without a guide.

Michael Garrett (he actually *was* called Michael) arrived about twenty minutes later. He was a couple of years younger than me, no more than sixteen or seventeen, with fair hair and wearing a dark blue thick woollen donkey jacket. He apologised for the delay in answering the phone. He'd been fixing up a day's skiing with a school friend in Somosierra, north of Madrid.

I followed him out to the taxi rank. We put the luggage into a taxi and got in. Michael took a piece of paper out of his pocket and gave it to the driver, who nodded, and we took off.

'Very odd,' I thought. 'Why doesn't Michael just tell him where he lives?'

In fact, as we headed into the city centre down the impressively named Avenue of the Generalissimo, it dawned on me that we might not be heading to the Garretts' place. After all, as far as Peter Garrett was concerned, I was a nineteen-year-old adult being employed to do a job, not some school exchange student arriving to get a taste of life in another culture.

'Where are we going?' I enquired.

'I'm not exactly sure, but it's around Callao somewhere.' He waved the piece of paper. 'I've got the address.'

'What is it, then?' I asked.

'It's a *hostal* in the centre that Dad's booked for you.'

'Oh, OK.' The meaning of *hostal* seemed obvious. They had booked me into some kind of hotel.

We eventually turned into a wide, busy street with restaurants and cinemas and a large department store called Galerías Preciados. We then headed around a square.

'This is Plaza de Callao,' he explained. 'We're nearly there.'

I felt a flutter of anticipation in my stomach.

We drew up in front of a tall building with large shuttered windows. There were steps up to the entrance and a sign in red neon letters proclaiming it to be the Hostal Roma.

'Not bad,' I thought as we went in. Immediately inside there was a doorkeeper in a little office who, when Michael spoke to him, waved towards the flight of stairs at the end of the entrance hall. The steps were thickly carpeted and looked very plush, so I almost bounded up after him to the first floor, suitcase in each hand. We stopped outside a large door off the landing with a sign on it that again announced the Hostal Roma.

Michael rang the bell and a lady instantly appeared, as if she had been lurking just behind the door awaiting our arrival. There was a quick mumbled conversation, then she shook her head and gestured vaguely upwards.

Michael turned to me.

'It's up there, apparently,' he said, pointing up the cavernous stairwell.

I looked up and saw that the staircase wound on round for several more flights. So I was in the attic, not the master bedroom.

As we headed up – no bounding now, just trudging – the carpet gave way first to thin lino and then to bare wooden boards. Two floors above the Hostal Roma was the Hostal Rincón – it still managed a small brass plate next to the door, but the difference in star rating was obvious.

Michael rang the bell and, considerably less swiftly than at the Hostal Roma, a middle-aged woman opened the door. I never discovered her name. She was called Carmen or Conchita or something similar. She was in her thirties or forties. I was insufficiently experienced in the world at that time to hazard more than a vague guess about women's ages. Females were either girls or nearly as old as my Mum. She had a large, kind-looking round face and permed brown hair and shuffled along in furry slippers. I was suddenly very tired and daunted by it all, so I just followed her in.

Michael turned to me and grinned.

'Goodbye, then,' he said briskly. 'My father will ring you.' And then he was gone.

I allowed Carmen/Conchita to usher me into a tiny reception area and take me down a hallway to a door marked

No. 11. She opened it with a key she took from her pocket then placed the key in my hand and said very slowly and distinctly,

'*Esta es su llave a usted.*' 'This is your key.'

I nodded and stepped into my new home.

II

Because the building wasn't square but came to a point on one side, and my room was where the point was located, it was triangular in shape. Not only that; it also wasn't very big.

There was a single bed along one wall. Near the point of the triangle a large window opened into the room like a pair of doors. As we were several floors up there was a waist-high iron railing across it to stop any sleepwalkers plummeting to the street below.

There was a wardrobe, a set of drawers and a small sink in the corner. A rickety table and chair and a tiny rug were positioned in the middle of the lino-covered floor. Beyond that there was nothing, except for a tiny heater attached to the wall just behind the door. I didn't take much notice of it or how small it was until a few days later when a midwinter cold snap sent temperatures way down and the heater's inadequacy became all too apparent.

I opened the windows and looked out. It was already starting to get dark, and the streets were coming alive. The *Madrileños* lived in the street just like their Mediterranean counterparts, even when it was only two degrees above freezing in January. There was an air of hustle and bustle, the honking of car horns, and the raised voices that accompany the activity of busy streets.

Suddenly I realised that I was hungry. But before I could think of eating or unpacking there was a knock at the door and Carmen/Conchita appeared and told me that *el Señor*

Garrett was on the phone.

I followed her as she padded along the narrow corridor in her furry slippers to the reception area and picked up the receiver.

'Hello,' I said.

'Hello, Michael. Peter Garrett here,' said a brusque, commanding voice. 'Sorry I couldn't meet you today, but I'm glad you've got here.'

'Oh, yes, everything's fine, thanks,' I replied, even though I was not absolutely sure that it was.

'I had hoped to come and eat with you tonight, but I'm afraid it's the Day of the Kings here. The sixth of January is a big family day. I'll meet you tomorrow at about twelve for a drink, if that's OK.'

'That's great,' I said, trying to hide my disappointment.

'I'll come round to the Rincón to pick you up. If you go out tonight there are lots of places to eat round there.' With that he was gone as abruptly as his son.

I unpacked a few things, walked round the room several times, and then, with a deep breath, made for the door and down the staircase to the street. My stomach was rumbling.

It was about seven o'clock and very chilly, but there were people everywhere, looking into shop windows, chatting in the street and walking in and out of steamy cafés and bars. It was exciting, but I didn't know what to do. I was hungry, but where should I go to eat? How much was a reasonable amount to pay for food? How did you order? And, most importantly, how conspicuous would I seem, a very young man – and obviously a foreigner – all on my own? I had a vision of being turned away from the first restaurant that I tried to enter while the well-fed patrons looked on, laughing as I slunk away.

In fact, as always, it was easier than I imagined. There was a sign at the bottom of a flight of stairs with the name of a restaurant. It offered a set menu for one hundred pesetas, which was exactly the amount of the highest-denomination note that I was carrying.

I went upstairs. No one laughed or pointed at me, and I was ushered to a table on my own. I looked at the menu and chose an *ensaladilla Rusa* – a Russian salad – as a starter, and a pork chop to follow. I wasn't really sure what a Russian salad was but it seemed a good bet.

In fact Russian salads had taken Madrid by storm that season. Subsequently, everywhere I went there were heaped displays in restaurant windows of cubed vegetables all held together by oily mayonnaise. Sometimes they were sculpted into incredible animal shapes. I saw swans and fish and even an elephant all made out of peas and carrots and potato.

I could have lived on Russian salad if I had wanted to, and some days I nearly did. It was cheap and readily available, and the quality didn't seem to vary. I imagined that there was a vast factory somewhere nearby churning out tanker-loads of the stuff.

After my successful foray into the restaurant, and feeling slightly embarrassed by the effusive thanks of the waitress for having given her a tip that was obviously far too much, I stepped out into the street again.

I was reluctant to go back to my bleak little room just yet. I needed cheering up, and a film seemed a possibility – both as entertainment and as a reason not to go back. There were a number of cinemas in the streets and squares nearby and, confident that I could find my way back to the Rincón, I struck out.

There were plenty of Spanish films with names that I couldn't translate – the colloquialisms hadn't been on my A level syllabus – but then after a few minutes I went past a small cinema showing *Family Life*, a film by a British director called Ken Loach. It was in English with Spanish subtitles and it was about to begin.

I bought a ticket. A nice, untaxing little comedy along the lines of the *Carry On* films would lift the spirits and remind me of home, but at the same time help combat any pangs of homesickness.

How wrong I was. Ken Loach was a radical left-wing director whose take on middle-class British society meant that he was highly unlikely to have put together a modest suburban farce. As I sat in the darkened room, anxious to be comforted by cheery visions of home, the sad story of a teenage girl and her descent into mental breakdown unfolded. She was a rebellious teenager with a confrontational attitude. Her overbearing, callous father and uncaring mother drove her towards self-destruction with her unsuitable boyfriend (who, as I recall, wasn't so unsuitable, anyway). Then she became pregnant and had an abortion.

There was a particularly poignant scene where she and the boyfriend spray-painted the front garden of the impeccable family semi bright blue, laughing as the roses turned a colour that could never be achieved naturally. I can't remember if this was pre-abortion or post-abortion, but it was an amusing scene as the young couple enjoyed themselves splattering paint everywhere. But, as I remember, it led to her parents having her committed to a mental hospital. She was taken there, kicking and screaming, by men in white coats.

I can't remember exactly how it ended but I know that I came out of the cinema into the cold Madrid night in a very different mood to the one I had anticipated when I went in.

Later on I realised just how open Spanish society was becoming. It would have been unthinkable to have shown such a film ten years earlier.

I trudged back to my little room at the Rincón and lay down on the bed staring at the ceiling. I felt cold and miserable, and suddenly the next six months seemed a very long time.

Finally I sat up, found a sheet of paper and started writing a letter home.

*

The next day was a Sunday and, as I was a good Catholic boy and this was Spain, I found a church where Mass was being said. San Ginés was suitably ornate and I sat through the liturgy, gaining some comfort from the thought that Mum was probably sitting through exactly the same thing at that moment in the church in March.

Mass seemed to be a less formal affair than in the UK. I sat still, paying attention, but most of the congregation were using the occasion to catch up on gossip with their neighbours. There was a knot of old ladies in black in the first few pews either muttering their way through their rosaries or gazing rapturously at the altar, but many people were promenading around the church arm in arm as the priest intoned the Kyrie and the Gloria. The hard core of worshippers at the front responded, but others seemed to dip in and out of the whole thing. The door at the back was constantly swinging noisily as people came and went.

I guessed that this was because Mass was such an everyday part of life that it did not need the hush and reverence that the much smaller Catholic community in the UK afforded it. It didn't matter if people didn't listen or made a noise or came and went. The Catholic Mass went on anyway, day in and day out, as it had without interruption for more than a thousand years.

Peter Garrett collected me from the Rincón at midday, as promised. His voice suited his appearance: he was tall with short brown hair and a neatly clipped brown moustache, and he was wearing a blue blazer with brass buttons, a shirt and tie and grey trousers. He took me to a bar around the corner – the smarter sort that I would never have gone into on my own. I was hoping for lunch but should have realised that in Spain midday is only just after breakfast, so it would be a drink only.

He ordered a Cuba libre – I had no idea what this was (it turned out to be a rum and Coke) – and I settled for a Coke. He told me that he had been at Oxford in the late fifties at St Edmund Hall, right next to Queen's, where I was bound the following October. After that he came out to Spain, met a Spanish lady and settled down.

His institute had a lucrative contract with the Diplomatic School to teach English to aspiring young diplomats (he didn't actually say that it was lucrative but it soon became apparent that it was). I would not be let loose on such high-profile clients. I would be teaching those who were coming in increasing numbers as learning English became a fashionable thing to do. General Franco was ageing rapidly; the controls that he had remorselessly imposed on Spanish society were slackening, and interest in the outside world was increasing. The craze to learn English was just one manifestation of this.

'Come along and I'll show you the Institute,' he said as he drained his glass.

We walked back past the Rincón and turned left into Calle Arenal and then into Calle de las Hileras and were almost immediately there. It was a large building with brass and wooden plates announcing the names of the various businesses based there. The Instituto Garrett was on the second and third floors. At least it would only take me about two minutes to get to work every morning. If I leant out of my bedroom window I could probably see it.

As Peter marched into the building the doorkeeper came out to greet him obsequiously. This man – apart from being about sixty, and therefore very old, as far as I was concerned

– was distinguished by having only one arm. Try as I might, I couldn't help staring at his left side where the empty sleeve of his dark blue jumper was pinned, flapping gently as he moved.

He was only the first of a series of such men that I came across. I learnt later that they were all victims of the Spanish Civil War, and all, seemingly, were employed to sit and watch in little cubbyholes at the entrance to buildings.

As I looked at him I recalled my glee at school when I learnt there were specific adjectives in Spanish for people missing various body parts – *tuerto* meant one-eyed and *manco* meant one-armed. To us in our sixth-form Spanish lessons this esoteric vocabulary had seemed outlandish. Now I could see that it was very useful in describing the thousands of casualties of the civil war.

Having explained to the doorkeeper that I would be turning up the next morning at nine o'clock and should be let in, Peter led me upstairs to the second floor. Behind a door with a glass pane with *Instituto Garrett* etched into it was the reception area. Leading off were doors into a series of small, windowless rooms. Peter gestured to one on the right.

'This will be your room,' he explained, and I peered inside. A desk and chair, obviously for me, and several chairs with folding armrests were placed around the side walls. Apart from that there was a blackboard and chalk, and that was all.

'Mariuca will be here tomorrow,' said Peter. 'She's on reception in the mornings and Elena is here in the afternoons. This is your schedule.'

He handed me a piece of paper with my timetable. I could see that classes ran from nine thirty in the morning until two and then from four in the afternoon to ten at night. The Spanish day certainly ran at a different rhythm to the Fens. I liked how different my life was going to be already.

'You'll have Tuesday and Thursday mornings off, so

you won't need to come in until four on those days. In fact there's another chap here from your neck of the woods – Tim Hewitt. He's from Peterborough. You'll meet him tomorrow.'

I managed an interested-sounding 'Oh,' as I gazed at my timetable. I could see that the following day I had Jaime Sancho from 9.30 for a double lesson.

Peter followed my gaze.

'Yes, you've got Jaime tomorrow. He's coming in three times a week for one-to-one lessons with you. Just go through the Martin and Jane books with him. He's very bright and will soon pick it up.'

I nodded. I had bought the series of textbooks that the Institute used to teach the first rudiments of English and had acquainted myself with Martin and Jane, their main characters. Suddenly I realised that, in order to fill a two-hour period three times a week with a very bright young man, I would need a lesson plan. It was just as well that Peter Garrett had to rush off for family duties on that particular Sunday.

We said goodbye and I headed off in search of lunch, which undoubtedly included a Russian salad, and then for a spell of serious preparation.

III

Predictably I woke early the next day, with thoughts of Martin and Jane and their make-believe world going round in my head.

I had looked through the first few chapters again the previous afternoon and planned a little of what I was going to do with Jaime. Martin and Jane were stick figures who did very repetitive things. What they were doing was written clearly on the page beside them. So Martin would watch the birds as he sat on a bench and then Jane would join him, and they would both watch the birds as they both sat on the bench. Inevitably a dog or a teenager or some other distraction would arrive and the birds would fly away.

'What a shame,' was Martin's reaction. 'The birds are very pretty.'

'Yes,' agreed Jane. 'I think the birds are very pretty too.'

Two hours of this three times a week… I thought I might be able to improve on it. Perhaps Jaime liked Genesis or football or we could talk about his girlfriends, which I was sure he would have many of.

Already feeling very well assimilated into city life, I had a quick Madrid breakfast of *churros*, little deep-fried curly sticks of fatty dough, and a cup of chocolate, then walked down to the Institute. It was about nine fifteen, chilly but with a blue sky overhead.

As I entered the building and made straight for the stairs to the second floor the doorkeeper came hurtling out from his room, the empty arm of his jumper unpinned and flapping madly. He overtook me with a surprising burst of speed and stood defiantly barring my way, a stern look on his face.

'Where are you going?' he asked me.

'Up to the Institute,' I said innocently.

'You must see me first. I don't know you. I don't know who you are,' he said furiously.

Did he really not remember our introduction less than twenty-four hours earlier? Or had I offended the established etiquette of informing him of my arrival, and he was pretending not to know me to demonstrate the importance of his role in keeping out unknown visitors? Whatever his reasons, he eventually let me go up. For the next three months my carefully directed '*Buenos días*' to him every day was met with nothing but a scowl.

As a result of this confrontation my carefully constructed confidence began to crumble and I approached the Institute with a churning stomach. My Madrid breakfast had definitely not been a good idea.

I pushed open the door gingerly and went into the school. It was completely deserted. Instead of the hive of activity that I had expected there was complete silence. It was so profound that my senses seemed to switch around and all I was aware of was a strong, musty smell of highly polished wood. I looked behind the reception desk as if expecting to find Mariuca, the morning receptionist, curled up in a ball on the floor. Unsurprisingly, she wasn't there, so I went into my little room on the right, immediately facing the reception desk. I unpacked my bag and took out the Martin and Jane volume and sat down nervously to wait for something to happen.

After a couple of minutes I heard the door open and someone entered the reception area.

I realised that I couldn't just lurk in my little room. I would have to go out. I opened the door and startled a small, young woman with her hair in a bun, wearing a large woollen coat and a scarf.

'*Usted es Mariuca*?' I asked. 'Are you Mariuca?'

'Oh, no. No, no, no,' she replied emphatically, and in a very obviously English accent. 'I'm Anne. Mariuca's Spanish.'

I had already guessed at Mariuca's nationality but didn't comment.

'And you must be Michael,' she continued.

I nodded and was about to speak, when she bustled past me and into the room beyond mine while pulling off her scarf and coat and continuing to talk.

'Yes, I'm a teacher here. We knew you were coming.' She stuck her head around the door again, with the scarf still trailing. 'You know – after Susan said she wasn't coming back. But you'll soon get the hang of it.'

This was the first I'd heard of Susan and her failure to return. Return from where? And why had Susan not been able to 'get the hang of it'? I hadn't realised that I was a replacement for someone who maybe hadn't made the grade. I'd assumed that I was an addition to the roll call of teachers. Peter Garrett hadn't mentioned it the day before, and it hadn't dawned on me until then that he would have tried to ensure a full complement of teaching staff in September and not start hiring again until the following year. The *churros* and chocolate lay heavily in my stomach as disturbing theories took shape.

Luckily, before I could dwell on them, people started to arrive and I had to concentrate on speaking Spanish and teaching English.

The real Mariuca was the next through the door – dark-haired, wearing very red lipstick and probably over forty. Her heavily made-up face broke into an insincere smile as

I introduced myself. Further conversation was impossible, however, as now a youngish man with unkempt fair hair and a baggy sports jacket that marked him out as Anglo-Saxon in origin came in. He was talking intently over his shoulder to a teenager who followed him in. The teenager was slightly younger than me and undeniably Spanish, dressed in a stylish green overcoat and brown cord trousers.

'Ah, you must be Michael,' said the sports jacket man to me in English. They had all obviously been primed for my arrival. He held out his hand and, without waiting for a reply, switched immediately into Spanish. 'I was talking to your pupil Jaime,' and he nudged the teenager towards me.

'This is Señor Jaime Sancho,' said Mariuca in reverential tones. Señor Jaime and I shook hands, both of us looking rather embarrassed like a boy and girl being pushed together by over-eager parents.

After that it was straight into the classroom and on with Martin and Jane and their iterative exploits on the park bench. I don't really remember how I got through the first two hours. Apart from Martin and Jane and their observations about birds and dogs and personal pronouns, I asked Jaime a few questions about himself, which he managed to answer in very passable English.

It was obvious to me by the end of the session that, if I had at least a loose structure to the class that I could fall back on, there would be every opportunity to digress into many different subjects in order to extend his mastery of spoken English. It was just as well, as while bidding me goodbye at eleven thirty he reminded me that he would be back in two days' time for another two-hour session – and he was just one of the many names on my timetable. Nevertheless I felt calmer and more in control after this first experience of the classroom from the other side of the teacher's desk.

I had no more lessons that morning. Lunch was from two

until four p.m., so at least I had some more time to swot up on the evening classes. My timetable told me I had two of them – each an hour and a half long. I managed a timid smile at Mariuca, who was perched on a stool behind the reception desk staring at me under heavily made-up eyelids like some exotic member of the crow family. Just as I was preparing to step back inside my little room the man in the sports jacket came out of a room opposite, bidding an effusive farewell to his pupil. Once the pupil had gone he turned round to me.

'We didn't have a real opportunity to say hello this morning. I'm Tim – Tim Hewitt.' He brushed back a couple of errant blonde locks that had fallen across his forehead with his hand – a gesture I noticed he repeated at frequent intervals. It appeared to be the only way to keep his hair in check. He then held out his hand for the second time and I shook it again.

'Peter tells me that you are from my neck of the woods. My family live in Peterborough,' he continued. 'Neck of the woods' … wasn't that what Peter Garrett had called it? I could see that it was possible that this man could turn into a fair-haired version of Peter Garrett if he ditched the sports jacket and bought a blazer. Would it happen to me as well?

'Oh, yes,' I replied. 'I know Peterborough well. I come from March.'

'Yes, March,' he said non-committally. 'I went through it on the train every time I came back from Cambridge. Tell you what… What are you doing for lunch?'

'Nothing,' I replied.

'Well, come with me and I'll introduce you to Milan and Tibet,' he said.

Again confusion clouded my overtaxed mental processes.

'We're in Madrid and he's talking about getting to know Milan and Tibet,' I thought. But before I could even answer yes or no or look confused the main door behind us opened and Tim sprang round me to greet his next pupil even more effusively than he had bidden farewell to the previous one.

'Francisco, how are you? And how was the hunting? How many boars was it this time?' he enquired, pumping Francisco's hand up and down.

'Oh, no,' said Francisco as they passed through. 'This time it was little birds – many little birds.'

'Oh, well, yum yum,' said Tim, releasing Francisco's hand to brush back his hair. 'You must be the scourge of the sierras. See you here at two, then,' he said over his shoulder to me and disappeared, talking furiously to the rather confused-looking 'scourge' about game and rifles and partridges and not muddling up the pheasants and peasants when out shooting. I caught a glimpse of Francisco's look of blank incomprehension as Tim shut the door.

I went into my room to prepare both for my evening pupils and also my whirlwind lunchtime visit to Milan and Tibet. Presumably pasta and yak would be on the menu, rather than Russian salad.

*

At two o'clock precisely Tim ushered Francisco out with a similar mixture of quaint English and bonhomie and we went to lunch. The *churros* and chocolate were a distant memory, and I was starving. I felt a bit like the heroes of the sixteenth-century picaresque novels by Cervantes and other Spanish authors that I had had to read for the Oxford entrance exam. They were all hidalgos – seemingly well-dressed but impoverished scions of the nobility without any income who paraded around town in their finery with empty purses, desperate to impress, and got as far through the day as they could without having to spend any money on unnecessary items such as food.

I still had some of the money that I had brought out with me, but I knew that I would not be paid until the end of the month. I was hungry but also anxious that my Milanese/Tibetan lunch should not be too extravagant. In my grubby mackintosh I furthermore could not be said to be dressed in anything approaching finery. All in all it was a pretty invalid comparison, but I liked it nonetheless.

'We'll take the metro,' said Tim as we went down the stairs and out into the street. 'It's only a couple of stops. You'll like Milan. He's quite a card.'

Aha! The penny dropped. I had been sensible enough not to mention my confusion but it was now obvious that Milan was a person – in fact a man. Tim's understanding of what would constitute him being a card was a little unnerving, however. I imagined a 1920s roué straight out of P. G. Wodehouse – this was a world that was as far removed from March, Cambridgeshire as you could get.

We went down the metro at Ópera and, such was the efficiency of the metro system, had emerged again within minutes at a station called Bilbao. I had gathered from Tim that he had lunch every weekday with Milan, who was some sort of émigré from the Balkans with some indeterminate job at the university. He had clearly fallen out with the left-wing regime of Marshal Tito in Yugoslavia and had sought refuge under the right wing of Generalissimo Franco. I never did find out, however, how Tim and he actually first met. Neither did I broach the question of Tibet, but felt reasonably certain now that there would be a logical though undoubtedly eccentric answer.

We met Milan in a bar opposite the metro station. Tim introduced me to him. He was an elderly, stooping man wearing wire-rimmed glasses, a trilby and a tweed suit under a heavy coat and scarf, and with the dyspeptic look of thwarted ambition on his face. I later realised that he must have been a considerable intellectual in his day, but the course of political events had meant that he presumably had left behind whatever career he had had and now he eked out a living teaching – history, as I later found out – to uncaring undergraduates. I was sure he would give it the slant that both he and the Generalissimo required it to have.

He spoke English to Tim and me and Spanish to everyone else with absolute precision, fashioning carefully every word and using outdated phrases as only long-term expatriates and those in isolated communities can.

We ordered drinks at the bar. I had not been expecting this pre-lunch aperitif and, as with Peter Garrett two days before, was thrown into confusion about what to have and also as to whether I could stretch to an aperitif as well as lunch. Milan, on seeing my indecision, immediately proposed that I join him and Tim in a drink whose name I have now forgotten. It was red and Campari-like but with an astringency that made me wince as I took my first sip.

Milan laughed, not in an unkind way.

'Welcome to Spain. It's all barbarism here – the food and the drink as well.' He later remarked frequently and unfavourably on the quality and refinement of the Spanish diet but, I began to realise, it was one of the only countries in the West in which he would feel comfortable.

'So,' Milan continued, 'I understand that you are going to Oxford University. What are you going to study?'

I looked slightly surprised at the question.

'Why, Spanish, of course.'

'Pah!' Milan was unimpressed. 'Why not study something interesting, like history? There is nothing interesting in Spain.'

'I disagree with you there,' Tim said. 'There's a lot going for this country. It's changing, even as we speak.' He looked around vaguely, as if to prove his point. 'Anyway, let's pay and get off to lunch. I'm starving.' He gestured for the bill.

Milan mumbled something as he dug into his little leather purse and I put twenty-five pesetas on to the metal plate where the waiter had placed the bill. It was fully 25 per cent of my lunch allowance.

We walked out and down the road a short distance, with Milan still lecturing me on the superiority of the study of history over all other subjects. He was actually quite charming in a way and I soon realised that, although fervent in his beliefs, he managed not to take himself too seriously all the time. His stern features would sometimes rumple into a knowing smile and it was clear that he had a sharp sense of humour. He also had a genuine interest in me and what I was doing, and in all things British.

We arrived at the restaurant. And there, over the doorway, picked out in ornate gold letters against a backdrop of majestic Himalayan peaks, was the name *Restaurante el Tibet* – so I was really going to Tibet for lunch.

As soon as we got in Milan made his way directly to a table in the corner, which was obviously set aside for him and Tim. He called a young waiter over immediately and informed him that an extra place should be set. He then started a slow and elaborate procedure of unwinding his scarf and taking off his trilby and coat as Tim and I sat waiting. I was already struck by the almost ritualistic aspects of the meal. I later understood that they repeated this routine Mondays to Fridays almost without fail. Presumably the only variation was seasonal, marked by the number of layers that Milan had to peel off as the freezing Madrid winter turned to roasting summer.

A small round surly man in a white apron came over to us with menus. Neither he nor the interior of the restaurant gave any clue as to why the name Tibet had been chosen. Both were definitively and authentically Spanish. Milan, who was occupied with folding and hanging up his outer garments, did not see him at first, but Tim and I took the proffered typewritten sheets. When he was eventually offered one Milan brushed it aside.

'Ah, *Jefe*,' he said as if greeting a favourably regarded domestic servant. '*Hay lentejas?*' 'Are there lentils today?'

The *jefe* gave a curt '*Sí.*'

'So,' said Milan, still without a glance at the menu, 'I will have lentils and a chop.'

I looked at the day's specials and saw the lentils were quite a bit more than I wanted to pay for a starter, but I had never eaten them before. So, quite possibly under the influence of the abrasive red aperitif that we had just drunk, I ordered the same.

Tim and Milan talked throughout the meal and I, slightly in awe, listened. I learnt about Milan's disagreement with Marshal Tito and how he had decided to leave Yugoslavia. He spoke about it in a sufficiently vague way to leave the impression that the falling-out had been personal rather than the result of him being unable to function under a Communist regime. There were no details given about the nature of his relationship with the Marshal – an oversight that was not, I think, accidental.

Tim, meanwhile, chuntered on about his classes and some of the other teachers at the Institute that I had not yet met – Moya and Hilary and Chris, and a new girl from Cordoba called Madeleine. He also let slip that he had a Spanish girlfriend called Carmen, who lived somewhere outside Madrid. I sat there, only one month out of a school classroom, soaking it all up.

The lentils arrived. They were a sort of stew with little pungent slices of sausage and kidney in them. They were also very tasty and so I ate them quickly, but I began to get the drift of Milan's comments about the nature of the Spanish diet. The food here was basic, without the slightest pretension to refinement.

Once we had finished it was time to return to the Institute so, having parted with much more money than I had wished, Tim and I took the metro back. He continued to talk more or less the whole time about Milan and teaching English and how he was now entrusted by Peter Garrett with taking some of the young hopefuls who were trying to get into the Spanish Diplomatic School and needed to have passed the Cambridge Advanced English exam.

This qualification was the worldwide gold standard for non-English-speaking adults with pretensions to demonstrating their fluency in the language. These young men – and I never saw a woman among them – were the most highly favoured clients of the Institute, and Peter Garrett was at pains to ensure that the Institute's excellent reputation for turning out fluent English-speaking diplomatic candidates was maintained.

I, needless to say, was never allowed near any of them.

IV

When we got back to the Institute it was approaching four o'clock. After running the gauntlet of the doorkeeper's vitriolic glances we opened the door to find it much busier than when we had left. I soon realised that it was like that every day. The Spanish only really started coming to life about an hour or so before everyone in Britain was thinking about winding down for the evening.

There were several students waiting around for their classes to begin. Behind the reception desk Mariuca had been replaced by another, younger woman with speckled brown and blonde long straight hair and a pretty face – which gave the impression that she was always smiling, although sometimes she was not. This, I soon realised, was Elena, the receptionist who worked from four until ten, and who rapidly became one of my mentors and confidantes.

Two other English women, both only a couple of years older than me, came over. One had long, dark hair and big horn-rimmed glasses. She introduced herself in a strong Yorkshire accent as Christine and told me that she had been there since the previous September. The other girl was Hilary, who was bubbly and with curly fair hair. She was a recent graduate of Leeds University and, like Christine, had been teaching in Madrid since the previous September. Anne, whom I had met in the morning, was somewhere in the background as well, greeting students and chattering in the easy way that all the teachers seemed to be able to do.

My Reign in Spain

I didn't catch sight of Moya or the mysterious Madeleine as I was ushered into my room by Elena, along with the three student nurses who were my next students. Their names were Juana, Alma and Maria and, although the term 'student nurse' implies youth and a certain abandon to some people, these three ladies had obviously discovered their vocation a little later than many.

Juana had short grey hair and, although probably not much past thirty, seemed to nineteen-year-old me to be someone of my mother's generation. Alma was a little younger, possibly, but her features were obscured by a pair of enormous glasses and, although very slight in build, her manner was so uncompromisingly severe that I was frankly terrified of her from the beginning. Maria was a softer, sweeter girl with long brown hair tied back in a ponytail, but unfortunately she was so cross-eyed that I could never tell if she was looking at me or the blackboard or out through the door.

I never found out how good they were at nursing. Juana must have had the wisdom that extra years bring and Alma the discipline that is needed on the ward, but as for Maria, I really could not see her administering an injection with any degree of accuracy. They were all nevertheless very kind and always showed concern about how a young man like me would fare in Madrid so far from home.

So for the next two hours and twice a week for many months afterwards I struggled to get them past Martin and Jane on the park bench. During the first lesson we all took it in turns to say,

'Yes, the birds are very pretty,' with varying amounts of success. At last, and in desperation, with three quarters of an hour still to go, I put my chair next to one of theirs, mimicking the bench, and they each came out in turn to play Jane to my Martin.

They had told me at the beginning of the class – in Spanish – that they all wanted to visit London as soon as possible, and that this was one of the reasons that they had decided to learn English. So after that first lesson I was happy to think that I had at least given them the ability to hold a conversation on a park bench when they got there. The usefulness of repeating,

'Yes, the birds are very pretty,' to all and sundry, particularly if the birds in question were the normal scruffy London pigeons, was not something I dwelt on. However I did imagine the three of them sitting there, being given a wide berth by everyone, as they chanted their little phrase endlessly, unable to ask directions or even buy a sandwich, Juana looking motherly, Alma shooting severe glances at everyone and Maria looking in at least two directions at once.

In truth so much was happening to me that, as soon as the class had ended, I forgot all about them until an hour or so before the next time we were due to meet, but their appearance twice a week did both scare and console me as time went by. I did not know how to get them to make any progress, but they were a genuine and kindly trio and seemed happy to come back for more.

My next lesson was not until eight o'clock, so I had two hours to spare. The reception area was quiet but I did get better acquainted with Elena who, I learnt, shared a flat with Judy, yet another teacher at the Institute. Judy seemed to be second in command to Peter Garrett and therefore dealt almost exclusively with Diplomatic School candidates. She taught in the rarefied atmosphere a floor above, next to Peter Garrett's office.

Then the phone rang and Elena became engrossed in a conversation with someone, so I sat in the waiting area by the reception desk and starting leafing rather aimlessly through Martin's and Jane's adventures.

'Are you browned off?' a voice asked me.

I looked up and saw a young man with a large black moustache in front of me. He was wearing a pair of round wire-rimmed glasses and a huge, friendly smile. I must have looked confused, as he went on.

'I mean, are you completely cheesed off?'

I was still a bit nonplussed. I hadn't seen him come in and I was sitting near the door, so he must have been there all the time. He was very dark and obviously Spanish-looking, but his accent was faultlessly English. Perhaps he was another of the P. G. Wodehouse-type eccentrics who inhabited this expatriate world where time and English phraseology stood still.

'I've got two hours until my next class,' I explained.

'Oh, well, I'm Sabin.' He held out his hand. 'I'm Chris's boyfriend.'

'Oh. I'm Michael.'

'Yes, I know. You've just started, haven't you? You're replacing Susan.'

'Yes. It all happened at quite short notice,' I explained, unsure of whether or not to pursue the question of Susan's failure to return. I decided not to, but sensing that it would not offend, and relying on his name as a clue, I leant forward and asked quietly,

'Are you Spanish?'

He smiled broadly again.

'Yes, I'm Spanish, but I'm also Basque. Sabin is a Basque boy's name. I'm from Bilbao. That's where I met Chris. She spent a year there at the university.'

I immediately hit it off with Sabin. He was a complete Anglophile who was intrigued by the language and culture of the UK, and he was always a bright, witty companion. He had not been able to find a job and so had adopted the role of housekeeper in the flat that he and Chris shared, while she was the breadwinner – a most un-Spanish arrangement at the time.

The other two teachers at the Institute were introduced to me shortly afterwards. There was Moya, an English lady whose speech and mannerisms indicated a middle class Home Counties upbringing. She was kept busy by a group of loyal Spanish students who all seemed to be friends with her. She was also living with her boyfriend Carlos who, I was reliably informed, was one of the props in the nascent Spanish national rugby team.

I only met him once. He was a softly spoken giant of a man with a dark beard and the largest hands that I think I have ever seen. He was ideally built for the role of prop. Moya grabbed his left pectoral in her hand on the one occasion I met him, stating,

'*Tiene más pecho que yo.*' ('He's got a bigger chest than I have.')

He was also very demonstrative in his affection for Moya. This may of course have been due to the fact that she was obviously, even at first sight, extremely pregnant. Her pregnancy was probably also the reason that I only ever saw her in huge, shapeless three-quarter-length smocks and trousers with her bump shifting loosely underneath.

Moya stopped working at the Institute very soon after I arrived, and I remember being quite astonished at how Spain must have been changing for her pregnancy not to have precluded her from normal society. The well-manicured and coiffured middle-aged Spanish ladies who seemed to make up most of her student roll did not seem to be at all put out by her unwedded state. In fact I think that Moya was more cordially greeted and cosseted by her pupils than any other member of staff. They certainly returned her enthusiasm and energy in a way that Tim's baffled students did not.

(Before she left she told me that her brother was at Oxford studying Egyptology and that I should certainly look him up when I got there. Needless to say, I never got round to it.)

And then there was Madeleine – slightly mysterious and newly arrived from a previous teaching position in Cordoba in the heart of Andalusia. She was the same age as Chris and Hilary, more or less, with fine brown hair, a thin face and a prominent, aquiline nose. She was very slim, a fact accentuated by her preference for wearing close-fitting jumpers and flared trousers in the winter and skimpy tops and skirts when the weather warmed up.

It may have been her capacity to eat endlessly and still stay thin or her twenty cigarettes a day habit that coloured Chris and Hilary's view of her, but they obviously seemed to think she had had some sort of mysterious and racy past down there in the south of Spain among the passionate flamenco dancers and *caballeros*. They alluded to this on various occasions and were a little concerned that I should not be too exposed to her influence. In fact, though, it was through Madeleine and her circle of Spanish friends that I had some of the most enjoyable times over the next few months.

There was, furthermore, nothing very exotic about Madeleine. She was actually from Northampton. She had been a good convent-educated Catholic girl. However, as with so many young ladies brought up to strict religious observance, once she was old enough to be free of family supervision she had decided to try out all the things previously forbidden to her. In her case the scene of her exploration of these supposedly illicit pleasures had been Exeter University, where she had taken a modern languages degree, and then the south of Spain.

There was a natural affinity between us as the newcomers and she, like Elena and Hilary and Chris, showed a motherly concern for my well-being and encouraged me to go out and see as many things and meet as many people as possible. They were like a group of older sisters or aunties who ensured that I was well-looked-after and had a source of advice and support, which helped me enormously to make the most of my time in Madrid.

So, back to the Institute and my final class of the day: a very small bespectacled gentleman with a pencil moustache. His name was José, he was a native of Alicante in south-eastern Spain, and he was possibly even more nervous than I was. He fidgeted throughout our eight to nine thirty session and his nervousness spilt over into his speech, as he struggled to end a sentence in either Spanish or English.

I don't remember the exact course of the lesson because my mental processes were fast approaching burnout by nine o'clock. I had been awake very early, consumed a large and heavy lunch of lentils and chops and then strained every neuron and brain cell to find a way to move the three nurses forward from their sole English sentence. I do remember, however, that I came out at the end of the day quite exhausted and with something approaching a nervous tic after an hour and a half of José's spluttering, staccato delivery, so when Sabin suggested that I join him and Chris for a drink I jumped at the chance.

V

We went to a bar just around the corner from the Institute and had a very pleasant evening. I got the opportunity to find out a bit more about Chris and Sabin and they, likewise, found out more about me. I was also able to order a couple of *raciónes* of meatballs and *patatas bravas*.

(A couple of *raciónes* of something or other was my mainstay in the evenings. They were bigger than *tapas* but smaller than a full-scale meal. Nevertheless, two or three of them normally satisfied me on most evenings, and, most importantly, were within my budget.)

Chris and Sabin didn't eat as they were going back to their flat in the north of Madrid – something which I immediately envied them, faced as I was with my bare little room at the Rincón. According to them it was only a tiny basement with a kitchen, a living room, a bedroom and a bathroom, but it seemed infinitely cosier to me than my triangular living space at the top of the winding stairs.

We stayed for some time, drinking small glasses of sharp red Ribeiro wine from Galicia in the north-west of Spain. I finished a third one and Sabin, grinning at me from over the top of his glasses, suggested,

'*Pedimos otra ronda?*' which was a literal, though never used, translation of: 'Shall I get another round in?' He was so imbued with the British way of life, and the accompanying language, that he was speaking in the vernacular of an English pub rather than of a Madrid city centre bar.

He had spent a couple of years in the UK while Chris finished at university and had, I think, only reluctantly come back to Spain. I did wonder, nevertheless, in which particular part of the UK he had come across people who spoke about being browned off or cheesed off. Probably not Chris' native Barnsley.

So we had another *ronda*, and eventually I wobbled back up the road to my room and they headed off to the metro for the short hop home. I heaved myself up the staircase past the Roma all the way to the top and let myself into the Rincón. It was very quiet, with just a small lamp alight on the tiny reception counter. I went along the narrow corridor and off to bed, dizzy from the wine and the climb.

*

During the first week lunchtimes were spent with Tim and Milan listening to slightly bizarre conversations about the oddities of the Spanish way of life or Tim's strange relationship with his so-called girlfriend (they actually hardly ever seemed to see each other) and sampling the best that the *jefe* had to offer in the Tibet. He served some unusual yet tasty combinations, and during that first week I became increasingly bold at trying them.

When I asked Tim and Milan what *arroz a la Cubana* (Cuban style rice) was, they had no idea. So I ordered it and was served a plate of rice, fried eggs, stewed tomatoes and (the Cuban bit, I suppose) a banana cut lengthways and artistically placed across the top of the little metal tray in which it was all presented. It actually tasted very nice and, the next day, I was gratified to be there when Milan ordered it for the first time, apparently expanding his culinary horizon by a substantial margin.

I also introduced them to kidneys Jerez style, which they

likewise had not tried before, and which was, predictably, kidneys sliced up and fried in sherry but with, inexplicably, more fried eggs. Again, very tasty, and falling gratifyingly within my budget.

(One of the ladies from the Banco Hispano Americano, which offered places at the Institute for any of its workers who wanted to join in the latest craze for learning English, admitted that the Madrid diet was not the most sophisticated.

'Two fried eggs followed by a pork chop and chips,' was her verdict on the typical midday or evening meal. Tim and Milan had seemed destined for this tradition before I started investigating the *jefe*'s menu.)

One thing that I don't remember ever having at the Tibet was the ubiquitous Russian salad. But that didn't matter. I had plenty of opportunity for a *ración* or two in the evenings.

In fact the evenings were difficult, and I was always glad during that first week if someone suggested a drink after work. I inevitably stayed until the last lesson was finishing, even if I did not have a pupil, although timid José from Alicante favoured the late spot twice a week and there were several others whom I taught until nine thirty or ten. When leaving at that hour the streets were still lively and exciting, and made the interior of my room seem all the more depressing by contrast.

On the second or third evening I had a drink and something to eat with Madeleine, and she told me about how she had been teaching at the British Institute in Cordoba but that it had all started to break up due to internal rivalries between teachers. This was why she had come to Madrid in the middle of the academic year.

I did not probe further into what it had all been about. The whole field of office politics and the tangled human relationships that underpinned or destabilised them was something still unknown to me. But I got the impression that it had been a very happy place where something had then gone horribly wrong. I also got the impression that Madeleine did not expect the Instituto Garrett to provide her with the same level of challenge or satisfaction and she stated quite baldly, as she blew smoke rings into the air, that she put herself on a different plane intellectually to the other teachers.

I could only nod and acquiesce to her views at that time. I had never met anyone like her before and she was, in some ways, as strange as Tim Hewitt or Milan in her talk and her mysterious, post-Northampton background. She had, furthermore, already found herself a Spanish boyfriend in Madrid despite only having been there a week (there were raised eyebrows and an upward roll of the eyes from Hilary and Chris when I told them the next day). He was an engineering student called Manuel and was from Huelva, way down on the south coast in Andalusia. I could not have seen Madeleine with a calm and practical Basque boy like Sabin. Passionate and unreliable was definitely what attracted her.

I got into a rhythm with the lessons as Jaime Sancho came and went a total of three times during the first week and we talked about his life and what he did and my life and what I did. Occasionally we talked about Martin and Jane as well, but he was very bright, and as bored as I was with their tedious and repetitive lives. He was only two years younger than me and perhaps I was hoping for a friendship of sorts but, although talkative, his interest in me was definitely confined to the four and a half hours a week we sat in my little classroom.

The three nurses came again, as did Nervous José from Alicante and two ladies from the Banco Hispano Americano. It was one of them, a comfortable matron called Conchita, who had confided to me the awful truth about the lack of imagination in the Madrid diet.

I had more trouble remembering anything that the other one, who was called Rosa, said. That was because I immediately fell in love with her. She was young, slim and possessed of a gorgeous mane of long blonde hair which she would shake carelessly from time to time. She hailed from Huesca on the southern slopes of the Pyrenees, and I thought her achingly beautiful. I was therefore desperate to impress right from the beginning but my efforts, so forced and obvious as they were, had if anything the opposite effect. One of our first conversations was, as far as I can recall, about my investigations of the menu at the Tibet. I'm not sure why I thought that would impress her.

'I had Cuban rice for lunch today,' I told her. 'Do you like Cuban rice?' I asked in my clearest tone

She gave me a bemused look.

'Rice is from China,' she told me. 'Bacardi is from Cuba'

'Oh.' A slight hesitation. 'Do you like Bacardi?'

'I do not drink alcohol.'

'Oh.' Try again. 'Well, what is your favourite pastime?'

'I like to go skiing. Do you go skiing?'

'Err, no. I haven't been skiing yet – but I'd like to go'

'Oh.' She seemed to lose interest and looked at her nails. Abashed, I turned my concentration to Conchita, who was genuinely interested in the Cuban rice concept.

Conchita stayed with me throughout my short teaching career at the Institute. Rosa did not. Despite more half-hearted attempts to impress her over the next weeks Conchita eventually came along alone, telling me that Rosa had made other plans for Wednesday evenings. I was saddened but not surprised. Conversation flowed easily with Conchita. With Rosa I was tongue-tied and bereft of ideas.

When Friday came around I was relieved that I had got to the end of my first week and all my pupils had apparently accepted me – no complaints, as far as I knew – but was also daunted at the prospect of a weekend on my own and more solitary treks through the streets, passing the time and eating alone.

There was a general exodus earlier than normal that day and I found myself alone at the reception desk with Elena as she was packing up. Only Tim was still in his room with a pupil.

'What are you doing this weekend?' she asked as she stacked papers and tidied pens.

'Nothing much. I'll just have a look around Madrid, I suppose.'

'There are many places that you must see,' she told me.' Toledo, Ávila, Segovia, the Escorial…'

'I know. Perhaps I'll go out to see one of them.' I perked up at the thought of a bit of exploration.

Tim's door opened and he came out, bidding his normal, effusive farewell to a bewildered-looking Cambridge Advanced English candidate.

'I was telling Michael that he must visit one of the cities near Madrid or go out to El Escorial,' said Elena.

'Oh, absolutely. Yes, indeed,' agreed Tim. 'I really must get round to doing that myself sometime.'

'But you have your girlfriend to keep you company,' I said.

'Well, yes, that's true,' he said.

'So are you seeing her now?' I asked, curious to know more about the relationship, which he only ever mentioned intermittently. During our lunchtime discussions I gained the impression that he hadn't actually seen her all week.

'No. I'm off to dinner with Milan,' he replied. 'Tell you what. Why don't you come as well?'

I had found one daily meeting with the two of them enough. Even after a week I was starting to consider alternative lunchtime venues. Hilary had mentioned that she knew a number of cheap restaurants from her student days and she would be happy to show them to me. Nevertheless I accepted Tim's invitation. It was certainly better than a solitary evening in one of the local bars. So we headed off.

'Are we going to the Tibet again?' I asked as I trotted down the metro steps next to him.

'Oh, no,' he replied. 'We normally eat at another place in the evenings.'

'You meet him every evening too, then.' I had had no idea, and they had never said anything about it at lunchtimes. I realised that I had always been talking to the others in the evening and, when I left, Tim had still been in his classroom so I didn't know where he headed off.

'Oh, well… Nearly always, yes. I should go home and cook but I can't ever be bothered. We normally meet up at the Tipico – it's just up the road from the Tibet. We meet at the same bar and then head off.'

Oh, dear. Another one of those tonsil-grating aperitifs. I was becoming used to them after a week but I was also becoming more adventurous in my tastes, and so I decided to have a beer instead.

We met Milan and I broke the mould by asking for a beer. Milan raised an eyebrow at this but said nothing more as the drinks arrived. The talk was the same inconsequential chat as at lunchtime and, listening rather than talking, I quickly downed the beer. As we left to go to the restaurant Milan held the door for me. I opened my mouth to say a quick thank you but, to my surprise, an uncontrolled and unexpected burp came out instead as the gassy beer fermented in my stomach. Milan raised both eyebrows this time.

'You see, Spanish beer – it's barbarian,' he said.

I didn't reply but followed Tim sheepishly down the road. It had seemed rather unfair to blame the beer.

The Tipico was just that: typical. I don't remember much more – just a small restaurant that I only visited once. What was memorable about it was the chicken breast in a white sauce that I ate. Even as it went down I felt uneasy – it didn't taste quite right. Nevertheless I finished it, along with a glass of sharp white wine. I said goodnight to them both and made my way back to the Rincón.

VI

I went to bed, aware that all was not well. I slept only fitfully, and woke to all the nocturnal sounds from the street below. It was cold in the room and the little wall heater was proving painfully inadequate to the task of heating the room, so I pulled the bedclothes tighter round me and hunched up, knees to my chin.

As it got light I woke again and felt a sharp pain in my stomach. The foetal position I had adopted was no accident. It was by far the most comfortable, or I should say least painful, position to lie in. I felt bruised as I lay there, and as I straightened up the pain became more intense. It was obvious that something was wrong in my stomach and I immediately thought of the strange-tasting chicken.

I got up, had a cursory wash and got dressed. I did not feel like doing anything at all so lay down again on the bed and listened to the ominous gurgling coming from my stomach. I resolved never to eat with Milan and Tim in the evening again and, for the third or fourth time that week, propped on one arm, I wrote a letter home. I did not mention my current predicament but told Mum and Dad about the happenings of the last couple of days.

It made me feel a little better for a while but after I'd signed it and addressed the envelope I found myself concentrating on the pain again. I knew from a few similar incidents through my childhood that whatever it was would pass, but the process of it doing so would be painful and probably last for at least all of that day.

So I was cold and already feeling very sorry for myself when there was a knock at the door. I got off the bed and looked at my watch. It was nearly ten o'clock and I knew that the room was cleaned every day, so assumed it was Carmen/Conchita who had come to do just that.

I opened the door. It was indeed her, but what she said came as a real shock as I stood there feeling bruised and vulnerable and just a little like I was eight years old.

'What time will you be vacating the room?' she asked me.

I wondered if I had heard her correctly.

'When am I leaving?' I repeated the question, totally nonplussed. I certainly did not intend to go anywhere that day.

'Yes,' she went on. 'I agreed with the English *señor* that we would rent the room for a week. Now I have another student who wants it.'

This news sent my stomach into even greater uproar – which could have proved potentially disastrous, bearing in mind the state it was already in. I looked down the corridor towards the bathroom and let out something like a groan as a spasm went through me and I leant forward.

'Are you all right?' she asked, seemingly genuinely concerned.

'I have a problem with my stomach,' I said. 'I ate some bad chicken last night. I didn't know that I had to go today.'

Bent forward and explaining my condition in poor Spanish, I must have looked a pathetic sight to her. She walked me back across the room to the bed and sat down next to me.

'The English *señor* said that you would need a week here and then you would be finding an apartment to live,' she explained. 'Have you not found one?'

'No,' I said. It hadn't even occurred to me during that first week to seek out alternative accommodation. I was fully occupied with surviving my initial classes and navigating my way around all the rest of what I had to do. 'I can't go today. I feel really ill.'

She looked at me for a few seconds and then seemed to decide.

'I will call the English *señor* and see what we can do. Do you have his number?'

I was relieved that she was taking the initiative and pleased that I had kept the piece of paper with the seven-digit number on it that had been with me ever since I left Britain. I handed it to her and she shuffled out to call Peter Garrett.

A few minutes later she came back.

'He wants to talk to you to explain,' she said.

I got up and went out to the reception area. I picked up the phone.

'Hello,' I said in a small voice.

'Hello, Michael. I'm sorry you're not feeling well and for the mix-up with the room. I had assumed that Mariuca had told you about it. She certainly should have. We only book a week for our teachers, normally, as they sort out somewhere to live for themselves.'

'Oh,' I said. 'I didn't know that.' I must have sounded very young and confused at that point because he went on to explain that he would talk to Carmen/ Conchita and make sure that I still had a room for as long as I needed it even though it might not be the same one.

I readily agreed to this, glad only that I would not be thrown out.

Carmen/Conchita took up the phone again and they began talking as I trudged back to my room and lay down once more. The thought of finding my own apartment to live in, possibly as cosy as the one that Chris and Sabin had described to me, took my mind away from my intestinal tract for a few minutes. It was an exciting possibility. But then another bout of pain pushed through me with a menacing rumble and I got up and rushed along the corridor to the bathroom.

Eventually it was decided that I could have the only spare room for the next few days, which was a double and so more expensive. And the following weekend I could move again into another single, which would become vacant then. Carmen/Conchita was very concerned about me and helped me to put my things in the two suitcases and transfer them down the corridor. She made me lie down on the bed and pulled the bedspread over me. I half-expected a goodnight kiss but she just said,

'Tell me when you feel better and I will make you an omelette.'

'Thank you very much,' I replied, although the thought of an omelette at that moment brought on a mild, sweaty panic.

As it was I slept for most of the afternoon and then awoke. The problem had passed. I began to feel much better and quite hungry so I rang the bell on reception and took Carmen/Conchita up on her offer of an omelette.

*

The world seemed slightly better the next day. My stomach problem had gone, I had a room for as long as I wanted and there was the tantalising prospect of my own little apartment at some time in the future. Even the barren room that I was now occupying, which was identical to the previous one except that it had two beds and therefore less room for the few items of other furniture, did not look so grim.

It was sunny and warm so I bought a copy of the Sunday edition of *ABC*, Madrid's longest-established newspaper, and went and sat in the park opposite the huge white facade of the eighteenth-century Palacio de Oriente. I leafed through the pages, then stared up at the icing-sugar front of the palace and told myself in a rather over-theatrical way that I could do this. Yes, I could stay in Madrid and make a success of the next six months. I would be resolute and brave and it would work out like a movie screenplay with me surviving the ups and downs and coming out of it stronger and wiser.

I kept up my mood until the end of the day, when I had to go back to the Rincón and think about my second week of lessons, which would start the following day.

I did not approach Mariuca the next morning about her omitting to tell me that the room was booked for only a week. She apparently knew that I had not been well.

'Yes, Peter told me,' she said, pursing her brightly made-up lips, and was busy telling anybody else who came in as well. So when Jaime Sancho had gone and I had a free period that coincided with one of Chris's she also asked me how I was.

'I'm fine now,' I said. 'But how did Mariuca know?'

'Well, she's Peter's sister-in-law, you know,' said Chris.

'Oh, I didn't realise that.' I looked over towards Mariuca. She was perched on the stool behind reception, filing her nails in a caricature of the underemployed assistant.

'Yes, and what's more she used to be a nun,' Chris told me. 'Can you imagine it?'

The thought of Mariuca – whose very being, for me, was defined by thick mascara and violent crimson lipstick – having ever inhabited a nunnery was too much. I erupted into giggles and Chris joined me.

'She couldn't be a nun, looking like that,' I whispered hoarsely. Mariuca had stopped the filing and was now looking straight at us. It was obvious that we were talking about her. 'They must have thrown her out for having a dirty habit.' A silly comment, worthy only of a nineteen-year-old.

There were more suppressed giggles before we started talking about something else.

Hilary didn't get to know about my stomach problem until the afternoon, as she worked Tuesday and Thursday mornings rather than Monday, Wednesday and Friday. She was very concerned and determined to broaden my horizons beyond the Milan and Tim lunch club. She had been a student in Madrid and knew lots of cheap but hygienic restaurants around the centre. We would meet up for lunch even on those days when she was not working and try them all.

Madeleine also came in with an offer to prevent me from falling foul of unclean kitchens again. Manolo, her newly acquired boyfriend, had already taken her to several bars that did good food as well, so she would likewise ensure that I was taken care of.

So it seemed my weekend of pain and uncertainty had been worth it. I had two mentors taking me under their wings and, that afternoon when Elena arrived and learnt of my recent predicament, she joined the sisterhood in proclaiming that I must be more closely supervised. I needed to look for an apartment, make sure that I was properly fed and have enough to occupy my weekends.

I, of course, was delighted with this development.

VII

One of the results of my first weekend, which had been spent debilitated by a stomach upset and threatened with eviction, was to place the matter of finding a flat to share higher on my list of priorities. Certainly the others – Hilary, Chris, Madeleine and Elena – encouraged me to do this. It was, they told me, cheaper, and I would have company in the form of flatmates. This was a very normal way of living, particularly for young foreigners and students such as me.

I started to look at the adverts in the *ABC* newspaper. I had no set location in mind. It would be price that decided just where.

Meanwhile, lunchtimes became more interesting. Following Hilary's offer to show me some of her former student haunts I was becoming gradually less well-disposed to lunchtimes with Milan and Tim. The ritual wince-inducing aperitif and sombre Spanish-bashing conversation in the Tibet was beginning to pall. I had very quickly run through all the menu had to offer and was slipping apathetically back, with them, into a routine of fried eggs followed by chop and chips.

What really decided me to take Hilary up on her offer was what happened one lunchtime in the second or third week, when I managed to miss eating altogether. Tim had, quite startlingly, suggested an alternative venue for lunch for the next day – a restaurant they did not use very often but which both he and Milan knew. Milan took a long time to mull over this rather risky proposition and was still doing so as he wrapped layers of outer clothing around himself and we left the Tibet. He finally succumbed to it, however, with a gracious smile and the comment,

'It will be no better than the rest of these barbaric establishments.'

Tim was not going to be in the Institute on the following morning – something about a dental appointment – so he gave me the name again that evening before going home. It was easy to find, he told me.

'Right opposite the metro station. Come out and the Buena Suerte restaurant is straight in front of you.'

'Which metro station?' I asked as he sped past towards the door.

'Oh – it's Alonso Martin...' and his voice trailed off as he went out.

I made a mental note and then went out for my nightly *ración* of something or other. I can't remember if I was on my own but I do remember traipsing back to the Rincón and moving my things into yet another bedroom there as Carmen/Conchita tried to accommodate me as an extra unexpected resident who was spoiling her carefully drawn up room planning.

The next day, as lunchtime drew near, I tried to remember the metro station that Tim had talked about. I went around the corner to Ópera, the nearest station to the Instituto, and consulted the large map at the entrance. I struggled to remember the name of the station. I recalled that it was two words, obviously someone's name and, of course, very Spanish-sounding. He had also said it was only a couple of stops away. So, working outwards from my current position, I scanned the map.

My eyes alighted on Menéndez Pelayo, two or three stops away. Yes – that was it, I decided. It was definitely Menéndez

Pelayo. I trotted down the steps, bought myself a ticket and got on a train.

When I emerged at the other end I expected to come up to see the Restaurant Buena Suerte straight in front of me. It wasn't. In fact I could tell immediately that this was a very different sort of area altogether. Although only just south of the Calle Mayor, the old principal street of sixteenth-century Madrid, there was a seedy look and feel to everything – shops, people, even the couple of scruffy dogs wandering aimlessly by. I could not imagine Milan, wrapped in layers of tailored tweed, or Tim, in a smart sheepskin coat, walking around here.

Although unappealing as a streetscape I did not feel unduly worried. I was already getting used to the fact that one advantage of living under the last real Fascist dictatorship in Europe was that the crime rate was low and there was therefore very little attendant anxiety about straying into unpleasant or even dangerous areas. The concept of a no-go zone did not then appear to exist at any time of day or in any place.

Nevertheless I hesitated to explore and to see if I could find the Restaurant Buena Suerte. I first of all walked a hundred yards or so in one direction and then retraced my steps, not wanting to stray too far from the reassuring presence of the metro station. I tried not to appear lost but was aware of several fearsome, muscular-looking matrons and hard-faced old men staring at me as they lounged in the doorways of the large dilapidated apartment blocks.

It was obvious that I could not find the restaurant just by looking, so I ambled as nonchalantly as I could a bit further down the street. There was a slightly less intimidating-looking group of people standing outside what appeared to be a hardware shop a few doors down. There was an old lady and what could well have been her daughter and a very fat child of indeterminate gender standing just underneath a long line of pans and buckets suspended on a wire and obscuring the name of their shop.

So I took a deep breath and went over and asked them, in my best Spanish, if they could direct me to the Restaurant Buena Suerte. The daughter, a sharp-faced middle-aged lady all in black, looked at me suspiciously and then burst out laughing – a horrible, grating cackle. She turned her head and shouted something back into the dingy shop interior. I could not hear clearly but it was something about a *muchacho* – that is, a boy – wondering about his good luck. (*Buena suerte*, I should explain, means 'good luck' in Spanish.)

The old lady, also clad entirely in black, opened her mouth and said something that I did not understand at all. But I did not even try to as I was transfixed by the three solitary teeth that she had in her mouth, one at the top in the middle and one on each side in her lower jaw. All three teeth were almost as black as her widow's weeds. She looked just like the picture of the wicked queen, disguised and tempting Snow White with the poisoned apple, which I remembered from a childhood picture book.

The fat child – a girl, I think – also started sniggering and, both embarrassed and unnerved, I spun around, ready to flee back to the metro. It was as I did so that I felt something tapping me on the leg and I looked down to discover yet another unattractive inhabitant of this menacing quarter staring up at me.

He was an old man. Presumably, I thought later, he was another casualty of the brutal civil war. In fact what made him so repulsive to my now tender-to-the-touch sensibilities was the fact that he was actually only half a man. His bottom half was entirely missing and his torso, with arms and head attached, sat on a little wooden trolley. He had two blocks of wood that he held, one in each hand, and that he could push against the ground to propel himself around on. It was with one of these that he had been tapping me on the leg.

I almost tripped over him as I turned and then recoiled as he put down one block and held out his cupped hand in the universal gesture of the beggar. My nerves were taut enough to snap, and I felt no sympathy for the plight he had suffered for probably nearly forty years. I uttered a strangled gargling sound, which actually surprised me for a second or so, and then, with what seemed the raucous laughter of the whole neighbourhood echoing in my head, I raced back down the metro.

I didn't eat anything that lunchtime. I felt too upset both by the cast of grotesques that I had seen and also by my uncharitable reaction to the poor little man, who was only half there, pushing himself around on his trolley and relying on the donations of a public much more hardened to his predicament than I was.

I saw several more trolley men like him over the next few months in Madrid and in some of the other towns of central Spain. They had been young men, perhaps like me, when the civil war had begun, looking forward to many different things, as many different people will, but all of them with lives circumscribed by the tragic events that they experienced and that maimed them so horribly.

Tim explained to me later that day that the Restaurant Buena Suerte was near Alonso Martinez metro – the opposite direction to Menéndez Pelayo. When I lingered by the reception desk and told Elena what had happened there was a sharp intake of breath and she told me that she wasn't surprised if I went down to the neighbourhood near Atocha railway station, which is where I had been. If I was looking at flats to share I wasn't to go down there.

I never got to the Good Luck restaurant. I was never really interested in going after that. Its title seemed completely inappropriate, as far as I was concerned.

So later that evening I agreed with Hilary that she would meet me at two o'clock the next day (she wasn't working in the morning) and she would take me to lunch.

*

Hilary was blonde, with a figure which my mother would have called 'amply proportioned' and an attractive, vivacious personality. She had graduated from Leeds University the previous year and was now sharing a flat somewhere just outside Madrid with her boyfriend Nigel. Before we were introduced on my first day at the Institute I remember her regaling everyone with the tale of how she had been in her native Cheshire during the Christmas break, trying on clothes in a boutique changing room when the lights went out, thanks to the power cuts.

'And when I stepped outside to get a proper look there I was in bright blue fun fur,' she screamed as Chris and the others laughed at her shopping adventures.

Lunchtimes with her were much more jolly occasions than with Milan and Tim.

'I'll take you to the Cat Restaurant,' she said purposefully.

'OK,' I replied, sounding a bit doubtful.

'It's very good *and* cheap,' she said. 'As long as you don't mind the cats.'

'All right.'

'And we'll have the *sopa de verduras* to start with. Cheap and nourishing.'

I looked blank.

'What's that?'

'Vegetable soup. Are you sure you're going to Oxford?'

'Oh, I see. *Verduras* means 'greens', doesn't it?'

'Exactly.'

So we went to the Cat Restaurant. It was just off the Plaza de Dos de Mayo – the Second of May Square, named after the Spanish heroes who had resisted Napoleon and been shot as a result, presumably on that day.

There were certainly a lot of cats – black, brown, tabby – sprawled around in various poses of inactivity in a way that would have sent any UK public health inspector into a frenzy.

'At least there won't be any mice,' was Hilary's comment as we went in.

I don't recall the restaurant's real name. In fact, as we always called it the Cat Restaurant, I don't think I ever knew it. It had the typical interior of a Madrid eating and drinking establishment that never ceased to impress me. The walls were tiled in blue and white with swirling designs that had drawn their inspiration from the Moors, and there was a long tin-topped bar where men stood drinking coffee and glasses of wine. Although the tiles made it seem chilly in the cold January air they would make a welcome contribution to cooling the place when the summer heat set in.

('*Tres meses de invierno – nueve meses de infierno*,' 'Three months of winter – nine months of hell,' referring to the violent swing from winter to summer, was how I had heard the Madrid climate described on several occasions. It did not trip off the tongue in the same way in English due, I suppose, to the lack of alliteration. Personally, after experiencing the *invierno*, or winter, in my room at the Rincón with just the tiny warm air heater on the wall, I could not wait for the 'hell' bit to begin.)

Presiding over the Cat Restaurant was a tall, thin middle-aged woman with a pencil moustache and her hair tied up in a bun. She had a permanently sour expression on her face as if, frustrated in her dream career of whatever description, she was now reduced to running this modest eatery.

I experienced many restaurants and bars during those first few weeks as I sought company and sustenance – in fact my life then was punctuated by decisions about where to go at each mealtime – and I don't think I ever entered one to be greeted by a smile. The most excited reaction I ever got was from the waitress on the first evening after I arrived when, utterly naive and full of Russian salad, I gave her a tip equivalent to half the cost of the entire meal. Obviously the restaurant trade in Madrid in the last years of the Franco era was a tough one.

So we had the vegetable soup on that, and on many other occasions, and we talked about the Institute and the other teachers and Elena and Mariuca. (Hilary confirmed to me that Mariuca was Peter Garret's sister- in-law, she had been a nun and – yes, as, I had suspected – the suffix -uca was normally added to a word or name to denote its unpleasant or pejorative nature. In the most uncharitable fashion Mariuca could be translated as something like Odd Little Mary.)

She then told me about her boyfriend Nigel and the flat that they shared.

'He's working for the British Council here and he's a year older than me. I didn't actually like him at university but he's turned out OK. We live a little way out and I get a bus to the last stop on the metro. It's nice because we can see the sierra from the living room window.'

'Oh.' I listened, taking it all in and picturing the two of them looking out at the snow-topped peaks where Michael Garrett was skiing and Tim Hewitt's pupil (Francisco, I think – aka the scourge of the sierras) was busy bagging game.

'We're going to try to get a car as soon as we can so that we can go out a bit more and see the countryside at the weekends. Nigel can't drive but I'll try and pass my test. I had quite a few lessons back home.'

'That'll be good. I failed my test just before I came out

here so I'll have to take it again some time.' I cast my mind back to three days before I had set out for Madrid and the embarrassing near miss I had had with the cyclist as I had taken my test on the teeming streets of Wisbech.

'We've got these really odd neighbours, though.' Hilary leant forward slightly and I unconsciously mirrored her action. 'They're American – Waldo and Martha – and they drink.'

I looked blank again.

'You know,' she made a drinking gesture with her hand. 'The bottle.'

'Oh, I see. What are they doing in Madrid?'

Hilary leant in again and so did I. We were obviously going to exchange confidences.

'I think he used to work at the U.S. Air Force base at Torrejón and when he retired they stayed on. Probably couldn't work out how to get home. He says he was an engineer of some sort, but I'd hate to get in a plane he'd serviced.' She made a trembling motion with her hand.

'What are they like?' I asked, intrigued.

'Well, they're both about fifty, I think, although it's difficult to tell – what with the drinking and the skin problems,' she added by way of explanation.

'Skin problems?'

'Yes. It's psoriasis or something. When you talk to them they're both scratching all the time. It's very off-putting.'

I had a vision of Hilary, laughing and joking in her bright blue fun fur with these two elderly people who would be swaying gently from the effects of the drink and scratching at their arms and legs as flurries of discarded skin floated gently down into two little piles on the floor.

'The thing is,' she continued, 'they seem to have adopted Nigel and me as a sort of substitute family, so they're always knocking on the door with something or other. They don't speak Spanish very well, so last night they came round with a letter that was actually a final demand for payment of the electricity bill. We told them what it was and how to pay it, but I don't know if it sank in. They both smelt terribly of drink, and had a real bad bout of the itches. It took ages to get rid of them.'

'Well, don't do too much for them or they'll expect you to do more,' was all the advice I could give.

It was at that moment I think that the *sopa de verduras* arrived and we were silent for a while, fishing around for the bits of cabbage and beans.

I didn't hear any more about Waldo and Martha for some time as Hilary then changed the subject to her new private pupil – a real catch from one of Madrid's foremost families.

I had already been made aware by her and the other teachers that the way to make a considerable amount of extra money was to find a private pupil or two. The going rate was to charge two hundred pesetas for an hour – the equivalent of approximately two lunches in the Tibet – and the format was really very similar to lessons at the Instituto.

Hilary was very lucky because her pupil was Jaime Sanchez de Toledo, scion of an ancient – and wealthy – family who were used to paying top rates for whatever they wanted, in this case double the going rate at four hundred pesetas for an hour, five days a week. The only drawback was that the hour that *el Señorito* Jaime had chosen was from eight to nine in the morning, which meant Hilary had to get up at about six thirty and leave the apartment promptly to get into the centre of Madrid in time. As she did not sometimes finish until ten in the evening, like me, and in any case life in Madrid mainly inclined towards activity late in the day, this was a tiring regime.

'Still the money's good – and I sometimes get breakfast there,' she said.

'They give you breakfast?'

'Not always. But if he hasn't finished his when I arrive we start the lesson at the breakfast table and I get a cup of coffee and a bun or something. Bit difficult sometimes, though, if I haven't got to bed until midnight or more the night before. Nigel just says, "Goodnight, then," from under the covers as I slip out in the morning.'

I thought this very funny. I was a nineteen-year-old admiring the sharp wit of someone older.

Hilary chattered on about her university days, her home life somewhere in rural Cheshire and how it was such a relief to have the private pupil subsidising her obsession with shopping for clothes.

We went back to the Cat Restaurant several times over the next couple of weeks. I always had the hearty *sopa de verduras* with various other dishes to follow and was glad that there was no re-occurrence of my previous gastric problems. My visits to the Tibet (and time with Milan and Tim) got less frequent as a result.

Although my stomach remained, at least temporarily, in fine fettle, I did wake up one morning with a very embarrassing rash – on the palms of my hands. It didn't itch and, if I kept my fists lightly clenched, it couldn't be seen. I half-wondered whether I had somehow been infected telepathically by Hilary's curious neighbours with their skin complaint.

When, at lunchtime, I showed it to Hilary she raised her eyebrows and quipped,

'Well, what have you been up to, then?'

I feigned ignorance, and in the end we put it down to some shellfish that I had eaten one evening when having another few rounds of Ribeiro wine with Chris and Sabin. She came with me later to a chemist's and we got some cream, which soon took effect.

VIII

Towards the end of January I had my first payday.

The phone in the reception area at the Instituto rang one Friday afternoon and Elena told me that I was summoned to Peter Garrett's office on the second floor. I went up there expecting it to be something like the headmaster's study, but was disappointed to find that it differed very little from my own classroom except that it was bigger, with a window and more seats.

'Here you are, Michael. Take care of it and put it straight in the bank,' Peter said, tearing the cheque out of the book and handing it to me. I looked at it reverentially. Thirteen thousand pesetas. I was going straight around to the bank to put it into my newly opened account.

With money now in my bank account I started to get a bit more adventurous at weekends, and one Sunday I caught the train out to the great stone palace in the mountains to the north-west of Madrid that Philip II, that most Catholic of monarchs, had built in his declining years.

In fact El Escorial, as it was named, was more monastery than palace. Philip had withdrawn here to lead an ascetic life and ponder on why his dreams of defeating the Reformation and, in particular, the realm of his former sister-in-law, Elizabeth I of England, had failed. He had built a monument that must have perfectly reflected his state of mind. It was impressive in size but cold, gloomy and joyless, with little of the luxury that is normally associated with a monarch, particularly such a powerful one.

There was snow on the ground when I visited and, while standing in the chapel, where Philip had allowed ornament and decoration to the glory of God, I could almost hear the murmuring of the clergy intoning the rosary and the gentle thud of the faithful falling to their knees on the cold stone floors. A faint howling of the biting wind coming down from the mountaintops added to the penitential feel of the building, and I pulled my coat around me as I walked from chamber to chamber.

I looked at a portrait of Philip hanging in one of the lofty halls. His face was hard and purposeful, his dress dark and without ornamentation – as if he had seen what life had to offer and did not want any more of it. He reminded me somehow of Milan – but without the ability to laugh at life.

'If I'd been you,' I thought, 'I'd definitely have done my penance and prepared to meet God somewhere down near the Mediterranean coast.' I would have been humbled – but warm – in his presence.

When I had finished my tour there was an hour or more before the train that would take me back to Madrid was due. Suddenly the sun came out so I climbed up a small slope from the road above the palace and sat on a rock watching the it set as the grim walls of the palace took on a lighter hue.

The sunshine seemed to change the mood of the place from menacing, inquisitorial harshness to a more melancholy, spiritual one. I felt peaceful and once again found myself reaffirming my determination to see my time in Madrid through, despite being cold and lonely. In fact it was colder and lonelier in my room in the Rincón than it was out here on the hillside with the sun going down over the gaunt monastery-cum- palace. But it would have been cosy and warm in my parents' living room back in March, so why had I been so determined to leave there?

The small Fenland town and my former classmates seemed further away than ever on that evening as I walked down to the station to catch the train back to Madrid. I still felt a connection with them but I was sure that the world was large and exciting and, though chilly and a little sad, I still wanted to explore all its possibilities, which I knew were beckoning. My life was going to be an enthralling one and this was a training ground for all the adventures to come. The golden glow in the west promised golden tomorrows.

The train arrived in the little station of San Lorenzo de El Escorial exactly on time and my mood was buoyant as we headed back down the branch line towards Madrid where lights were starting to twinkle in the cold, clear air.

*

Madeleine seemed to be having a great time in Madrid. Her former colleagues in Cordoba had alerted several *Madrileños* that she was coming, and there had been the beginning of a circle of friends already awaiting her when she had arrived early in January. It was via one of these friends of friends that she had met Manuel – Manolo – and he had soon become her boyfriend. Hilary and Chris were sure that Madeleine had never been short of a boyfriend for more than a day or two, wherever she went.

Madeleine continued to view herself as the cultural doyenne of the Instituto. When Elena told her that she had a new pupil for her, a man who was a professor at the university in the suburb of Moncloa, Madeleine very loudly proclaimed that it would be good to talk to someone at last who would be her intellectual equal. She furthermore sought to raise her capital in my eyes by telling me that, while I would have Oxon after my name as an Oxford graduate, she had Exon after hers as a graduate of Exeter University. The inference was obvious – only one letter away from an Oxford degree. Leeds and Sheffield, where Hilary and Chris had studied, did not even merit a mention.

They both got their own back when discussing birthdays. Madeleine had been born in August 1949 but Hilary and Chris were a year younger. Both had been born in 1950.

'It's only a year, I know,' sighed Hilary, smiling her sweetest smile, 'but I think there's such a difference in being able to say that you were born in the 1950s rather than the 1940s. After all, the 1940s sounds such a long time ago.'

Madeleine blew a smoke ring and smiled back.

'Yes, but it also means one has so much more experience of life and can discuss things on an altogether different level.'

I stayed silent and went back to the three nurses and stick figure conversations on a bench. No worries for me that I would struggle with the cosmic significance of things in the classroom.

Madeleine's interest in me was genuinely altruistic. She knew that I was lonely and away from the support of my family for the first time, so she decided to introduce me to her circle of friends. Hilary and Chris were unable to fault this genuine gesture of friendship, but made one or two veiled comments about enjoying myself but being wary of not going too far.

I looked blank when this advice was handed out, but when I told them I was meeting Madeleine's friends in a bar near her flat one Saturday evening they both looked at me as would a pair of aged aunts when told that their favourite niece had a date with the town gigolo – half-envious of my luck and half-disapproving of my outrageous lack of morality.

Madeleine lived in the suburb of La Prosperidad. (By chance it was the same area as Tim Hewitt, although their paths were very unlikely to cross other than by chance. There was a mutual lack of common ground or interest between them, which meant that they only ever exchanged the briefest of niceties.) It was in the north-east of the city on metro line no. 4, and it only took me about twenty minutes to get there.

She had told me that they were all meeting in a bar called the Tankstelle where Manolo, the boyfriend, and his friends often went. It was apparently run by a German (hence the distinctly un-Spanish name) who had married a girl from Madrid and decided to settle there. It was very much a German-style bar, Madeleine told me, with sauerkraut, which I had never actually heard of at that time, and lots of different beers.

So on the Saturday night following my previous weekend excursion to El Escorial, and with the address and instructions on how to get to the Tankstelle on a piece of paper firmly clutched in my hand, I made my way out there.

It was easy to find, not far from the metro, with light and noise spilling out from its half-open doorway and window into the darkened little side street. It seemed to illustrate my situation perfectly as I peered in. There was light and warmth and people standing at the bar or perched on stools, all having a good time. I was outside in the chilly night, peering through the steamed-up window and trying to pluck up the courage to join them.

I couldn't see Madeleine, and it was difficult to make out individual faces in the smoky air. The words 'Bar Tankstelle' were also painted on the window in red, edged in green, so I had to try and see through the centre of the first 'e' of Tankstelle, which was at about head height.

It would have been easy to walk straight in for some. But it seemed for all the world to me like a private and very sophisticated party, at which I knew no one. I imagined a sudden hush descending and a hundred pairs of eyes looking at me as I entered, leaving me awkward and stranded just inside the door. I took a deep breath, nevertheless, and prepared myself.

Just as I was about to take my eye away from the letter 'e' and conquer my paralysing shyness a group of three or four young people came round the corner just along from the entrance, laughing and joking. They gave me a quick glance, showing momentary curiosity, and then opened the door and bundled inside. I stayed rooted to the spot, looking in the direction of the doorway. My resolution evaporated like the steamy air leaking from the half-opened door and I realised I couldn't do it.

I walked quickly away towards the metro, cold and confused. Why couldn't I just go in and look for Madeleine? No one would notice me for more than a minute. I'd come all the way to Spain on my own and then, on this night, all the way out to the bar, where I stood a real chance of making some new friends.

Nevertheless, although returning alone to the Rincón and the tiny wall-mounted air heater was by far the less attractive option, it was the one I took. I was angry at myself for my ridiculous inability to go in, which compounded my misery, and, rather than go straight back to my room, I wandered aimlessly around the El Corte Inglés department store near Plaza de Callao for about an hour. It was warm and light and full of people, just like the Tankstelle.

I didn't really 'shop' in any meaningful way. I just walked round and round for a while, riding up and down the escalators and, for all I knew, probably arousing the suspicion of the security staff. My feelings couldn't have been further from the ones I had experienced only a week before on that chilly hillside as the sun went down over El Escorial.

I saw Madeleine later on the following Monday and made some excuse about not being able to find the bar.

'Oh,' she said. 'What a pity. We had a great night. We all went off afterwards to a flamenco place off the *Plaza Mayor*.

Didn't get home until four o'clock.'

It was all such an obvious contrast to my sad evening that I had to go back into my classroom straight away, unable to speak.

I was distracted from my thoughts of how pathetic I had been, and how I had lost a Saturday night – never to be recovered – by my next pupil, who was starting her first lesson.

Her name was Dolores. She was probably about forty-five to fifty with short, black hair combed back over her head and plastered down with some sort of hair cream. She was wearing the same violent shade of lipstick favoured by Mariuca but, with bushy black eyebrows and a severe expression, she could not help looking like a man dressed in a twinset and pearls.

Elena ushered her into my room with a broad grin on her face.

'This is Dolores, who is coming to you twice a week,' she said. 'She has been here before.'

'Oh good – so she knows Martin and Jane,' I remarked, perhaps a trifle flippantly.

Dolores fixed me with a stare.

'I do not talk about Martin and Jane. I have finished with them long ago.' Her voice was a bass rumble that perfectly matched my preconception of her as a cross-dresser.

I was again flummoxed, as I had been by the three nurses. This time it was not the lack of comprehension and vocabulary, but the obvious range and depth of both that I found hard to deal with. Dolores had little reason to come to me for lessons. She was almost fluent. I could talk about any subject and ask her opinion and she would then pause, stare at me intently, and proceed to talk for up to fifteen minutes at a time.

It was even easier than with Jaime Sancho – he had moods

– but Dolores was always exactly the same: stern, forbidding (I don't ever recall a smile), but very eloquent. I really began to look forward to our twice-weekly encounters. All I had to do was find a subject from the newspapers and she would expound her theories on it in her basso profundo voice at length, all the while staring at me from under her beetling brows.

Elena told me that she booked in to the Instituto every year for several months for something to do. She had plenty of money and did not work. She was unmarried, due to some vague incident in the past with an unsuitable man who her family had disapproved of, so she had ended up a bored and lonely spinster in a country that still did not have many outlets for a wealthy unmarried woman. I was probably her eighth or ninth teacher over the years. (It was a few months before I found out a few details of the vague incident that changed my view of her entirely.)

The only subject that was a no-go area with Dolores and, I was warned, with anyone else at the Instituto, was politics. Although the most repressive policies of the past were vanishing Spain was still a dictatorship, and it was unwise to express any opinion other than one of solidarity with the regime. Dolores was certainly an avid supporter of Franco, from what I briefly gathered – but it was an area I never explored with her or with any other pupil.

*

That week, possibly due to the chilliness of my room at the Rincón or because I had got very wet one evening walking to one of the bars I sometimes ate in, I developed a cough. It was not serious enough to keep me away from work. In any case, staying in my room for several days was most unappealing. I came to work for company as well as to earn money. But it was enough to be an inconvenience in the classroom. Elena, Hilary, Chris, Madeleine and even Tim rallied round and showed concern. Hilary went down to the pharmacy with me again (the same one where I had obtained the cream for my embarrassing hand rash) and we were given some capsules by the pharmacist, which he assured me would start to solve the problem within hours.

It was a surprisingly large package that I was given but I went straight back to the Instituto, eager to benefit from its curative effects. I went along the passageway on the first floor to a small kitchen and filled a glass of water from the tap. I unwrapped the package and took out one of the tablets. It was very strange: rather large, and shaped like a little torpedo with a waxy feel to it. I didn't take it straight away but went back to the reception area where several teachers were gathered around Elena's little reception desk, as we often did if we didn't have a lesson at that particular time.

'Have you taken it?' Elena asked.

'No, not yet,' I replied. 'It's quite big. I don't know if I can swallow it.'

'Well, let's see,' said Hilary.

I showed her the capsule.

'Did you try to swallow it?' said Madeleine, in Spanish.

'Yes,' I replied, although I hadn't actually got as far as putting it in my mouth, and Elena collapsed into giggles.

Hilary took the packet.

'I thought so' she said, pointing to some writing on it. 'Look - they're suppositories.'

They were all laughing by this time, but the word meant nothing to me.

'You don't swallow them,' Hilary continued.

I was confused.

'Well, what do you do with them?' I asked.

The four women looked at each other. Who was going to

tell me?

'You put them in the other end,' said Madeleine tactfully.

I still didn't get it and stared at them blankly.

'You push them up your bottom,' Chris said quietly with characteristic bluntness.

I felt myself go bright red.

'That's why they're covered in wax,' said Hilary. 'To – you know – make them go in more easily.' More giggles from all.

'You take them that way so that the medicine can get into the bloodstream more quickly,' explained Madeleine. 'They're very effective,' she assured me.

I was dumbstruck, both with embarrassment at the topic of conversation and with trepidation at the thought of what I had to do. I was suddenly six years old and needed my Mum to sort things out. I wasn't sure I could do it myself.

Nevertheless, after a few very carefully chosen words of encouragement from my four substitute aunties I plucked up courage, went down the corridor to the toilet and, eventually, after much fumbling, managed to 'take' my medicine in the correct manner. It still seemed ludicrous to me that something to alleviate the symptoms of a cough should be introduced into the body at the very furthest point from where those symptoms were found.

We ascertained from the packet that the suppositories had to be taken every four hours until the problem was solved. I therefore had to creep furtively away once more that evening to administer the remedy.

It was actually very effective, as they had told me it would be. My cough quickly subsided. I nevertheless went to bed that night with a strange mix of feelings, somewhere between guilt and relief.

IX

I got the opportunity to try again with Madeleine's friends the following weekend. I had arranged with Chris and Sabin to go to Ávila for the day on the Sunday, but Saturday was still stretching ahead, long and empty, when Madeleine said that they were all meeting up again in the evening. This time, determined to avoid the fiasco I had inflicted on myself the previous week, I arranged to meet her first in a large, city centre bar. I had continued with my story about not being able to find the Tankstelle so she suggested, very generously, I thought, coming into the centre of Madrid, meeting up a bit earlier and then going back to the Tankstelle together.

I moved around all day, making far more of the forthcoming occasion than was really necessary, excited and nervous about meeting some 'real' *Madrileños* outside the confines of the Instituto. It might even mean that I would start to have a social life.

Because I was so nervous I had one or two *Chinchóns* too many before we went up there.

I had discovered *Chinchón* as an authentic local drink a few weeks before on one of the periodical post-work outings that Chris, Sabin and I shared in the bars near the Puerta del Sol. It was an aniseed-type liqueur, thick and sticky-sweet, made in a village of the same name about twenty miles south-east of the capital. Its relative lack of fame elsewhere in Europe, and, I discovered, in other parts of Spain may actually have been down to the fact that it was yet another example of what Milan would have termed the barbarism of the Spanish diet at that time. It was the type of drink that did not travel well. A bottle bought in Madrid and transported home to northern climes would undoubtedly have stayed untouched in the drinks cabinet in a way that a fine cognac would not. Nevertheless it had a calming effect on my nervous system that was welcome at the time.

In order to steel myself I therefore drank several with Madeleine before taking the metro out to La Prosperidad. She, perhaps as a result of previous experiences, declined to drink them, and made one beer last for an hour or so.

When we arrived at the Tankstelle I found, as a result of my *Chinchón* consumption, that my nerves had disappeared, and I strode in behind Madeleine to meet the assembled gang.

There was a group of people at the bar who immediately recognised Madeleine, and we went straight over to them. A small, chubby man with lots of dark curly hair kissed her on both cheeks. Madeleine took me by the wrist and pulled me forward – even with several *Chinchóns* inside me I was hanging back – and introduced him.

'This is Manolo,' she said. 'My boyfriend.'

I shook his hand, somewhat taken aback. He was several inches shorter than her and did not look like the tall and haughty castanet-clacking Don Juan that Hilary and Chris had guessed he would be. He was dark and very comfortable-looking, and his broad grin and round face were as far from haughty as you could get.

'Hello,' I said, and then, stuck for what to say, 'Madeleine has told me a lot about you,' which was partially true, as Madeleine seemed genuinely excited about this new man in her life.

'She has also talked about you,' he said. 'She tells us that you have come to Madrid on your own and you are only just nineteen. That's very brave.'

I felt suddenly very proud, firstly because Madeleine had taken the time to talk about me and secondly that Manolo would consider my determination to get to Spain as a courageous act. Yes, I was brave. Far more so than my contemporaries, who had simply gone to the much closer and safer environments of university straight away. Lonely weekends haunting the sales floor of the El Corte Inglés department store suddenly seemed romantic and worthwhile.

Madeleine then introduced me to someone called Enrique, who slipped down from his bar stool to shake my hand. He was about the same height as Manolo but fairer and the exact opposite in build – thin and almost delicate in appearance. He sported a thick head of hair, which was brushed back from his forehead, and a large moustache, which prevented him from seeming too doll-like, which he could otherwise have done.

When he spoke, as if to further emphasise his masculine qualities, he had a very deep and penetrating voice, which seemed too large for his frame. He was wearing a short-sleeved shirt and I noticed that he had the hairiest arms that I think I had ever seen.

'Hello, Mike,' he boomed, grasping my hand firmly. 'What do you think of the Tankstelle?'

'Oh, it's great,' I said gazing around. 'It's very popular.'

'Oh, Peter's got the best bar in the whole neighbourhood,' Enrique told me. 'I come here every weekend. Peter,' he turned to the bar and addressed a heavyset man, obviously the Germanic bar owner, 'let's get Mike a drink.' He turned back to me. 'Big or small?' he asked, indicating his own enormous beer glass – which seemed twice as big as him – by way of explanation.

I didn't hesitate. This was Spain, land of the *macho*, and despite his slight frame, Enrique was obviously the embodiment of that virile ideal.

'Oh, a big one, of course,' I replied with a conspiratorial laugh. It looked like the night would go with a swing.

I met others that night in the crowded bar and ate my first plate of sauerkraut. Enrique's brother Antonio was there and another friend of theirs, called José Carlos. There were also some teachers from the British Council, one called Susan who brought to mind for the first time in weeks the lady who had preceded me at the Instituto and whose reason for departing suddenly I had never found out. I was also introduced to Peter the owner and his wife, who were both behind the bar along with Roger the barman.

I had a long, rambling conversation with Roger. He must have been very bored talking to a now very drunk and incoherent teenager but he did tell me that he was a male model who had achieved brief fame as the man in the Big Fry advert on television. I recalled, when young, seeing this advert for Fry's chocolate in which a strapping young man with chiselled features strode across a dockside with a packing case full of something held on his shoulder (cocoa beans, perhaps?) to a catchy tune. I think he was then subject to the admiring glances of various females as he held the case aloft and looked rather nobly up and out across the water and a voice-over made a suitable comment, equating chocolate with the desirable physical qualities that Roger embodied. This, I gathered, had been the high point of his career, and he was now in Spain pursuing other opportunities.

I was surprised afterwards that he had bothered to tell me the story and not just told me to get lost, but then if the Tankstelle was as far as opportunity had led him perhaps he was only too glad to recall his former life to anyone who would listen.

The other memorable event of the evening that I recall was a bout of drunken posturing between two Americans, servicemen at the Torrejón U.S. Air Force base just outside Madrid. Both were very large and probably naturally bellicose. Having consumed several of the large tankards of the beer that Enrique and I favoured, they decided to see who could push the other back using just the force of their beer-inflated bellies.

They squared off in a friendly way against each other, unbuttoning their shirts and displaying a large area of taut, rounded stomach and responding to the cheers of the onlookers with hands above their heads. They approached each other and both bounced backwards as their stomachs collided. Egged on by us, they squared up again. But this time one of them, seeking the element of surprise, I suspect, charged at his opponent before the opponent realised he was coming and started to push him rapidly across the room.

The other man, literally caught on the back foot, recovered and started pushing back. A snarl came across his features as he pushed, and it was obvious to all that it would soon get out of hand. Anxious not to see his bar wrecked like some Wild West saloon, Peter came quickly round and broke them up.

'It's gonna get nasty, guys. It's gonna get nasty if you don't stop,' he said in a heavily accented American-English voice. 'I've seen it happen before.'

I looked at Madeleine, who gave a little giggle. This was certainly the liveliest time that I had had since arriving in Madrid.

I talked mainly to Madeleine and Manolo that night. Enrique seemed preoccupied with Susan, and José Carlos and Antonio disappeared very shortly after the servicemen's joust. I drank some more beer, probably had more sauerkraut, and staggered out sometime in the small hours. I was still sufficiently coherent to know that the last metro back to the centre was just before two o'clock so I weaved my way back to the station, having promised that I would be up to the Tankstelle again very soon to reconnect with all my newly made friends. Madeleine disappeared up the street with Manolo, his arm hooked firmly round her shoulder. His feet only just touched the ground as a result.

I got back to the Rincón, fumbled with my key in the main street door downstairs and then, as quietly as my drunken state would allow, let myself into the *hostal* and fell asleep, fully clothed, on the bed.

I had had a great evening out.

X

I slept badly with *Chinchón*, beer and sauerkraut circulating inside me, and woke at about eight o'clock. I felt predictably awful and lay on the bed, trying for a few moments to piece together the events of the previous evening. It then dawned on me that I was still in my clothes and furthermore that I was due at the Estación del Norte, the North Station, at ten o'clock to catch the train to Ávila with Chris and Sabin.

I got undressed and had a shower in the little bathroom down the corridor. After that I felt better, got dressed again and went out to get some breakfast. I avoided the *churros* and chocolate option and had a coffee and a bread roll instead at a little cafe on the way to the North Station.

There were quite a few trains to Ávila, which lay about fifty miles to the north-west of Madrid. It was on the old main line north which eventually snaked its way up to the French border at Irun despite initially setting out in the wrong direction. I had actually arrived from Irun two months earlier on the new 'high-speed' route that had been driven across the Somosierra mountains. The route via Ávila was anything but high-speed, and took many hours to traverse a lot of that part of north-western Spain.

I got to the station early and was reading the Sunday edition of the *ABC* newspaper when Chris and Sabin arrived. They were both as talkative as usual, and I'm sure that Sabin was raring to try out a few more phrases that he had come across recently.

'Apparently Ávila is about five degrees colder than Madrid,' he informed me. 'It's about another three hundred metres higher up just under the Sierra de Gredos. It'll be rather parky.'

To counteract the expected 'parkiness' both he and Chris were swathed in coats and scarves. I was wearing a jacket with a furry collar but regretted not having dressed more warmly as it was a chilly morning, even in Madrid.

'It's a very old city, I think, with ancient walls all around it,' I told them in return, having asked Elena at the Instituto what it was like. 'It's the birthplace of St Teresa, who founded the something or other nuns.' I'd got that snippet from Mariuca when I had informed her of our proposed day trip. 'Mariuca said it's a very special place.'

'Unsurprising, that,' was Chris's comment.

The train was indeed a main-line one, but its rate of progress was so slow that to have travelled anywhere further than Ávila would have been a mistake if the purpose was a day trip. As it was, the fifty miles took an hour and a half, climbing slowly through the treeless, wind-scoured landscape.

As I got off the train I could see how right Sabin had been in his prediction of the temperature. It was the beginning of March and it was literally freezing, as snowflakes floated gently down and settled on our coats.

Nevertheless my spirits were high as we strode into the city. It was impossible not to be affected by Chris's down-to-earth humour and Sabin's boyish enthusiasm for everything, and the stark outline of the high walls against the grey Castilian sky was very impressive. The snowflakes stopped falling as we walked through one of the gateways in the thick ramparts and began our exploration of the narrow streets.

The cold, harsh aspect of the ancient stone buildings and the bleak surrounding landscape of the high Castilian plateau, known as the *Meseta*, acted on me in a strange way. It may have been in some part due to my tiredness and the lingering after-effects of the *Chinchón* and sauerkraut, but this city and its museums devoted to the ascetic life of contemplation of its most famous daughter, St Teresa, made me distinctly light-headed. Any slightly humorous remark – and Chris and Sabin were both quite capable of making these – brought on a severe fit of the giggles.

The first eruption of mirth was in the St Teresa museum where several other intrepid and snugly upholstered tourists were, like us, inspecting various artefacts and exhibits associated with her life. For some reason these were labelled in three languages: Spanish, of course, English, understandably, but also in Dutch.

What French or German, or even Italian visitors would have made of this I do not know, but the translations provided us with much amusement. Two scraps of paper under glass contained two of St Teresa's signatures written in her own hand. The Dutch translation of this was '*Twee handschriften*', which for some reason caused Chris and me to double up with laughter. The use of the word '*twee*' made it sound as if St Teresa had deliberately made these signatures nauseatingly charming or kitsch.

We also showed a total lack of respect at what was purportedly a piece of her forefinger, described in English as: 'Big bone small part holy finger'. Finally, Sabin's phraseology caused much amusement when, while reading a résumé of her life that was posted on the museum wall, he commented that, as she had died in 1582, she had 'hit the bucket' nearly four hundred years ago. The idea of this twee little nun bashing a metal pail with her bony fingers was too much for me. I started giggling in the way that a schoolboy does in assembly when all around are listening to the headmaster and the urgency of stopping only serves to make the laughter more unstoppable.

We left the museum, with disapproving glances from the handful of other visitors, in search of lunch. We found it in a little restaurant where a valiant attempt at translation had again been made, this time with the menu. I settled for 'Pig side bone meat', which turned out to be a very juicy pork chop and 'Rice with milk in oven', which was a cold rice pudding that had long since left the oven. There was also 'Lamb with tinsel', but none of us felt up to tackling whatever that was. Of course eating was difficult due to the constant laughter the mistranslations produced and Sabin's assertion that the restaurant was 'totally spiffing'.

We ended the day in a little bakery buying the tiny yellow cakes known as *Yemas de Santa Teresa* – translated, correctly this time, as 'Saint Teresa's Yolks' – which again provoked wild guffaws, for some reason.

I went on another couple of day trips during the weekends immediately after that. I visited Segovia and its castle on my own. There was no great merriment on this trip, of course, but the weather was more clement and I began to get the first hint of the arrival of spring on the high Castilian plain.

I went on the other day trip, to Toledo, about thirty miles south of Madrid with a lady called Jenny. I met her when she joined Tim and Milan for lunch on one of the increasingly infrequent days that I also lunched with them. We went to the Tibet as usual after the searing red aperitif, and Jenny joined us there. She knew Tim via the English-teaching community in Madrid and was at one or other of the institutes that rivalled Peter Garrett's. She was in her late thirties, I would think, although my judgement in these matters was imperfect at best.

It was Milan who suggested that Jenny and I go to Toledo together. He did not pay much attention to me during the meal – being taken up with Jenny, who was a new interest for him. I suppose that the endless repetition of routine aperitifs, lunches and dinners combined with his seeming disdain of the Spanish, their diet and their way of life, made any newcomer a welcome diversion, particularly if female and possessed of a charming, tinkly laugh such as Jenny's. Nevertheless, at the end of the meal, he turned his attention to me and asked where I had been.

'Oh, Ávila and Segovia and the Escorial,' I explained.

I think he had been referring to my lunchtime meal arrangements, so he looked surprised.

'I mean that's where I've been at weekends,' I explained. 'Not lunchtimes.'

'And you haven't been to Toledo yet?' He enquired. 'Pah! It's the only one worth seeing.'

He then gave his opinion on the savage and uninteresting nature of the Spanish countryside around Madrid and the lack of inspiring monuments in the cities that I had visited. I could not agree with him on this but stayed quiet, as always. Tim told me afterwards that he did not believe that Milan had in fact ever visited Segovia or Ávila – or Toledo, for that matter. His prejudice seemed to be based yet again on a personal history that had seen him washed up against his will in Madrid as the only place where he could feel comfortable, a comfort he was unwilling to admit.

Then Jenny chimed in.

'I've never been to Toledo either,' she said.

'Then you must go together,' said Milan.

'Oh, yes. That would be nice,' said Jenny, looking at me across the table. 'Much more interesting to have a companion,' she added, and gave another tinkly laugh. So it was decided.

On the following Sunday we met up at the station – Atocha this time, on the south side of the city. It was near to Melendez Pelayo, where I had had my unfortunate experience with not finding the Buena Suerte restaurant but encountering the man with no legs.

Toledo was a little closer than Ávila, about thirty or so miles away from Madrid. The journey still took about an hour, and I learnt something of Jenny's background: she was the only child of ageing parents, had been born and raised in Bath, had lived in Madrid for several years and was earning a good living teaching English.

There was something a little sad about her, though, a kind of rootlessness and impermanence that her lifestyle betrayed and which, to some extent, the tinkly laugh may have been designed to counter. After all, surely she had better things to do on a Sunday than go on a day trip with a nervous nineteen-year-old? Perhaps she saw it as exciting and reconnecting with youth. I didn't care. I had a travelling companion and would not have to look around Toledo on my own.

We duly arrived and walked up to the city. Toledo had been the capital of Spain before Philip II had moved it to Madrid, so had considerable significance in the Spanish psyche. Perched as it was, high above the River Tagus, it had always had an *alcázar*, or fortress.

The city's significance to the modern Franco-supporting Spaniard was all the greater, due to the long and bitter siege that his supporters had endured there at the hands of their left-wing rivals at the start of the civil war. They had refused steadfastly to abandon the huge square fort to the opposition and had restored it after the war was over.

The most famous inhabitant of the city during its sixteenth-century Golden Age was undoubtedly the painter El Greco. I read, when there, what his real Greek name was, but found myself unable to pronounce or therefore remember it. El Greco – the Greek – was a much more sensible alternative.

So Ávila had been devoted to a saint who had in turn devoted herself to God. Toledo seemed devoted to a painter who was devoted to devotional paintings – and therefore to

God as well.

We went to El Greco's house and we looked at examples of his work. They were nearly all religious subjects with the elongated faces and bodies that were the hallmark of his compositions. The temperature was warmer than Ávila by some margin and I didn't have a hangover but, in spite of this, or perhaps because of it, the trip was not such an amusing one. No giggling in the cathedral or titters over the badly translated menus.

We saw all the sights and I bought a miniature sword-shaped letter opener made of the famed Toledo steel and a small enamel brooch with a pattern of a damascene rose for Mum, but it was a sombre day out. Jenny was a lot older than Chris and Sabin and did not seem to share my nineteen-year-old sense of humour, so the conversation was by turns sparse and then intense.

At the station while waiting for the train back I had an encounter that I did not at first understand. Because I was bored and wanted something to do I decided, like a toddler, that I needed the toilet. I went to the end of the platform where one was indicated and went inside. Almost immediately afterwards a man, whom I had not noticed before, entered and stood beside me. In the most masculine tradition I stared straight ahead at the wall but he peered round at me and asked me something in Spanish which I did not understand. I caught several words that did not seem to make sense when put together and, because the scene seemed to me to be generally very unwholesome, I left quickly.

'What does '*majo*' mean?' I asked Jenny as I got back to her.

'It means handsome or good-looking for a boy,' she replied. 'Why?'

'Well, a man just came up to me in the loo and called me '*majo*' and then said something else to me that I didn't understand,' I said.

'Oh,' then a long silence from Jenny. 'Well, perhaps he was just being friendly. But if I were you I wouldn't go to the toilet on a station again.'

The train pulled in at this juncture and we got on. I looked around to check that the man wasn't to be seen. He wasn't. But the whole incident cast a bit of a pall over our trip to Toledo. I went on numerous other trips to various parts of Spain, often by train, but I never visited any public convenience on a railway station again.

I only saw Jenny once after that, and it was by accident. It was at the cinema several months later and I had to look twice because, while it was undoubtedly her, she had dyed her dark hair a very bright shade of blonde, and she was on the arm of a thickset, middle-aged man wearing dark glasses.

Tim Hewitt told me that he was a property developer with a large house in the sierra north of Madrid, and she had practically dropped out of sight. She certainly had no further need, therefore, of the company of a teenager.

XI

I was increasingly aware of the foolishness of continuing to stay in my little room at the Rincón. Common sense dictated that I should find a flat-share. It would, Elena and all my other 'aunties' told me, make financial sense as it would be cheaper, and I would no longer be forced to eat every meal out. I had some very basic cooking skills, which I was sure I could employ from time to time – even if, like Tim, I continued to frequent restaurants and bars for meals during the day. If chosen carefully it would also give me some new social connections, and the company that I missed so much still at weekends and during the latter part of the evening. I could even stay in from time to time, rather than feeling obliged to go out endlessly when I wasn't working.

So I started to scour the pages of *ABC* every day along with Elena or Chris or Hilary or Madeleine, depending on who had free periods at the Instituto at the same time as me.

Elena was always available after lunch, perched on the stool behind reception that Mariuca vacated every day at two o'clock. She had some firm opinions on where was suitable and where was not. I went to look at one flat quite near to Atocha station, which was advertising for people to share. It was not far from Melendez Pelayo, the scene of my fruitless lunchtime search for the Buena Suerte restaurant, and Elena shook her head in disapproval.

'You won't like it,' she said. 'Not around there.'

She was quite right. The building it was in was dingy in

the extreme, with badly lit corridors and stale, oily cooking smells. The lady in charge was an ageing hippy wearing a bandanna and lots of chains around her neck and wrists. She chain-smoked three cigarettes as she showed me the interior, which was cluttered and dirty. When I enquired how much exactly it was per month she waved her hand vaguely in the air and simply exclaimed,

'*Aqui, todos pagamos lo mismo.*' ('We all pay the same here.')

This was less than helpful to me as I knew I could afford an upper limit of about four thousand pesetas per month and when I told Elena she scoffed.

'This woman must be mentally deficient,' she said. 'Either that or a socialist.'

Elena, I should add, like almost all Spaniards at that time, was not given to overt political statements and she was sufficiently liberal to be living, at least part of the time, out of wedlock with a considerably older man, so I took her comparison to be uncharacteristic of her general opinions … the more so when I later learnt that she had been left an orphan when her parents had been killed in the civil war, presumably by Franco's troops.

Nevertheless I agreed with her on that one. The woman had had a slightly crazed look to her, probably from nicotine poisoning, and I didn't want to take a chance.

I looked at other flats, in particular one very nice one on the borders of the Salamanca district, the most fashionable part of central Madrid, which I could not hope to afford. I knew that it was around there that Hilary's private pupil lived, and I just wanted to glimpse inside the opulent world that she visited every day. There was another where I was shown a room that had no windows, (I had a panic attack just standing in it), and another where the entrance to the bedroom that was being offered seemed to be via a bathroom-cum-kitchen of sorts. There was someone having a wash in there as the landlord showed me through.

I started to get a little despondent. The flat in the Salamanca district had been very good, but way out of my league. The others, though well within my price range, were, to me, almost uninhabitable. I still kept phoning, and one evening got through to a number that was in an advert looking for students to share a large four-bedroomed apartment in a quiet neighbourhood near the city centre. The voice that answered the phone had what I could already by then distinguish as a South American accent. His name was Santiago and he was very keen to meet me, as he liked having British students in the flat very much. He and his other flatmates were, he told me, clean, quiet and reliable payers.

When I asked where the flat was he gave me the address – no. 68 Calle de Canillas, *segundo derecha* (which meant it was the right-hand flat on the second floor). When I asked where that was he told me that it was in the area of La Prosperidad. What a happy coincidence – just along the road from the Tankstelle, and where Madeleine and all her pals lived. It all seemed providential, and I arranged to go up the next evening to have a look. I had a two-hour gap between classes, after the nurses finished and before Nervous José arrived, which was more than enough time to get there and back.

Elena provided me with a checklist (which I promptly forgot to take with me) of things to ask, such as how often the dustbins were emptied and what the cleaning rota was, and I set off on the metro.

As I had found with my trip to the Tankstelle it was only fifteen minutes from the Ópera metro station to La Prosperidad. Calle de Canillas was a long, gently curving street lined with modest apartment buildings, some with small balconies, all built within the preceding twenty years or so as Madrid expanded ever outwards. It was probably best described as a respectable, blue-collar neighbourhood for those on low to middle incomes, which made it quite attractive and within the reach of many students.

I found no. 68 with no difficulty. There was, inevitably, a caretaker who came hurrying out of a ground-floor flat as he heard the front door opening. I was almost reassured to see that he too had only one arm but, proud of the fact, he allowed his empty jacket sleeve to swing, rather than pinning it up as the surly doorkeeper at the Instituto did. As well as being more smartly dressed than his Instituto counterpart he was immediately much more friendly, and directed me upstairs to where *el Señor Santiago* was waiting for me.

I went upstairs, rang the bell and, my heart beating a little faster, waited. Footsteps echoed along the corridor on the other side of the door, which then opened to reveal a small man with jet-black hair, a bushy beard and large, dark eyes peering at me through tortoiseshell-framed glasses. He introduced himself as Santiago and invited me in.

There was a long corridor running along to the right of the front door to another door at the end.

'Come along and I'll show you around,' he said. I followed him along the corridor and through the door at the end.

'This is my room,' he explained. I thought it an odd way to start off a tour for a prospective flatmate – I was more concerned with my accommodation than his – but it seemed a cosy, lived-in bedroom, which he had personalised with many reminders of home. There were lots of photographs of a very large family, and I asked him if they were his.

'Yes,' he replied. 'I am the oldest of twelve brothers and sisters. All my family live in Ecuador.'

'You're a long way from home, then,' I said politely, to fill the conversational gap more than anything else.

'Yes, this is my sixth year of studying engineering,' he told me.

It struck me that he must be either very clever, having taken his studies to a level far beyond that attempted by other students, or not very clever at all, needing to endlessly repeat them before being able to graduate.

'Which is my room?' I asked.

'Oh, of course, you want to see it, don't you? It's through here.' He ushered me out and into the room next door. It was large with a double bed in it and various items of furniture.

'This is Dr Gutierrez's room,' explained Santiago. 'The spare room is through here,' and he opened a pair of glazed double doors into a smaller bedroom. I had not at first realised that Dr Gutierrez's room was windowless, but I could now see that the light that did come into it came through the frosted panes in the double doors. The bedroom beyond, my prospective room, had a window on to the street below, but could only be entered through the doctor's room. This was a considerable disappointment, and I began to doubt if this was really a home for me.

'This is the only way into the bedroom, is it?' I said, stating what was obvious.

'Yes,' said Santiago, 'but,' he continued, reading my thoughts, 'you'll like Dr Gutierrez. He's in the living room. I'll introduce you.'

He led the way back down the corridor past the front door and into another room, which was sparsely furnished with a large table and six chairs, a cabinet, a television and one or two bookcases and cupboards. Sitting in one of the chairs, apparently staring into space, was a middle-aged man with short dark curly hair and big black-rimmed glasses. I could not help but notice that he was in a dressing gown and pyjamas, even though, particularly by Spanish standards, it was quite early in the evening.

He looked round at us balefully as we walked in.

'This is the young Englishman who I said was coming over to look at the other bedroom that Tomas is vacating,' Santiago explained, as if addressing an elderly relative who was hard of hearing.

It seemed to take a moment or two to register with Dr Gutierrez but then his face broke into a smile, which immediately had the effect of making him look several years younger. He held out his hand and I shook it.

'Hello,' he said. 'I am Clemente Gutierrez, the foremost heart surgeon in the Dominican Republic.'

'Oh,' I said. 'I'm Michael – Michael Giddings.' I couldn't think of a superlative to describe myself so I just said, 'I'm coming to live here.' It wasn't what I had really intended to say, I don't think. If he had not added the surprising information about his medical rank I don't think I would have said anything about taking the room. In truth I hadn't until that moment decided. But there it was – I was now coming to live in their odd little household.

Santiago took me through a door on the other side of the living room where there was another corridor with the kitchen to one side and then, at the end, a bathroom and another bedroom.

'Whose bedroom is this?' I asked, attracted by its relative distance from the others.

'That belongs to Alberto, another student. He's leaving soon as well. I'll be advertising for this one next week.' Santiago told me.

'Oh, well,' I made a snap decision. 'Can I have this one instead?'

Santiago pursed his lips and frowned slightly.

'It's not free for another two weeks, and I'll be losing the rent on the other one,' he said.

'Oh, well, I can pay a bit extra to cover that,' I said. The idea of passing through the bedroom of the heart surgeon with the doleful countenance on a daily basis did not appeal to me much. This room was far better.

'OK,' said Santiago. 'I'll need payment up front, though.'

I was prepared for that and handed over a month's rent in advance, which I had withdrawn from my bank account that day.

'And this is to cover from now, even though you can't move in for two weeks,' he went on, counting it.

'Yes, I realise that. I'll stay where I am for two weeks and then come over.'

It was straining my finances to do this but I was very interested in securing the bedroom at the back of the flat. So we decided on dates and I said I would ring again just before I arrived and Santiago handed me a receipt for my deposit.

I noticed that his name was Santiago Jurado Cobo – two surnames, one maternal and one paternal, which was the norm in the Spanish-speaking world.

'Oh,' I said, just to appear interested. 'That's an unusual name. Whereabouts in Spain did your family originate from?'

He looked at and again the lips pursed and a frown appeared.

'I am not Spanish,' he snapped. 'I'm Indian – pure Indian.'

I had apparently insulted him without realising. As I found out Santiago had some very strong views on the Spaniards and the exploitation of South America. It was the one thing that could be guaranteed to ruffle his gentle manner.

Anxious not to offend any further, and mindful of the need to return to work, I said I would be going.

'OK,' said Santiago, his annoyance having immediately abated. 'Just say goodbye to Gutierrez. He'd like that.'

We went back to the living room but Gutierrez wasn't there.

'He's in his bedroom, I should think,' said Santiago.

I could not think where else he would have gone in his pyjamas and slippers and indeed, he was lying propped up on the bed, staring into the middle distance.

'Nice to meet you,' I told him, 'and I'll see you soon.'

He looked at me through the thick black framed lenses.

'I will look forward to it, young man.'

I decided to venture one last comment.

'You're resting, I suppose, before a big operation. You need to be very alert at the hospital.'

He stared at me and there was another momentary pause when the comment did not seem to register, and then he smiled and sighed and told me,

'Oh, no. I don't do heart surgery any more. I got bored with it. Always the same thing every day.'

I didn't have an answer for this. I didn't realise that being a prominent heart surgeon equated to drudgery, so I just smiled and followed Santiago out of the bedroom. I felt quite relieved that I would be the other end of the apartment from this medical anomaly, wracked as he was with boredom and worn down by the tedium of his profession.

When I got back to the Institute and told Elena all about it she just laughed – particularly about Dr Gutierrez.

'Don't let him near you with a knife,' she giggled. 'He's probably out of practice.'

Hilary and Chris both thought it sounded a bit odd, but probably all right.

Hilary was preoccupied, anyway. She had had another encounter with her dipsomaniac American neighbours, Waldo and Martha. Despite clear written instructions from Hilary and Nigel they had somehow failed to pay their electricity bill and had knocked on Hilary's door late the previous evening to say that they had been sitting in the dark for hours.

'They both reeked of booze, though,' said Hilary to those

of us assembled by Elena's reception desk. 'I think they'd been sitting there in total darkness knocking back Bacardi and Coke. I was going to give them a couple of candles but Nigel said no in case they set the building on fire.'

'So what did you do?' I asked.

'We just took them back over to their apartment and Nigel said he would phone the electricity people this morning. He made Walt give him a bundle of cash and I think he's going to try and pay it for them,' she shook her head, 'but it's just getting worse. Apparently they've got a car. We didn't know that, and now Walt's saying that they need to go to the American embassy or something to get some papers signed in order to be able to go home. I think he's going to drive there.'

'Probably won't be worse than most of the other drivers on the road,' was Chris's comment.

Sabin, who was sitting in the reception area, as he did on many evenings, expressed an opinion that being a bit squiffy did not always mean you were a bad driver.

'Squiffy? They're not squiffy. They're pissed as farts,' Hilary retorted, in an uncharacteristically brutal manner.

When Madeleine appeared from her classroom after one of her deeply intellectual exchanges with the professor from Moncloa University, she was genuinely pleased that I had at last found a flat to share, despite the eccentricity of my flatmates.

'It's much better, and it'll all be fine. When I first got to Cordoba a couple of years ago,' she announced, 'I shared a flat for a while with a one-legged Moroccan girl who danced flamenco for the tourists near the Mezquita. She was a bit odd, but it all worked out OK.'

There was no real possibility of topping that in the 'Weird-flatmates-that-I-have-shared-with' storytelling session that could have ensued, so we all exchanged a look and Elena reached under the desk to press the bell that she rang to announce the beginning and end of classes. We all trooped back to our classrooms to continue the education of the population of Madrid.

XII

With the prospect of moving home and an improvement in the weather – which was particularly welcome, as the wall heater in my room at the Rincón seemed to be gradually expiring – time seemed to pass more quickly. I would soon be moving into the flat with Santiago and Dr Gutierrez, plus whoever they found to occupy the front bedroom that I had managed to avoid.

However, just a few days before I was due to join them in Calle de Canillas, Madeleine came up to me and asked what I was doing over the weekend. It was extended to three days due to a public holiday.

'I'm moving into the flat,' I told her.

'Oh. I'd forgotten. Well, can you put it off for a couple of days – say until one of the days when you've got no lessons until four o'clock? It's just that we're going to go down to Enrique's flat in Gandia tomorrow for the weekend, and it's the *Fallas*, so I wondered if you'd like to come. It'll be a bit of an adventure. We're going to hitch-hike down the N3.'

This was a lot of information, a considerable part of which I didn't understand. What were the *Fallas*? Where was Gandia? Was Enrique the same one that I had met in the Tankstelle who, despite the gravitas his voice lent him, did not look old enough to me to own a flat anywhere? And, finally, was it really safe to hitch-hike in Spain?

Madeleine explained it to me. It *was* Enrique from the Tankstelle. His family owned an apartment in the resort of

Gandia, a town on the Mediterranean coast about thirty miles south of Valencia. In that region the feast of San José, which was 19 March (and the cause of the public holiday), was celebrated with great fervour and numerous fiestas, culminating in processions of large papier mâché statues full of fireworks – which were then ignited in a spectacular evening display. This light-hearted Mediterranean version of Guy Fawkes Night was known as *Las Fallas*, and was renowned throughout Spain. It would be a great shame to miss the opportunity to see it, particularly with free lodging available in a seaside apartment.

Hitch-hiking aside, which I was still not too sure about, it did sound like a bit of an adventure, so I agreed immediately. I rang Santiago, who was quite happy for me to come a few days later because I had already paid, and I also negotiated with Carmen/Conchita to keep my things at the Rincón for a day or two more. I was probably her longest remaining resident by that time, anyway, so we were quite well-acquainted, and when I explained what I was doing she actively encouraged me.

'Ah, the sea, the fireworks, the paella...' she sighed wistfully. 'You must go – but,' she looked at me sternly, 'be careful of the girls. They are very beautiful – but,' and she wagged her finger in warning, 'do not touch.'

With all this firmly in mind I told Madeleine that everything was arranged.

Hilary and Chris were also consulted, and it also seemed to them to be a great thing to do. I was expecting some well-meaning advice about the perils of hitching rides in Spain but they seemed to be slightly envious, if anything, which I took as a good sign.

As with all things organised by the Spanish, particularly young men under the age of about thirty, there was a fluidity to the arrangements that was at odds with my Anglo-Saxon need for detail and precision. It was not finally decided who was going or where we were meeting until the very last moment on the Friday (which was taken as a public holiday as part of the San José celebrations).

Madeleine met me at lunchtime – this much we *had* arranged – and told me to go back to the Rincón and pack a bag. I was to be outside the Retiro metro station at 4 p.m. The Avenida del Mediterráneo and the start of the N3 road to Valencia were nearby and it would be convenient to begin our hitch-hiking attempts there. Manolo was definitely going and she thought that José Carlos would be as well. Enrique was already in Gandia and greatly looking forward to our arrival.

I could recall what José Carlos looked like from our encounter at the Tankstelle but he had left with Enrique's brother fairly soon after I had arrived, so I had a memory only of dark, swept-back hair, a cheeky grin and a large pair of black-rimmed glasses. That was all. If Madeleine and Manolo were going together then I would inevitably be teamed up with José Carlos. I hoped that we would get on well.

We met at the Retiro metro station as agreed – though José Carlos was, inevitably, late. Timekeeping was something that only applied to official activities in the Spanish consciousness and I had already begun to appreciate that, in their leisure time, the accent was on spontaneity and not on planning.

After a quick beer in a little bar we trooped down to a convenient place to stand, by some waste ground, where the traffic gathered and the N3 to Valencia started. Manolo and Madeleine walked some distance further down from José and me. We had agreed that whoever got the first offer of a lift would try to negotiate to get the others on board as well, but if we had to split up and travel independently then that is what we would do. I was sure that Manolo and Madeleine, obviously travelling as a couple, would appeal more to motorists than two young men.

I had exchanged a quick *Hola* and a handshake with José Carlos when we met, but after that we had not really spoken other than for him to tell me where to stand and the correct angle to hold out my thumb at. He was obviously about my age and seemed friendly, but I did not know what to talk about. The atmosphere was very different to that in the Tankstelle when I had first met him, and anyway the task of securing a lift kept us occupied.

After about ten minutes of standing there, traffic roaring past, and with no success, Madeleine and Manolo walked back to us.

'We're going to buy some tobacco,' said Madeleine. All three of them smoked. I was the only one who did not.

'Good idea,' agreed José, and we went back to the bar where we had had the beer.

'Just time for another one,' said Manolo, indicating the beer tap.

'Good idea,' said José again, and that was it for about half an hour. We all had a beer, and then José and Manolo had another, and they all smoked cigarettes. The lack of a sense of urgency was palpable. Manolo and José rattled off a string of jokes and inconsequential banter, Madeleine put her hand on Manolo's chubby thigh and looked adoringly at him, and I glanced anxiously out of the window at the traffic, imagining one after another of our potential lifts hurtling past.

Eventually we went back again for another fruitless wait by the side of the road until Madeleine and Manolo walked back up to us again and announced a change of plan.

'This is not working,' said Manolo, stating the obvious.

'We're going to get the train,' said Madeleine. 'There's one in about an hour.'

'Good idea,' I said, before José could get in a response.

No one had even slowed down during the previous twenty minutes, and I was beginning to feel light-headed as my lungs took in tobacco fumes mixed with carbon monoxide.

'Yes,' said José, looking at me, faintly amused. 'That's a good idea.'

So we went to Atocha station, bought tickets and got the night train to Valencia.

Although one of the nearest spots on the Mediterranean to Madrid, at a distance of about 220 miles, the train journey to Valencia still lasted all night. As with the older trains going up to the French border through Ávila, the original railway line to Valencia also left Madrid initially going only vaguely in the right direction. It made its way across the plain known as La Mancha in a more southerly direction than the one in which Valencia lay, and very gradually made its way back around in a long loop.

There was, as for the journey to and from France, a more direct high-speed Talgo route in place, but this was more expensive. And anyway it did not run at eight in the evening, which was the time at which we got to Atocha station after making another stop for supplies: four bottles of red wine, some beers, some bread and sausage and more cigarettes.

As a result of the less than direct route and the speed of the train, which seemed to average only slightly faster than walking pace, the journey took about ten hours. We had no couchettes, just a compartment of six seats … but that did not matter, as José Carlos and Manolo had no intention of sleeping anyway. My northern European preoccupation with getting a good night's rest – or even a bad one – did not tally with the spontaneity of living for the moment, which José Carlos and Manolo displayed as true Spaniards.

We ate the sausage and bread and drank a bottle of wine and some beers and they talked and laughed and joked with each other and the inhabitants of two of the other compartments all night long. I could not always follow the banter and the punchlines of the jokes, as they spoke at such speed, so I stood, or sat, on the sidelines with Madeleine in awe of their capacity to smoke, drink and enjoy themselves and not to think of the consequences. There was, I learnt from Madeleine, a specific verb in Spanish for doing this: *trasnochar* – to stay up through the night.

I was feeling a little ragged at the edges as we drew into Valencia the following morning with the sun just coming up. Manolo and José seemed unaffected by the lack of sleep demanded by *trasnochando*, however, and the first thing that they suggested that we do was to find some breakfast.

José was still carrying two unopened bottles of wine, which he referred to as '*mis hijos*' – my children – and when we sat down in a cafe he promptly opened one of them and demanded a glass. I was most surprised when one was actually produced by the barman for him. So José settled down to his wine, Manolo ordered a beer and Madeleine and I both had milky coffees. I was quite hungry but nobody mentioned anything to eat, so I decided to let my stomach rumble on.

The general mood of levity continued throughout the morning as we made our way to the bus station to get the bus down to Gandia. It was, in contrast to the train journey, only a short ride of about forty minutes or so to the town, and I expected to see the Mediterranean immediately. However, Gandia itself was an old town, dating back many hundreds of years. It was about three miles inland, and the much more recent beach development where Enrique's parents had their flat was either a long walk or a short taxi ride away.

After another stop for refreshment, me still on coffee, Madeleine graduating to join Manolo in a beer and José finishing off the last of his 'children', we got into an ancient taxi and headed out towards the beach.

I gazed sleepily out of the taxi window at the lush landscape as we passed through the area known as *La Huerta* full of fruit trees and other market garden staples, before emerging at the small fishing port. To the left of us the road followed the line of the beach with modern blocks of flats either completed or nearing completion stretching away for a mile or so. (I don't think Gandia ever became a huge holiday destination with non-Spaniards, but it was nevertheless starting to look like many of its more well-known neighbours.)

Ahead was the sea, silver-grey and sparkling in the warm sunshine. It was still only late March but the temperature was in the mid twenties and there was a blue and cloudless sky. I inhaled deeply and felt a frisson of anticipation for something that I could not quite name. Here I was with friends, still a bit apprehensive about their behaviour and habits and unable to keep up with their language or iron digestion, but I was by the Med with the rest of the weekend to look forward to and, if José and Manolo did not flag, we would have a riotous time.

Inevitably we went to a bar. I now ventured to have a beer as it was around lunchtime but I also felt that I would pass out if I didn't have something to eat. The others joined me in a *bocadillo*, although José Carlos was too busy laughing to eat much of it. Manolo made a phone call in the bar and within about fifteen minutes or so Enrique appeared.

If anything he looked more delicate than he had in the Tankstelle when I had first met him and sampled the big beers. But again the fragility of his physical appearance was balanced by the deep, resonant voice as he embraced Madeleine and clapped the rest of us on the back.

'Hello, Mike, *macho*,' he boomed. 'Welcome to Gandia. It's good to have you here.'

'Thanks Enrique, *macho*,' I replied, emboldened to use the word '*macho*', which all self-respecting young Spanish males seemed to use when addressing each other. 'We had a long journey, but it was worth it.'

'Of course it was,' he said. 'I want you to meet Maica as well.' He looked around and, as if at a prearranged signal a strikingly beautiful young woman came into the bar. Enrique put a proprietorial arm around her and shepherded her across to us. It was obvious from the way that she greeted him that she knew José Carlos already.

'This is Maica,' said Enrique, proudly. 'The loveliest girl in Gandia.'

We all smiled in recognition of this fact, and Maica blushed. It was true that she was very good-looking. She had black, lustrous hair that hung down to her shoulders, and her features were clean and well-defined. She was wearing bright red lipstick that contrasted perfectly with her skin tone and dark eyes. We exchanged a quick kiss on both cheeks, and she did the same with Madeleine and Manolo.

As always on this trip, I was not really a party to the discussions about what to do next. There was animated talk between the three of them – José Carlos, Enrique and Manolo, (women had a noticeably lower level of involvement in such business, which Madeleine seemed to accept) – and the upshot was that we would go back to the apartment for a while to have a rest. José Carlos and Manolo in particular had been firing on all cylinders for about twenty-four hours with very little rest, and even they were now flagging. I was very glad of the suggestion.

As we walked along the seafront Enrique detached himself from Maica and trotted along beside me. He walked like a nervous racehorse – small, rapid steps with a suggestion that he would break into a run at any moment.

'Isn't she beautiful?' he said, nodding towards Maica.

'Oh, yes, she certainly is,' I agreed, quite truthfully.

'We don't get much opportunity to be together, with me

in Madrid and her with her parents here. They're very careful about what she does, but we have some time today.'

'Good,' I said, unclear as to what to say next. I did not know him well, was seriously lacking in experience with girls, and so felt myself to be totally out of my depth in offering any advice or opinion. 'Err, is the apartment near here?' I simply wanted something to say.

'Yes, not far,' he replied. 'But we must be very careful when we get there.'

'Why?' I looked suitably puzzled.

'My mother doesn't know that I am using it. She thinks I'm down here staying with friends, but I had another key made so that I can use the apartment whenever I come down. It's nice to be alone with Maica,' he added by way of explanation.

Inexperienced, and with nothing to offer by way of advice, I could nevertheless immediately appreciate the benefits of being alone with Maica.

'But we have to be careful,' he repeated. 'There's an old woman in the apartment beneath who would tell my mother if she knew we were there. I call her *La Cicuta*.'

'So we have to be quiet when we're there,' I said.

'Exactly,' he nodded. 'We don't want *La Cicuta* to know.'

Ever anxious to broaden my vocabulary, I asked what '*La Cicuta*' was. Madeleine, who had been within earshot and who had obviously been apprised of the need for discretion in the apartment, told me.

'It's hemlock,' she said. 'It's very poisonous. It's what killed Socrates, you know.'

I nodded sagely as Madeleine again flexed her intellect. It would have been so good to have Hilary or Chris there to exchange a knowing glance with. They may have known about hemlock, but would they have known about Socrates?

Enrique's apartment was close to the sea, just one street back, and in a building which was obviously almost new. We tiptoed up the stairs, José and Manolo making a supreme effort to keep quiet, all exchanging grins and putting our fingers to our lips – except Enrique, who looked very serious and frowned at José. He certainly did not want to jeopardise his love nest, and I did not blame him. Anyway, it had already dawned on me that having a pal with an apartment near the seafront in a Mediterranean resort was a friendship to be cultivated. I did not want him to be discovered either.

The apartment was small and unremarkable. We sat, or rather slumped, in the main living room on the available chairs and sofa, and even José and Manolo gradually subsided into silence. Enrique and Maica went into one of the bedrooms, primarily, I suspected, for a snooze – although, given the ban on any untoward sounds that could give us away to the loathsome *La Cicuta*, any activity, including sleeping, had to be undertaken in silence. I remembered wondering, as I dozed, if Manolo snored when asleep. It would be terrible if the twitching antennae of *La Cicuta* caught us out when we were asleep after all the trouble we had taken to be quiet when awake.

José and Manolo slept soundly and with the same spontaneity that they exhibited when awake (and Manolo did not snore). Madeleine curled up next to him and was also asleep in an instant. I took longer, but eventually the doze deepened and I fell into a dreamless sleep.

When I awoke it was getting dark. It took me a few seconds to recollect where I was. I could see in the half-light the others still asleep as before. None of them had stirred, but there was a light coming from the small kitchen. It would have been too difficult if *La Cicuta* could see as well as she could hear but I presumed that, from her apartment beneath, the light would not be visible.

I got up and went into the kitchen. Enrique was standing by the fridge, drinking from a bottle of milk.

'My ulcer,' he explained, on seeing my obvious bafflement. Milk was not big on the list of favourite tipples for a Spanish *macho*. 'It helps to soothe my stomach so that I can drink more in the evening. Do you want some?'

I shook my head.

'No, thanks,' I said. 'I'm not a big milk drinker.' This was only partially true but I wanted to retain my *macho* dignity in front of him – and I was sure that a *macho* only ever drank milk for medicinal purposes, and then only reluctantly. It was quite a shock that someone not much older than me should be suffering from something that I associated with old age. My grandfather had had an ulcer, but he had been ancient.

Still, I reflected, there was something slightly romantic about Enrique, sick with love and with a physical ailment brought on by a fast, hard life such as I had never experienced. He seemed to be a Spanish cross, somewhere between Shelley and Scott Fitzgerald. I definitely admired him.

The others were stirring in the living room and it was decided, again with no input from me, that we would go out and get something to eat. This was a relief as, apart from the bread and sausage on the night train and the lunchtime *bocadillo*, I had eaten nothing for twenty-four hours. Manolo, on his beer diet, and José with his 'children' in bottles around him seemed to thrive, but I was finding it hard going. Perhaps it was all the cigarettes they smoked that suppressed their appetite.

When I mentioned it to Madeleine she simply gave a laugh, tossed back her head and said,

'Well, that's the Spanish for you. They're a race apart. That's what I love about them. They know how to have fun.'

We descended the stairs as silently as we had come up them and then, relieved to have passed through the danger area, bounced out into the street. It was almost dark now. The temperature was warm and inviting, and gave the air a velvety feel. As we turned the corner on to the seafront the apartment blocks led away into the purple-tinted distance, each one now starting to glow as thousands of light switches were flicked on. Bars and restaurants occupied the ground floors of many of them, with seating areas spilling out on to the pavement where people were beginning to walk up and down, young and old, many arm in arm. I felt light-headed at the sight of it, a twinkling, magical penumbra that spoke of excitement to come.

Very soon we were seated outside one of the bars. I gazed around silently, drinking it all in.

'Do you like it here, Mike?' asked Enrique.

'Oh, yes. Very much,' I replied. 'It's a great place. We don't have anywhere near the sea like this in England.'

'It's not like Clacton, is it?' commented Madeleine, and I giggled.

'No. Nor Hunstanton, either.'

At that moment two more girls joined us. This was obviously prearranged and there was much kissing of cheeks and hearty greetings. They were called Rosa and Teresa and both were around twenty or so, with the same dark looks as Maica. They were very smartly dressed, one in long flared trousers and a light-coloured blouse and the other in a cheesecloth shirt and pleated skirt. José seemed to know them both, but again Madeleine, Manolo and I were introduced for the first time.

We ordered beers. The conversation increased in intensity and the laughter became quite raucous. I soon drank my beer, so another was ordered for me. I began to feel more relaxed as the alcohol entered my bloodstream. In fact the effect was immediately noticeable. The soft night air, the lights along the front and the endearing nature of my companions all played their part as well and I began to talk. In three minutes I had said more than in the previous twenty-four hours. It was all rubbish but everyone thought it very amusing rubbish as I mangled the Spanish language and threw in a few slang terms that I had learnt.

'I like it here,' I told them.

'Good,' said Enrique. 'So do I,' and he squeezed Maica's hand. 'It's the best place in the world.'

'Yes, I could be happy here, I think,' I said. 'In English we say I'm as happy as a pig in shit.' The translation of this into Spanish had them hooting with laughter.

'*Macho*,' said José clapping me on the back. 'I did not know you could talk so much. Not the quiet little Englishman any more.'

'Well, I'm on holiday. I've been working very hard with Martin and Jane.'

They looked blank, just as I had intended they should.

'Don't you know Martin and Jane?' I asked incredulously. 'They're about this big,' and I indicated a length of about two inches, which was the size of the stick figures in the English textbook, with my thumb and forefinger. 'Perhaps they're under the chair.' I turned sideways and pretended to inspect the underside of the chair.

There was more laughter and comments about this surprisingly eloquent side to their guest and I began to feel under some pressure to continue to perform.

'We'll have to get you a girlfriend, Mike,' suggested José. 'What sort of girls do you like?'

'Well, I like all girls,' I responded, and I used the term *chica* for girl. I looked around and, by chance, there were two girls at that moment strolling past arm in arm. One of them had a very elegant linen jacket slung around her shoulders. The word for jacket immediately jumped into my mind – it was *chaqueta* – and in a second I associated it with the diminutive for *chica* meaning a young, and attractive, girl – a *chiquita*.

'I really want to go out with a well-dressed girl – a *chiquita en una chaqueta*.' I delivered the line as gleefully as I could, with a slight wobble of the head to give maximum effect to the ridiculous alliteration.

It had the desired effect. Both José and Manolo were taking a gulp of beer at that moment and both choked on the mouthful as they were forced to try to swallow and laugh at the same time.

'He's really good,' Manolo managed to say. 'That's a great way of putting the words together. I'd never have thought of that.'

José was chortling as well.

'*Macho*, I thought you were really serious and dull when we were coming down here,' he said, clapping me on the back. 'But you make better jokes than me.'

I was extremely pleased with this. José's effortless facility to enjoy himself and live entirely in the present was something I knew I could never achieve, but to be congratulated by him like this filled me with a feeling of intoxicated pride. The crowds passing by, the smells of seafood starting to fry in the adjoining restaurant, the sensuous clinging of the night air – everything fuelled my desire to continue the communal good time that we were having.

'Well, Mike – *macho* – you can really speak Spanish better than a native,' said Enrique, smiling in an almost benevolent fashion. He did not give quite such full rein to his amusement as did José and Manolo. It was as if he needed to retain a certain dignity, which they saw no need to do. He was the doting boyfriend, the one whose feelings had obviously taken him to a different plane – one where he could observe our silly jokes and chatter with some detachment.

'Where did you learn to speak Spanish so well?' asked Rosa.

'Yes. You're very good at Spanish,' Teresa piped up.

'He's going to university in Oxford,' Madeleine told them. 'It's one of the best.'

'Oh,' was accompanied by a look of admiration on Rosa and Teresa's faces. 'You must not go there. You must stay in Spain, Mike,' Rosa continued. 'In fact you must live in Gandia.'

'Oh, I'd like that,' I said. 'I could live in Enrique's apartment. That would give *La Cicuta* something to talk about.'

'*Macho*, you could stay in the spare bedroom,' José encouraged me.

'Then if it got cold I could have Enrique to keep me warm,' I said, an image forming in my mind. 'He's so hairy it would be like going to bed with a rug.'

I used the word *alfombrita*, meaning a little rug or mat. I was quite pleased with it as it was a fairly unusual word, implying a wide knowledge of vocabulary in the user.

The effect was all I could have hoped for. José doubled up with laughter and almost fell off his chair. Rosa and Teresa giggled like a couple of schoolgirls – which they probably were – and Manolo almost squeaked as he took off his glasses to wipe the tears from his eyes. Madeleine looked at me unbelievingly and Enrique and Maica were forced to join in, although I'm not sure how genuine their enjoyment of the image of Enrique as a small scrap of shagpile really was.

'A little rug,' hooted José. 'That's it from now on,' he told Enrique. 'I'll always call you *Alfombrita* – Little Rug. Wait until I tell your brother and all the guys at the Tankstelle,' and he started laughing again.

Enrique's gravitas seemed somewhat deflated by my comparing him to a floor covering, but he took it in good heart. He was probably counting on José's short-term memory not being up to the job of remembering to tell everyone that he had acquired a new nickname.

We ordered more drinks, and they soon arrived. The

normal Spanish toast as far as I knew was *Salud, suerte y amor* – Health, good luck and love. However, with my brain racing and in an attempt to maintain my popularity at the centre of our little circle I now grabbed my glass, raised it in the air and said,

'As we say in England ... Bottoms up.' However, rather than translating it in a way that reflected the image of the bottom of the glass pointing upwards as its contents were drunk, I used the phrase *Culos arriba*. This had nothing to do with the bottom of a glass but meant, quite precisely, 'Arses in the air', or 'Stick your bottom up'. The idea that there was a toast in Great Britain that encouraged everyone to point their backsides uppermost as they drank created a further furore at the table.

'He's gone into orbit,' spluttered Manolo, banging the table with his palm as he squeaked and giggled.

'You can't tell them that,' Madeleine laughed. 'They'll all be arrested.'

'*Macho*, you should have your own programme on TV,' insisted José Carlos, taking off his glasses to wipe his eyes. 'Is that what you do when you drink beer in England?'

For the rest of the evening – and beyond – that was the toast as every round of drinks arrived. Perhaps more than the Little Rug episode, I bequeathed to certain of the youth of Gandia an immortal phrase to be employed – selectively, of course – on an evening out with friends that summoned up the image of those strange Anglo-Saxons indulging in the perverse ritual of pointing their bottoms in the air as they quaffed their foaming tankards of ale. For me it characterised the harmless, carefree atmosphere that was made all the more magical that evening by the inexact but amusing imagery and language that I had dredged up.

It was, nevertheless, a little difficult to sustain my success after that. There was a meal in a restaurant somewhere and I managed to continue to amuse and surprise with my observations and language-mangling metaphors, but as the evening progressed I began to run out of steam. It was hard work being the centre of attention, so I quietened down and ceded centre stage again to José and Manolo.

Rosa and Teresa left quite early. They had indulged in a little flirting with José, but I was far too nervous and unsure of myself to try to get much better acquainted with them. Anyway, I was busy acting the fool. They were well-turned-out, as were all Spanish girls, but the message was still very much: 'You may look but do not touch.' The heady abandon of the sixties that had infused Western youth had made far less impact in the relatively isolated and parochial society of Spain, as far as I could make out.

As further proof of this Maica was put into a taxi for home by Enrique as we tottered back to the apartment. She was definitely not staying the night. I began to understand at least some of the reason why Madeleine could be such an attractive girlfriend to a Spanish boy. Being frustrated in your ambition to be with your girlfriend on such a warm, romantic evening must have been hard.

However, Enrique seemed to be bearing it well. Before our silent ascent of the staircase there was much whispering between him and José. With Maica gone, Enrique adopted a more boyish demeanour. The voice was still resonating at its bass pitch but he was more attuned to the humour and language of the other two. They both looked at me, amusement in their faces, as the sleeping arrangements were confirmed. José would share a room with Enrique (further muted giggling and references to hairy rugs) while Madeleine and Manolo would sleep on the convertible sofa in the living room. I was to have the spare bedroom.

I looked at José and Enrique and the conspiratorial glance that they exchanged as I went into the bedroom. The door had a key in the lock so I turned it and it gave a satisfying click. Two minutes later, as I lay down with the room gently swaying around me, I heard the door handle quietly move and then a grunt and giggle of resignation as they realised that I had frustrated their little scheme, whatever it was.

Smiling at the memory of the evening, I went straight to sleep.

XIII

We slept until mid morning the next day and then gradually roused ourselves. It was again warm and sunny, so it was decided that we would go down to the beach. I had swum in the Mediterranean once before off Sorrento in Italy but it had been murky and uninviting there – we had stuck to the hotel swimming pool most of the time. Here the sea was shimmering blue and silver and I wanted to take a dip.

A pair of trunks for me appeared from somewhere and we proceeded silently downstairs and then to the beach.

'Is Maica coming today?' I asked Enrique.

'She has to go to Mass with her mother and father,' Enrique grunted in reply. He obviously was not in favour of this but I felt a pang of conscience as I suddenly thought of the assembled throng at Our Lady and St Peter in March. Mum would be there with lots of familiar faces. They seemed a long, long way away now.

We stayed on the beach for a couple of hours. I got my dip in the Mediterranean, although it was a very quick one. The Med was not warm in March. I also got sunburnt shoulders, which I was strangely proud of. It was further evidence of how far I was from my former life – spending Sunday on a sunny, sandy beach with friends was more exciting than anything I'd done before and offered tantalising possibilities, as yet not fully formed, about what my life could be like in future.

I was back to my quieter self now, but I felt more confident with them and the conversation was easier and more natural. I was still looking for opportunities to impress, but the pressure to do so had subsided. There were one or two references to Enrique's new name and the *chiquita en una chaqueta*, but the tone was less frantic.

Bursts of hilarity continued such as when José jumped on to Enrique and then rolled them both on to a large beach ball, shouting,

'Ay, Enrique, look at the egg you've made me lay.' Manolo kept up a stream of banter with José as Madeleine looked on and I walked up and down the beach a couple of times trying to look as attractive and cool as possible.

Eventually they came up with a plan for the day and we headed off to catch the bus into Valencia to eat some paella and see the *Fallas* processions.

It was two o'clock, early for lunch in Spain, when we got to Valencia. We heard firecrackers going off in the distance. Apparently they were let off every day at two o'clock in front of the town hall for the duration of the fiesta.

Enrique took us to a small restaurant with a big glass window in a side street and ordered the paella for eight of us. I wasn't sure how Enrique had arrived at the number of diners but Madeleine told me that Maica was coming along as well as two other friends. We were told that the paella would be ready in about two hours.

We went, inevitably, to a bar to while away the time until lunch. I was torn two ways about what I wanted to do. It was the *Fallas*, a great festival, and the streets were already full of people milling about and promenading as they waited for the processions to start. I also knew that this was the third city of Spain after Madrid and Barcelona, so there must anyway have been a lot to see. When we had arrived the morning before I had had a glimpse of the Plaza del Ayuntamiento – the Town Hall Square – and the huge bullring, but that was all. However, another part of me did not want to miss the atmosphere and excitement that Manolo and José and everyone else managed to generate when we were all together.

My mind was made up for me when Maica arrived with another couple, who were introduced as José Antonio and Maite. They were in their early twenties and they were very much a couple, quieter than the others, talking mainly to each other and – something I had not seen before very much – holding hands, even when sitting down.

I was intrigued by the names of the girls – Maica and Maite. They were not in the collection of names that I had ever come across for Spanish girls. I was accustomed now to girls called Nieves (Snows) and Inma, short for Inmaculada (Immaculate) – one was named after the Virgin of the Snows and the other the Immaculate Conception – but Maica and Maite were new. Madeleine, as ever, explained that Maica was short for Maria Carmen and Maite for Maria Teresa. All very simple, and less overtly entangled with Spain's Catholic faith.

Another lazy hour of drink and chatter followed. I paced my beer consumption more carefully than the night before and, as a consequence, had less to say.. I was content to soak up the atmosphere and work hard on understanding every comment, wordplay and joke that was circulating around the table.

We eventually walked back round to the restaurant and a few minutes after we sat down an enormous, dustbin lid of a plate was set down in front of us. It was a beautiful sight. The rice was a delicate shade of creamy yellow and the seafood, chicken and other pieces of meat were artfully arranged across it. We ate with relish – it was the first proper meal that I had had for about three days – and washed it all down with carafes of rough red wine which I, in concert with the girls – Madeleine apart – mixed with *gaseosa*, a Spanish version of lemonade. The conversation again became more noisy and boisterous, approaching the levels of the previous evening, and José felt it absolutely necessary to tell the new José and Maite how I had christened Enrique 'Little Rug'. There were other references to a *chiquita en una chaqueta*, which I was really quite pleased about, and every so often someone raised a glass and shouted '*Culos arriba.*'

Eventually it was time to go. We went outside as it began to get dark. The plan was that we would go along to watch the *Fallas* processions that were starting, so we turned into one of the main streets where people were gathering two or three deep and craned our necks over the top of their heads as the sound of a band drifted down the street towards us. Around a corner came the band – men and boys in white shirts and trousers with brightly coloured waistcoats playing assorted brass and percussion instruments in a strange medley that was not quite off-key but still far from the perfect tones that I would associate with a brass band. It looked quite familiar but sounded faintly exotic, giving a hint of Spain's mixed folklore heritage with the presence of the gypsy and the Moor still evident on these shores.

Behind them came the *ninots*. These were huge papier mâché figures – grotesque three-dimensional cartoon-like representations of various characters, which were held proudly aloft by the groups of men who had spent many hours fashioning them. I did not recognise who they were supposed to be.

Manolo pointed out one or two that were prominent local figures – apparently it was acceptable to lampoon the politicians in this way, although not Franco himself. In fact, I learnt later, the range of characters represented could be very wide – the living and the dead, and indeed the mythical as well. This became obvious when there was a roar as a figure wearing what appeared to be chain mail and a giant sword was paraded around. This was El Cid – who vanquished the Moors in the twelfth century from this part of Spain and reached mythic status as a result.

The parade dwindled and the crowds began to move. There were going to be more of them, I was told, and eventually the papier mâché figures would be burnt in a great celebratory bonfire with fireworks – all except for one, which was voted the best and kept in the museum dedicated to the *Fallas*. But we couldn't stay for that. We had to catch the bus back to Gandia or risk being stranded for the night.

It struck me as eminent good sense to ensure that we got to the bus station on time, but I later reflected on how great a change in the normal, spontaneous and unplanned activity the existence of a simple bus timetable had brought about in my companions.

*

The journey back was uneventful and we crept into the apartment, still anxious to stay under *La Cicuta*'s radar. We were all very quiet now, however. Even José and Manolo were subdued and Enrique was almost surly on account of Maica's need to go home as soon as we arrived back at the bus station in Gandia. She left with the other José and Maite, who were still holding hands. As we were heading back to Madrid the next day he would not be seeing her for a few weeks, so his lack of humour was understandable.

'What exactly is happening tomorrow?' I asked Madeleine. We had another day before returning to work, due to the generous provision of Spanish public holidays, but I now wanted to get back as soon as possible and move into my new flat.

'We're going to catch the coach,' Madeleine explained. 'It's cheaper than the train, and quicker.'

I certainly hoped that this was true. I did not want to sit on a coach for ten hours, although even that was better than another attempt at hitch-hiking.

'When have you arranged to move into your flat?' she asked.

'I thought I'd move on Thursday,' I replied. 'I don't work until four o'clock, plus I've been paying for it for a week already.'

'Well, you'll be near all of us, anyway,' Madeleine reminded me. 'We're just up the road, and José is on the Avenida de América.'

The Avenida de América was a major thoroughfare, bordering on La Prosperidad and no more than ten minutes' walk from Calle de Canillas. I did not imagine, however, that I would be visiting my new friends in their houses.

I had already learnt that Spaniards did not meet friends at home. Social life was lived in the streets – you met people outdoors, or at least in a bar or restaurant. A generally dry, if not always warm, climate in central, southern and eastern Spain meant that plans to be outdoors could be made with some certainty that they could be carried through – although, as I had now experienced, planning in the social sphere was at best very erratic. Still, I would be near the bars and places that they frequented if I needed a break from Santiago and the enigmatic Dr Gutierrez.

So we went to bed early and the next day left Gandia and caught the coach from Valencia back up the N3 towards Madrid.

I sat next to José on the coach – he seemed to prefer my company to that of Enrique, who was still moping about his enforced separation from Maica. There was a brief reference to little rugs and then, after some more pleasantries and brief descriptions of some of the details of our lives, José went to sleep.

I tried to doze, but was prevented from doing so by the strident tones of a young woman sitting with a companion several rows ahead. She had a penetrating, rasping sound to her voice that I had noticed in many Spanish women, predominantly the young, to which the Spanish language with its harsh, flat vowels and explosive consonants seemed to give an extra edge.

I could hear nearly every word and realised that, like many of her female compatriots, she also seemed to be able to talk endlessly about almost nothing. In the years since the end of the civil war, when Franco had established a stranglehold over the entire political and intellectual life of the country, I suppose there was little to talk about anyway. Until a few years previously tourism had been almost non-existent and Spain's sense of isolation intense. *España es diferente*, said the adverts, and yes, partly because of this isolation, it still was.

In the sixth form at school we had briefly looked at one of the most popular novels to be written in Spain during the period after the civil war. It was by a young writer called Carmen Laforet and it described her teenage life and that of her family and it was called *Nada – Nothing* – which neatly captured the emptiness of life in a country that could not talk about its immediate, catastrophic past but also had little contact with the outside world to provide any stimulation.

No wonder, then, that a generation of women, who had traditionally played a subservient role in national life, anyway, should have nothing of any significance to say.

So I dozed fitfully with *La Voz* – The Voice, as I dubbed her – grating on my subconscious until José awoke. He agreed with me that she had a voice that fitted a certain stereotype of Spanish female.

'You will see her when we get off,' he told me. 'She will be very beautifully made-up and have very smart clothes, but up here,' he tapped the side of his head, 'she will have nothing.'

When we got back to Madrid, before we said our goodbyes and went our separate ways, I caught a glimpse of *La Voz*. She still seemed to be talking to her almost silent companion – and José was quite right. She was very pretty and well-groomed. She was wearing a tight-fitting blouse and expensive-looking well-cut flared trousers but her face, as she lit a cigarette and continued to talk, betrayed no emotion or sign of any conscious thought pattern. She seemed to me like a life-size battery-operated mannequin.

XIV

I had so enjoyed my trip to Gandia and the warm, exciting embrace of the Mediterranean that I kept thinking over the next couple of days how I could get myself invited back there. Tuesday and Wednesday passed uneventfully in this way but then, suddenly, all thought of excursions to the coast were driven from my mind. It was time to move into my new home, Calle de Canillas no. 68 (*segundo derecha*).

I bade farewell to Carmen/Conchita and the Rincón. I glanced around my room before I left. It was the third one that I had occupied since early January but was identical in every respect to the other two – except that the second one had two beds instead of just one. I was particularly looking forward to living somewhere that was warm. It was still chilly in the evenings and the wall heaters that featured in every one of the Rincón's rooms not only looked identical but were all equally inadequate to the task of heating.

The one-armed concierge was there when I arrived at Calle de Canillas and greeted me enthusiastically.

'Señor Santiago is expecting you,' he said. 'Welcome to no. 68.' He held out his hand and I shook it gently. I imagined that if I shook too vigorously I might cause him to overbalance, but he seemed to cope.

Santiago was indeed there to open the door after I had lugged my suitcases and rucksack up the two flights of stairs. He seemed to spend a great deal of time in the flat and not very much at the university. Perhaps this was the reason that he had so far taken six years in his engineering studies.

I thought that I heard Dr Gutierrez moving around in his room but I headed straight into the living room and down the corridor on the far side to my little bedroom at the end. I went over to the window and looked out, something I had not bothered to do when I had first put in my bid to occupy it.

Outside there was a small patch of wasteland with a large tree in the middle. It was coming into leaf and was a wonderful, soaring contrast to the urban landscape it was marooned in. Elena had impressed on me the importance of getting a room that looked out on to the street and not into the well that was at the centre of most apartment blocks. Rooms overlooking the central well were inclined to be very noisy and, in summer, very hot. In fact in Calle de Canillas no. 68 it was the living room that had a window with this perspective – the bedrooms were either overlooking the street front and back or, like Dr Gutierrez's, had no windows at all.

I unpacked my belongings and then lay on the bed for a short while, feeling very pleased. I was now living in a proper flat, albeit with a couple of slightly strange co-residents, and could do all the normal things associated with independent living, like cooking and washing my clothes – and life would soon become very exciting, I was sure.

The journey to the Institute took a little longer than before, but was still only twenty minutes or so – and I had the choice of metro with one change or the no. 1 bus, which started its route in Calle de Cartagena, just around the corner, and dropped me in Puerta del Sol, from where it was two minutes to the Institute. In fact, although it was a slightly longer journey, this became my preferred method of transport during the day. Observing the street life of the capital from the wooden seats on the bus was more interesting than the tunnels of the metro.

The domestic chores were, at least initially, something that I looked forward to. I bought some soap powder and washed my clothes in the large china sink in the kitchen and draped them around my room to dry. I also tried my hand at cooking.

I realised almost immediately, however, that I would still need the occasional restaurant trip. Apart from a fried cheese sandwich, sometimes enhanced by putting a fried egg on top, I did not have a very wide repertoire of dishes. Furthermore, in order to melt the rather rubbery cheese slices that I had bought to put in the fried sandwiches I had to increase the heat so much that the bread nearly always burnt and filled the kitchen with smoke.

'I can show you how to cook some things,' Santiago volunteered. 'I have a lot of rice and vegetables and sometimes some meat. It's very easy, and I sometimes cook for Dr Gutierrez.'

This was interesting, as during the first days I don't think I ever saw Gutierrez in the kitchen and I wondered just what he did for food. In fact on the second or third day – it was one of the days when I didn't start until four o'clock – I realised that I hadn't seen him. So I asked Santiago, who was in his room, as usual, where he was.

'Oh, he went to the hospital today,' he told me. 'There's an operation that they want to do and they need to ask him how to do it.'

I was stunned. The laconic Gutierrez was apparently so well-qualified as a surgeon that he gave advice to the doctors at a major hospital in Spain's largest city.

'Oh, he's very clever,' said Santiago, picking up on my evident surprise, 'but he gets very bored, operating. He did one operation and lost interest halfway through, so they had to get someone else to finish it. It caused a bit of a fuss, I think.'

A bit of a fuss … no wonder Dr Gutierrez did not have permanent employment. I would not want a heart surgeon with attention deficit disorder operating on me.

'By the way,' Santiago continued, 'we have a new lodger arriving next week to take the spare room.'

This was the room at the front that I had declined, as it could only be entered via Gutierrez's bedroom.

'He's a Bulgarian, called,' and Santiago picked up a piece of paper with a name written on it, 'Anton Ivanov. He's a scientist on an exchange scheme at the university.'

'Well, that's different,' was my response. So no run-of-the-mill Spaniard then with a nine-to-five or, as this was Spain, eleven-to-eight job. I was sharing with a Bulgarian, a Dominican Republican (if that was the right way of describing a citizen of the Dominican Republic) and an Ecuadorian. The little Fenland town that had encompassed almost all my life until a couple of months before seemed to fade even further away.

Everyone at the Institute (that is to say Elena, Chris and Sabin, Hilary and Madeleine, since they were increasingly my main circle of work friends) was amused to hear about the exotic cast of characters at Calle de Canillas no. 68, but in an increasingly cosmopolitan Madrid that was changing fast it was not thought particularly unusual. After a few days I was perfectly comfortable with living there, and became used to their eccentricities.

However, one evening, a couple of days before Anton the Bulgarian scientist was due to arrive, I came back at about eight o'clock (Nervous José having cancelled his late night class due to illness) and let myself in. Dr Gutierrez was there in his dressing gown and pyjamas. He passed me in the hall as I came in, carrying a cup of coffee. He had evidently made it as far as the kitchen on this occasion.

'Hi,' he said. 'Hard day at work?'

'Yes,' I replied. 'I've been teaching classes since ten this morning.'

He uttered a sigh which sounded like a mixture of disbelief and envy and padded back to his room with his coffee.

The door to Santiago's room was open as well. He was sitting at his desk and lifted his hand in greeting. I waved back and then went through the living room and down the corridor to my bedroom.

As I was earlier than expected, due to Nervous José's indisposition, I spent a few minutes sorting out some washing. Once ready I gathered up the dirty laundry and made for the kitchen with a packet of washing powder.

I entered the kitchen and let out a little involuntary cry. There in front of me, staring at me with the gaze of a maniac and brandishing a large knife, was Santiago. He seemed intent on doing harm. His face was contorted, his eyes were popping, and the knife was waving unsteadily in his hand as he started to take a step towards me like a zombie chef.

I gave a gasp as the air seemed to be pushed forcibly out of my body and my heart pounded against my ribcage. Wild-eyed, he continued to stare straight at me as he shuffled forward. I was instantly terrified. I dropped the dirty clothes and ran through the living room towards Dr Gutierrez's room, hoping desperately that he and Santiago were not part of a ring of desperadoes who lured innocent young foreigners to a grisly doom.

Dr Gutierrez was lying on his bed, as always, sipping the coffee.

'Clemente, Clemente,' I screamed. 'Quick, it's Santiago. He's gone mad with a knife.' I used the word '*loco*', meaning 'crazy'. I really wanted to say 'berserk' but didn't have the vocabulary.

'What?' Gutierrez looked puzzled and slightly annoyed. I

listened for Santiago's footsteps along the hall.

'He's in the kitchen with a knife and he's mad.' I pointed down the corridor. 'Go and see.'

Gutierrez got off the bed and slowly put on his dressing gown.

'Quick, quick,' I urged him. 'He'll kill us both.'

'I'm sure he will not,' Gutierrez reassured me and, with a swish of his dressing gown, went out towards the kitchen. I followed him, several paces behind, wondering if we would encounter Santiago coming at us with the knife.

We went through the living room and Gutierrez entered the kitchen. I stayed in the living room ready to run as soon as I heard any sign of a struggle, but there was no noise and Gutierrez came back out almost immediately.

'It's nothing,' he said. 'Just one of his epileptic fits. Come in.' He ushered me into the kitchen and there was Santiago sitting at the little table, now looking rather dazed, with the knife and a variety of vegetables in front of him, half of which had been cut up.

'He gets them from time to time,' explained Gutierrez. 'But this one must have taken him by surprise.'

Santiago looked up and his face seemed to reassume its normal, gentle mien.

'I am sorry,' he said. 'I normally have some warning and I sit down or lie on the bed until it passes, but occasionally it surprises me.'

'Oh.' I didn't know what to say, again being in territory that was totally new to me. I laughed nervously and said, 'I thought you were going to kill me.'

Neither of them thought this at all funny. Gutierrez rolled his eyes, uttered yet another small sigh and went back to his bedroom.

Santiago said,

'I'm sorry if I upset you,' and went back to chopping his

vegetables.

Feeling rather chastened, I gathered up my dirty clothes and got on with washing them.

That was the only time that I saw Santiago have a fit. He always withdrew to his room if he felt one approaching – they were fairly predictable, as he said. I did not like to broach the subject with him, but Gutierrez told me that this was the reason that his studies were taking him so long and why he did not go out very often. The medication he took was sufficient to alleviate the condition but could not give complete control over it.

Apart from filling the kitchen with smoke as I tried to perfect the fried cheese sandwich, my other early domestic disaster was melting my new yellow underpants as I attempted to iron them. This greatly upset me, as they were the first coloured pair that I had ever had.

Until only a year or two before all men's underwear had been uniformly white. The revolution in young people's dress in the late 1960s had started on the outside and only more recently had it reached the realm of undergarments. Only when Marks and Spencer's underwear had assumed various pastel shades had Mum thought it proper to invest in anything other than white Y-fronts for me, but before leaving for Spain I had persuaded her to buy a pack of three hipster briefs, two in shades of blue and one yellow. As with many items of clothing at the time, they were made primarily of the wonder material: nylon. So when I first ventured to use the iron in the flat and applied maximum heat to them they simply melted into a tacky yellow lump, which obviously ruined them and made rather a mess of the iron.

I learnt two things. One: adjust the temperature of the iron to suit the material. Two: don't bother to iron underwear.

XV

Shortly after the domestic disasters that marked my first week in the flat Anton the Bulgarian scientist arrived. He was short and very stocky with wavy fair hair, cut close to his head. He had a very limited knowledge of Spanish, so conversation with him was slow. His favourite phrase seemed to be '*Por supuesto*' ('Of course'), which was his answer to nearly every question or attempt at conversation.

So a typical exchange with him might be:
Me: 'Do you like the flat, Anton?'
Anton: 'Of course.'
Me: 'And how is the university?'
Anton: 'It is good. Thank you, of course.'
Me: 'Is the work interesting?'
Anton: 'Of course.'
Me (now struggling): 'What do you do there?'
Anton: 'It is science.'
Me: 'So ... very different from Bulgaria?'
Anton: 'Of course.'

It was perhaps unsurprising that after one or two exchanges like that I gave up and only took a very cursory interest in Anton and what he was doing.

My own life continued along the same lines as before. I grew rather more confident in my teaching techniques and spent less time on preparation. I knew the first few chapters of Martin's and Jane's exploits by heart, anyway, and had developed some exercises to take beginners past the dreaded

'Feeding-the-birds-on-the-park-bench' phase.

I could not, however, claim any success with the three nurses. They came diligently for every lesson, I even set them some simple homework – phrases that they could practise together – but it seemed to make no difference. They were quite happy to come along and learn off by heart little snippets which they would repeat to me in the lesson. Unfortunately they had no ability to retain anything. They would say in turn,

'The sun is shining today,' 'Madrid is a beautiful city,' 'I have two brothers and a sister.' (This last sentence was only applicable to Juana, I think.) I was convinced that I had made a breakthrough when Alma told me,

'I have three sisters and one brother,' signifying that something was sinking in and real thought processes were taking place. But no. Next time I started off hopefully, asking them how many brothers and sisters they had. I got three blank stares – one particularly unsettling one from Maria, with her two-directional gaze – and we had to start all over again.

Conchita, the lady from Banco Hispano Americano, was a delight, however. She had travelled widely throughout Spain, so I was genuinely interested in engaging her in conversation about the country. Following her previous revelation about the typical Madrid dinner of two fried eggs and a chop and chips, we started every lesson at seven o'clock, which she attended alone after Rosa had dropped out, with her telling me what she had had for lunch. The Banco Hispano Americano staff restaurant seemed to have a very varied menu and we both learnt many new words in our respective languages for everything, from hors d'oeuvres to desserts.

Dolores, the formidable spinster, was also easy to teach. She started every lesson with the same stern look on her face and I took it as a challenge to get at least a brief smile from her during the course of the hour.

One very interesting thing that she told me was that a friend of hers, a professional artist, wanted to learn English but could not spare the time to attend a class at the Institute. Could I give him private lessons? I answered, emphatically, that I could. This, I knew, was the best way open to me to earn some more money. Frustratingly, he would be out of Madrid now until after Easter, so I would have to wait until then to meet him and discuss the arrangements. I felt very flattered that Dolores had spoken to him about me. My instinct was to give her a hug in thanks - but I managed to suppress it quite easily.

I continued to have occasional after-work drinks with Chris and Sabin and lunches at the Cat Restaurant with Hilary. My trips to the Tibet with Tim and Milan became ever more infrequent, however, and it was during this period that they ceased altogether.

I also had another evening at the Tankstelle, which resulted in a rather drunken agreement to go on an Easter trip to Andalusia with Enrique's older brother, Antonio, who had never been to southern Spain, and another *macho* called Miguel, who was rumoured to own a car, and was therefore very much sought-after as a friend. I was actually hoping for another invitation to Gandia, but as far as I could tell Enrique had exams and had to stay in Madrid. As ever, the exact details of movements and timings were not fleshed out and I was reconciled to having to wait until the last moment before anything was decided.

One Sunday, soon after Anton had moved in, I went out after lunch for a stroll around the Retiro Park, just a couple of metro stops away in the centre of Madrid. It was a bright spring day, and as I came back again from the metro station towards the flat I could feel real strength in the sun on my neck and back. The 'three months of winter' were over and the 'nine months of hell' were obviously beginning.

As I ascended the staircase at no. 68 I could hear some kind of disturbance coming from above. All apartment blocks in Madrid, and throughout Spain, are noisy places at all times of the day and night. Spaniards are sometimes noisy people and the inhabitants of Madrid generally lived their lives amidst a constant hubbub of laughter, traffic noise and short-lived arguments, so I did not at first take much notice of it.

However, as I got nearer, it became obvious that the sound of raised voices and thunderous crashes was coming from our flat. I had a sudden, terrible thought that perhaps Santiago had had another unforeseen fit and run amok with the kitchen knife, but dismissed it almost at once. I knew little about his condition but Madeleine, when I told her about him, had assured me that epileptics did no harm to anyone but themselves.

I arrived at the front door as the noise stopped and everything went ominously quiet. The door was ajar and I pushed at it tentatively. It swung open and, feeling like a character in a television murder mystery, I went in. I could see straight into the living room and there were Santiago and Dr Gutierrez both staring at two small piles of wood and other fragments, which I immediately identified as the remains of two of the chairs that had been placed around the dining table.

'What's happened?' I asked, staring like them at the wreckage, as if it could answer my question.

'It's Anton,' said Santiago. 'He got drunk.'

'He got very drunk,' said Gutierrez emphatically.

'Then he got angry and started smashing the furniture,' Santiago went on.

'Why did he do that?' I asked, looking up.

'I don't know. I think he's been drinking in his room,' said

Santiago. 'I heard him earlier.'

'Yes,' said Gutierrez. 'At first he was singing very quietly and then very loudly and then he started shouting. He brought back lots of bottles with him yesterday,' he added.

'Where's he gone?' I looked around anxiously. Even armed only with a broken chair leg Anton would be a formidable opponent. Although no taller than Santiago he was about twice as broad. I suspected the three of us were barely capable of disarming an eight-year-old with a water pistol let alone an infuriated, blind drunk fifteen-stone Bulgarian with the build of a champion shot-putter.

'He's in the kitchen.' Gutierrez jerked his thumb back over his shoulder to indicate the direction that Anton had taken.

Santiago turned and went towards the door through to the kitchen.

'We'd better see if he is all right,' he said.

Gutierrez and I trotted after him and looked into the kitchen. It was completely quiet and everything was where it should be except that Anton was in the corner slumped on a kitchen chair, his great, broad head resting on his arms, which in turn were resting on the front gas rings of the cooker. He was sobbing gently and muttering to himself in what I took to be Bulgarian. I was further taken aback to see that he was wearing nothing but a pair of voluminous off-white underpants.

We just stood for a second and stared, and he saw us. He raised his head, gave a sniff and managed to blurt out,

'*Lo siento.*' ('I'm sorry'.)

Always one to break an embarrassing silence with an inappropriate question, I asked,

'Are you all right, Anton?'

'*Por supuesto,*' he breathed almost inaudibly, and then his eyes closed and his head fell with an almighty clang back down on to the gas rings.

'We'd better get him back to his room,' suggested Santiago. 'He can sleep it off.'

'He'll be heavy to move,' I said.

'I'll light the gas,' said Gutierrez, moving towards the cooker. 'That'll make him move.'

'No,' Santiago and I shouted in unison. Apart from the obvious immediate damage that this would do I could not help but think that a sober but badly burnt Anton would be likely to wreak terrible revenge on those responsible for his disfigurement. He needed to be treated with respect.

So we heaved and pushed and got him through the living room, around the pile of broken furniture, and back to his bedroom, where we dumped him on the bed and Gutierrez pulled a blanket over him.

Santiago went back to the living room and swept the broken furniture into a pile in the corner. I had something to eat and then, anxious to be out when Anton eventually came round, I went to see if anyone I knew was in the Tankstelle.

As it was a Sunday I drew a blank there but I stayed for a beer and exchanged a few pleasantries with Roger. When I got back later on the flat was all quiet. Santiago was in his room and told me that Anton had not stirred and he was sure that he would be very sorry for the damage in the morning. Nevertheless I went to bed feeling a little uneasy and turned the key in the lock on the bedroom door.

I did not see Anton during the following days. He left every morning early and did not seem to reappear until very late. Then on the Wednesday evening following his drunken rage he came into the living room where I was sitting, eating an enormous beef chop that I had bought in the market earlier.

'I am very sorry,' he said, looking very sheepish. 'I was very lonely and want to go home.' This was the longest sentence that I had heard him say. He must have been rehearsing it.

I suddenly felt sorry for him. I understood entirely the concept of homesickness. Many nights and weekends alone in a room at the Rincón had taught me that.

'That's OK,' I told him. 'We're all like that sometimes.'

'*Por supuesto*,' he said and slid quietly and sadly from the room.

*

Meanwhile, as Easter drew nearer, plans for the trip to Andalusia began to take some sort of shape, albeit still with a predictable element of vagueness. It seemed to be an essential part of the all-important *machismo* that no one bothered to think beyond the next hour or so. Planning for an entire week would have been a sign of hopeless inadequacy if not outright incompetence.

We intended going from Saturday to Saturday during the week before Easter. The Institute was closed for just one week, so my ability to compromise on the timing was limited. It transpired that Miguel, with the car, could only be away from Monday to Saturday, however. I didn't understand the reason why, but I soon gathered that a *macho* never enquired too closely about such things.

Antonio, nevertheless, wanted to take advantage of a full week to visit Seville and Cordoba and see the famous *Semana Santa* – or Holy Week – celebrations. I shared his wish to do this but was somewhat dismayed at his solution. We would hitch-hike down to Cordoba, and Miguel and José Carlos (who at the last minute decided he could come as well) would drive down on the Monday and join us. I left the decisions about exactly where and when to them. Despite their lack of coordination everybody always seemed to meet up in the right place sooner or later, anyway, so I decided that that was how it would be this time as well.

Because I did not know Antonio very well I asked Madeleine her opinion of our proposed trip. Would it be safe? Were they reliable? Was it a crazy idea?

'Of course it's not crazy,' she told me, over an after-work drink. 'You'll have a great time. All that sunshine, and Holy Week is a terrific sight. Where are you staying?'

I had to admit that I didn't know and that the itinerary seemed a little fluid.

'Well, that's how Spaniards are,' she said, blowing smoke leisurely into the air. 'You'll love Cordoba. I'll give you some addresses of people to look up when you're there. Don't worry about where you stay. You won't have much time for sleeping.'

So it was settled – as much as it could be, anyway.

Instead of the N3 to Valencia Antonio and I would set out for the outskirts of Madrid to join the N4 towards Andalusia, our thumbs at the ready, for a week in the sunshine of the south.

XVI

The sign said that the village was called Madridejos – a corruption, I supposed, of *Madrid Lejos* – Madrid Faraway… Except that Madrid was not far enough away for two hitch-hikers intent on reaching Andalusia by the end of the day. The *Despeñaperros* pass, which marked the border between La Mancha – where we now were, and Andalusia and the city of Cordoba, where we wanted to be – was still another 200 kilometres distant, and it was already half past four in the afternoon.

In true *macho* style Antonio did not, of course, seem very bothered. We had started out at nine o'clock that morning and got a lift in a lorry fairly quickly as far as this large cluster of buildings grouped around a church with the traffic of the N4 roaring past it. The driver had then pulled into the lorry park of the bar and restaurant in Madridejos, which seemed to serve as a way station for hauliers on this main north–south axis, and declared that he could not take us any further in case he was caught by the police. We got out and he promptly drove off in the direction that we wanted to travel.

That had been about four hours before. Since then we had had a drink in the bar and then stood disconsolately at the side of the road, thumbs out, being ignored by lorry and car drivers alike as they stopped for refreshment and then continued on their journeys. Antonio had even tried to 'chat them up', as he put it, trying to persuade several lorry drivers to take us as they climbed into their cabs. All shook their heads and gave the same excuse: if the police caught them they would lose their licence.

'I didn't know it was illegal to hitch-hike here,' I said, after another unsuccessful attempt at a lift.

'It's not. They're all idiots,' Antonio assured me.

He was older than his brother Enrique, with fairer, thinner hair that was cut short, rather than being swept back. He was also quite a lot bulkier and did not have the fragile, doll-like quality that his brother gave the impression of having. He too was studying at the university, although he was a little vague on exactly what the subject was. It varied from psychology to natural sciences to medicine, according to who he was talking to.

It certainly wasn't something that preoccupied him during our week of travels. He had brought no work – not even a book – with him, and carried only a small rucksack on his back. He did, however, share the customary lack of money that students exhibited everywhere. He told me that we had to hitch-hike as he had no money: Miguel's enforced stay in Madrid with his car until Monday had obviously been a considerable obstacle, but I had agreed to hitch-hiking as I wanted to visit Andalusia as much as Antonio did and I only had a week to do it in.

At a practical level hitch-hiking was now our only possible means of exit from Madridejos, anyway. When we had failed to get a lift down to Gandia we had simply gone back into the centre of Madrid and caught a train. There was no such option here. I could imagine that public transport in Madridejos was confined to a weekly bus to the nearest town.

'What can we do?' I asked, rhetorically. Stuck in the middle of this brown, featureless plain, miles from anywhere, quite possibly attempting to break the law, was unnerving me.

'We keep trying,' he replied.

He approached a middle-aged lady who was getting into a large saloon on her own in the car park next to the lorries. I couldn't hear what he said but she gave a little shriek, which I did hear, and waved him away with a shooing motion as if trying to dismiss an inquisitive dog.

He came back to where I was watching him.

'She doesn't like students, I don't think,' he said.

She drove out of the car park on to the carriageway, shooting us a venomous look as she passed. I could imagine her going straight to the nearest police station and reporting us. I did not want to tangle with the Spanish police – particularly the *Guardia Civil*, who patrolled rural areas. They had a fearsome reputation.

While musing on what conditions in Spanish jails for foreign lawbreakers might be like I failed to notice a small, olive-green Seat saloon chugging slowly out of the car park. Antonio must have stuck out his thumb – although it was obvious, anyway, what we were doing – and it stopped.

There were two men inside, both well-built and far too big for their tiny car. The one in the passenger seat got out.

'Where are you going, *machos*?' he asked from under a prodigious moustache.

'We want to go to Cordoba,' Antonio told him, 'but anywhere towards Andalusia will do,' he added.

Not confining us to one destination was a good move. I just wanted to get out of Madridejos to a town – any town – that lay vaguely to the south.

'Get in, then,' said the man, and pulled the passenger seat forward to allow us into the back.

We clambered in, with some difficulty. Accommodating two medium-sized hitch-hikers and their rucksacks in the back seats when the front is already occupied by two heavyweights was quite a feat. We sat, rigid, in the back with our luggage on top of us. The front-seat passenger climbed back in, pulled his seat forward a couple of inches and hunched himself up. It all added to the general impression that this was a Spanish version of a crazy competition to see how many people could be crammed into a very small car.

We set off - slowly.

'We're going to Granada,' said the driver.

'Oh.' Antonio and I exchanged glances. Without saying a word we were obviously in agreement. 'Well, that's fine for us,' Antonio confirmed. 'I've always wanted to go to Granada.'

It suited me too. I didn't want to do any more hitch-hiking. We would tell Miguel and José Carlos to divert to Granada on Monday.

'I'm Juan,' said the passenger.

'And I'm Javier,' said the driver. They both leant round to shake hands, which was both difficult and, in the case of the driver, extremely dangerous. After much manoeuvring of the rucksacks and twisting of limbs we managed a limp handshake with both of them.

'We've come from Barcelona,' said Javier. 'We're going to a wedding.'

'We're just tourists,' said Antonio. 'He's English,' he added, indicating me, by way of explanation.

'Oh – God Save the Queen,' said Juan in faltering English, and everyone giggled.

The journey passed uneventfully at first. The road was generally level but there was an occasional dip or rise, which meant a gear change as the little car struggled with its load. Antonio told us how some members of his mother's family were Catalan, from the region around Barcelona, and there were comments from all three of them about how awful Franco had been to the Catalans, forcing them to drop their language and culture.

The general opinion was that it would be a good thing when he was dead – which, they hoped, would be soon. This was far more extreme stuff than I had ever heard before. As far as I knew such comments could only be made in private to trusted counterparties. I looked around to check that no police car was following, ready to pounce on the illegal hitch-hikers with the extremist views.

My anxiety level rose ever higher when, shortly afterwards, Juan the driver took out a cigarette and lit it. It had a very strange smell and it was obvious what it was, particularly when he offered it to Javier, who took a long drag and then passed it into the back. Antonio, likewise, put it in his mouth and sucked in noisily, before exhaling and offering it to me.

I didn't know what to do. I didn't want to offend, or not appear *macho*. I was under no illusion, however, as to the severity with which the police dealt with those who indulged in illegal substances. When I had registered my presence in Spain at the British embassy a couple of months previously I had seen posters, prominently displayed, exhorting Britons to *Stay off the Grass*, with a picture of a luckless individual sitting on a bare bench in a cell.

Still, I was already an illegal hitch-hiker who had teamed up with political mavericks, so I took the joint and tried my best to inhale the smoke. This only resulted in a violent fit of coughing and much amusement on the part of the others.

'I don't usually smoke,' I gasped.

'Well, that's Moroccan Gold – the best,' Javier told us.

We must have looked a curious sight as traffic overtook us on the N4. A tiny car, travelling at about thirty miles an hour with four hulking men and their luggage squashed into it, gradually filling up with greyish-white smoke.

It must have looked even more comical as we approached the *Despeñaperros* pass, the gateway to Andalusia. The pass was about two thousand feet up and the brown plain of La Mancha, over which we had been chugging along, was already at a height of over a thousand feet, but the final relatively modest climb was nearly too much for the little olive-green Seat. We eventually crested the top in first gear at a speed of about eight miles an hour, with the engine revving furiously.

Inside the car, however, the atmosphere was relaxed. It was difficult in the back to see anything through the smoke and around the rucksacks, and this was undoubtedly a blessing. Any rational assessment of the risks that we were running – packed into a battered and unroadworthy smoke-filled car being driven by a doped-up driver over a rugged mountain pass – would have made the blood of any sane person run cold.

Somehow we made it to Granada. A few miles after the *Despeñaperros* pass we had opened a window and blown the last remnants of the smoke away and Antonio and Juan had fallen asleep. I stayed awake, both due to the discomfort that I was experiencing under my rucksack and as a precaution to ensure that Javier did not nod off at the wheel.

It was eight o'clock and dark by the time we got there and were dropped in a plaza near the city centre. There was a chilly wind blowing down from the Sierra Nevada, and the temperature was much cooler than I had expected. Finding somewhere to stay was an imperative and so we set off, looking for a *hostal* or a *pension*.

The first couple of *hostals* that we tried were full. It was the beginning of *Semana Santa*, the Holy Week celebrations that were a tremendous event in Andalusia and a huge tourist draw. I had naively assumed that we would find somewhere to stay immediately, but accommodation was going to be in short supply (as we would find later in the week).

Just when I was anticipating a night on a park bench we came across a sign at the entrance to a small courtyard, indicating that there was a two-star *hostal* inside.

Antonio did the talking and managed to ascertain from

the elderly man in a little room at the side of the courtyard that there was a double bedroom still free. Without even asking to see it he said that we would take it. The man gave us a key and directed us up a flight of wooden stairs to the first floor.

The room was sparsely furnished but it had two single beds and, as it was past ten o'clock, we both decided that we did not want to venture out again. I was hungry but Antonio had apparently used up his monetary allowance for the day and so, with rumbling stomachs, we went to bed.

*

I had some knowledge of Granada and its history. At school we had studied the poems of Federico García Lorca, one of Granada's most famous sons. His works were saturated with the imagery of the city: the Alhambra Palace built in the thirteenth and fourteenth centuries by Granada's Moorish rulers, the gypsies who lived in the caves of the Sacromonte area, and the brimming passions and blood feuds abounding in the surrounding sun-baked countryside that so often led to death. Spain, I had been told, celebrated death more than any other European society.

Antonio knew about the gypsies and the palace too, so the next day it was not too difficult to decide on an itinerary.

'Let's go to the Alhambra first,' he said. 'Then we'll see the gypsies, if we have time.'

'Probably best to see them in the evening, anyway,' I added, thinking that the atmosphere then would be better suited to the dances that they were famous for.

'Some of these Andalusian girls, *macho*...' Antonio whistled in appreciation. 'There are several staying in the rooms upstairs.' He pointed towards the ceiling. 'I'm going to see if I can chat one up.'

'Oh, me too,' I answered enthusiastically, wondering just how to do this. As a fully fledged *macho* I had to be ostentatious in giving full rein to my hormones, even if I really didn't want to. 'What about breakfast?' I asked, more to the point.

'Oh,' Antonio gave a wave of his hand. 'We'll pick up a couple of rolls at a bakery. That'll suit me.'

'OK,' I agreed. In fact something much more substantial would have suited me, but Antonio kept reminding me of the slender nature of his budget. Perhaps I was going to be like one of those hungry hidalgos that I had read about at school, proud of their status but broke.

We got dressed and went downstairs. No sunshine. In fact the air was cool and still and the sky was threatening rain. Oh, well. A quick refreshing shower and the gardens of the Generalife up at the Alhambra Palace would be looking their best.

We dropped off the key in the little room by the entrance to the courtyard. The man from the previous evening had gone. In his place, lying propped up on a makeshift couch, was a very old woman dressed entirely in black. She had one of the most wrinkled faces I had ever seen.

'*Quien es*?' she intoned. ('Who is it?') while staring blankly towards us.

'It's us, *Señora*,' said Antonio, instinctively raising his voice. 'We are in Room 12 and we're going out, so I'm leaving the key.'

'You're a good boy,' she shouted back, as if he was somewhere across the road.

'Thank you, *Señora*,' said Antonio smiling. He'd made a good impression on at least one of the ladies of Andalusia.

As we went into the street it started to rain. Big, heavy droplets just sprinkled down at first and then they gathered in force and number. We both had thin anoraks – thankfully we'd put them in the rucksack as we came out – so we put them on.

We stopped off in a bakery to get the rolls, as Antonio had suggested. I wolfed mine down, aware that it was insufficient to assuage my hunger, and we continued on towards the Alhambra. It was quite a walk – about half an hour – and the final leg to the entrance to the palace complex was a steep climb. So, with the weather acting as a dampener, literally, on our spirits, the whole journey passed in near silence.

By the time we arrived at the entrance we were both drenched, and the weather showed no signs of getting better. I had been expecting to see sun-soaked landscapes, but the only soaking was from the rain.

A further complication when we got there was that tickets were time-stamped, and there was a considerable wait before we would be able to get in. Even in the rain it was a popular destination for Easter week.

So we sat on a stone wall, under a dripping tree, to wait for the appointed hour stamped on our tickets. Antonio's budget stretched only to the ticket. I did also manage to afford a guidebook, which I looked at while we waited.

It told me all about how the Nasrid dynasty, the Moorish rulers of Granada, had built the palace in the fourteenth century, and the way that their engineering and design skills were far in advance of anything in the Christian West at that time. I read how the Islamic world particularly valued and cherished water as an essential feature of garden design, and the Generalife gardens at the top of the palace contained wondrous water features and ingenious small canals and drains to channel the 'precious commodity', as the guidebook termed it, in and out.

I was looking forward to watching the ancient drainage system working flat out to get rid of the deluge that continued to pour down. The 'precious commodity' was certainly not in short supply at the moment and, while looking up at the grey sky and wiping the drips from my face, I wondered if the Nasrid engineers' canals and rills would be able to cope after seven hundred years.

'*Macho*, no luck with the weather, hey?' Antonio remarked. 'Still,' he nodded towards the young girl in the ticket booth, dry and warm behind a glass screen, 'The view's not too bad. These Andalusian girls – wow.'

'Wow, indeed,' I thought, managing a weak smile, and went back to the guidebook.

We eventually went in and saw the wonders of the Alhambra and the little Generalife palace with its gardens and fountains. In the Patio de los Leones, the famous Courtyard of the Lions, with its stone statues of the creatures at its centre, I was most struck by the water pouring off the roof and splashing on to the stones beneath. It was an impressive and unexpected sight. I could not help but feel that we were not having the best of luck with our trip so far.

The rain continued all day, so that when we got to the Generalife and its gardens at the top of the palace the ancient rills and the stone gutters and drains were all brimming with water – not bringing it in, but desperately trying to get rid of it. The fountains were switched off, but had they been switched on I don't think we would have noticed them through the curtain of rain.

Somewhere along the way we managed a *bocadillo* of some sort. I don't remember what was in it, just the attempt to find somewhere dry to eat it.

Finally we traipsed around the Renaissance palace that Charles V had added to the site after the reconquest of Granada from the Moors. It seemed to me to be out of place there on that Moorish hillside, and our footsteps became leaden and heavy as we walked slowly round. It offered some shelter from the downpours, but by late afternoon we had

had enough and we headed back to the *hostal*, undecided about what to do next.

We got back and trudged into the courtyard, still dripping wet.

'*Quien es*? Who is it?' rang out from the little room near the entrance. The old woman was still there and must have sensed our presence.

'It's us, *Señora*,' replied Antonio, loudly and in the same baleful tone as the old woman. 'We've been out and we're coming back. We need the key to room 12.'

'You're a good boy,' she replied. 'It's on the hook.'

Antonio went in and took the key.

'Thank you, *Señora*,' he intoned plaintively.

'You're a good boy,' came back more softly this time, almost like an echo. The whole conversation was so ponderous and slow that it sounded like a lament between two disconsolate witches on a windy day.

There was no bathroom attached to our room, just one further down the corridor that we had to share with the rest of the floor. We both needed a shower or bath to restore the circulation and then some dry clothes, so Antonio set out for the bathroom first while I lay on the bed staring at the ceiling, trying not to think about how hungry I felt.

He came back about fifteen minutes later, towelling his hair dry.

'*Macho*,' he said. 'I just saw a couple of those girls going upstairs. They are *buenisima* – really lovely. We've got to meet them.'

'I know,' I replied, trying to get enthusiastic. 'I like the one with the long blonde hair.'

He looked puzzled for an instant.

'Don't think I've seen her,' he said, which wasn't surprising, as for some reason I had made it up on the spur of the moment – just to impress, I suppose. Remember: a *macho*'s hormones are always raging, so I was always alert.

I went along to the bathroom to shower and generally recover from the soaking that we had had all day. I did not want to return from the sodden south with a cold. It would be an admission that our trip had not been all it could have been. A light tan and a nonchalant air was what I was aiming for.

The bathroom was, inevitably, occupied. I waited along the corridor and looked through a narrow window out on to a small side street below. I heard the bathroom door open and the sound of footsteps going back along the corridor. As I looked around I caught a glimpse of the back of someone in a dressing gown just turning into the staircase to go up to the next floor. What caught my attention, however, was that this person was towelling dry her long blonde hair. The image of it remained in my mind as I went into the bathroom to perform my own ablutions.

So there was a young girl up there with long blonde hair after all. The only thing now, however, was that I, being a true *macho*, would have to pursue her with the same vigour that Antonio was intending to employ in chatting up one of the girls that he had so admired.

We didn't see any more of our fellow guests that evening. Hunger drove us out into the city. After another round of, '*Quien es?*' with the ancient doorkeeper, who seemed now to be on permanent duty, I suggested that we have a drink before eating. Antonio looked reluctant so I said I would pay, and he immediately agreed.

We went into a small bar not far from the Capilla Real, the church where Queen Isabella and King Ferdinand were buried a few years after reconquering Granada. It was small and rather cramped but, as there was still a fine, cold drizzle outside, we just ducked into it.

'I'll have beer—' said Antonio.

'And I'll have a *Chinchón*,' I said to the young boy behind the bar. I thought that the sticky aniseed liquid might actually warm me.

My request brought a look of consternation from the young boy, who was no more than twelve years old. He turned to an older man, who was sitting at a table by the door and smoking a cigarette.

'Papa,' he said, 'what's a *Chinchón*?'

The father took a long drag on his cigarette, obviously mentally perusing the back catalogue of his barkeeping knowledge, and told his son,

'It's gin – that yellow bottle at the back – and a tonic water. That's a *Chinchón*.'

I didn't like to contradict, and I had not yet appreciated the narrow geographical range of my favourite liqueur's availability, so I settled for a very strong gin and tonic. Unsurprisingly, the junior bartender did not seem very sure about measures. As an aperitif it was probably a more suitable drink anyway.

After this even Antonio had to admit that he was hungry. His instinct for a cheap meal meant that we were soon sitting in a small, noisy restaurant that smelt strongly of tobacco smoke, oil and sweat. It was several steps down from the Tibet and one or two even from the Cat Restaurant.

'I'll have the fish soup,' said Antonio, looking at the menu. 'That'll do me. Fish is very nourishing, so it's as good as a main course.'

'OK,' I agreed. 'I'll do the same.' I could, I thought, always fill up on bread.

When the two steaming bowls arrived we set about them with gusto. I had a nose now, or at least a taste bud or two, for what was more or less wholesome when eating out, and the flavour and the unidentifiable slimy lumps floating in this soup quickly alerted me to the fact that it was near the less wholesome end of the healthy eating spectrum.

I looked at Antonio, but he was bolting it down without a problem. I was very hungry and so I ate the lot as well but, as we left, I was sure that it was not the last that I had heard from it. (Madeleine, or Hilary, possibly, told me later that they deeply mistrusted fish soup. It was the repository for all the uneaten scraps of fast-putrefying fish that were left over from main dishes and could be left on the stove for several days to simmer and seethe).

We went back to the *hostal*, were greeted by the old woman in the customary way, and went upstairs.

'We'll need to tell Miguel and José Carlos where we are,' commented Antonio. 'I'll find a phone and call them.'

'OK,' I agreed. 'Oh, by the way, I meant to tell you I saw the girl with the long blonde hair from upstairs when I went to the bathroom earlier. She seemed very nice.'

'Did you talk to her, then?' he asked.

'Oh, yes. She's from somewhere in the north of Spain.' I thought of Rosa from the Banco Hispano Americano, who had soon tired of me and my classes. 'Her name's Rosa.'

'*Macho*, you don't lose time, do you? Are you going to see her, then, tomorrow?' said Antonio.

'She's – err – busy tomorrow. She's got to visit an aunt or something,' I stuttered, aware that I was digging myself in deeper but still desperate to impress.

'That's odd. You'd think she'd stay with her aunt, wouldn't you?' said Antonio, making an obvious point.

Before I could enmesh myself any further in this fantasy, however, he simply said,

'But that's girls. They do strange things. Honestly, *macho*, you English guys, you really work fast. We'll have to make sure you have time to see her before we leave.'

Happily the conversation then turned to the following day's agenda. We were going to see the gypsies in the caves of Sacromonte, so Antonio was particularly interested in trying to guess how much it might cost and whether some caves were more expensive to enter than others. Before that, however, he had to phone Miguel to tell him of the change of plan and where to find us, so he went downstairs to make the call and to try and find out from the old woman if there was a bed for our two travelling companions on the following night.

So, to my immense relief, the practicalities of my arranging a date with the blonde did not come up again that evening. Nevertheless I lay in bed that night, listening to the rain drumming relentlessly against the shutters and wondering why on earth I had invented my phantom female friend and if she would be called upon to put in an appearance at some stage.

XVII

The weather did not improve the next day. The clear light of Andalusia was matt grey and the glowing white of the buildings and the vibrant colours of the townscape were hidden behind a veil of fine rain. It imbued the day with a sense of sadness. The weather wasn't supposed to be like this.

Antonio told me that Miguel and José Carlos were arriving by midday, following a very early start from Madrid. They had apparently expressed a desire to visit the gypsies of Sacromonte as well. I could not believe that they would actually appear at the appointed hour, but Antonio made some rudimentary plans for the day based on the assumption that they would.

'We'll go to the bakers and get some rolls,' he told me, 'and then we'll wander round the city for a while and come back here at midday.'

After looking outside at the weather I would have been happy to stay at the *hostal* until they arrived but, once again, hunger – or rather a dry emptiness in the pit of my stomach – drove me out with him.

On leaving I was disappointed that the old woman was not in the little room that served as a reception. The man who had originally greeted us when we arrived on Saturday was there, so we skipped the ritual elements of depositing the key.

We had our customary rolls from the bakery, and sat in a park in the drizzle eating them. I felt tired and wet and miserable and there was an ominous loose feeling in my stomach thanks to the fish soup, but Antonio seemed able to keep happy whatever happened. There was a sort of stoicism about him that I quite admired. His Spanish nature seemed able to tolerate hardships and inconveniences and make light of them much more easily than mine. My demanding northern soul craved order and certainty. He, like his friends, seemed to live for the moment.

Quite remarkably, as we trudged back to the *hostal*, we spotted Miguel and José Carlos in the act of parking the car. It was a rather aged grey Seat with, I was delighted to see, four doors, which meant we would have slightly more room than in the previous vehicle we had travelled there in.

Miguel seemed a little distracted at first and made some comment to Antonio that I did not hear, but there was much backslapping and laughing from José Carlos and I told them both in my halting, colloquial Spanish about the journey down with the pot-smoking *Barceloneses*, which had José in an inevitable fit of giggles.

Miguel seemed to cheer up very quickly and it was decided, by them, that we would head straight up to the caves of Sacromonte to see the gypsies and – incredible luxury – we would drive there. I jumped into the back seat of the car and sank back, enjoying the stuffy atmosphere of the interior. Just glad to be warm and dry, I left all arrangements to the other three.

The caves were an obvious tourist trap. We were enticed into one of them by a persuasive young man who grabbed our attention and herded us into his cave before any of his rivals could reach us. Antonio insisted on a round of bartering, which reduced the price by a few per cent, and we handed over our cash.

Inside, the cave was well-furnished with irregular whitewashed walls. It was obviously someone's home. There were about twenty of us in all who had been persuaded to enter, and we sat on upright wooden chairs as a man in the ornate shirt and tight black trousers of the flamenco performer started to play a guitar.

I was not a sufficient connoisseur of the art of flamenco to know if any of what we saw was authentic. It was a show for tourists, discussed, rehearsed and timed beforehand. It certainly was not the spontaneous *juerga*, or party, at which singers, instrumentalists and dancers would be seized by the spirit of flamenco, the indefinable and unpredictable *duende*. This spirit welled from somewhere deep inside and drove those who had it to give electrifying performances of *cante jondo*, the emotional 'deep song' that spoke of grief and passion and violence. This much I knew already from our discussions of Lorca in the sixth form.

I'm sure we got a watered-down version, but I was impressed nevertheless. There were four young girls who stamped and whirled in tight flouncy dresses to a complicated rhythm of castanets and strumming on the guitar. There was an older man who suddenly burst into song, pouring out words that I could not follow but which were designed to give vent to the feelings and emotions harboured by the close-knit gypsy community for hundreds of years. Finally, the guitarist put down the guitar and danced, slowly and sensuously, with one of the girls. To a background of stamping feet and clapping hands they danced around each other with an elaborate arcing and bending of their bodies, which intertwined but never touched.

Authentic or not, we clapped madly at the end as a cap was sent around and we contributed further to the upkeep of the cave and its inhabitants.

My Spanish friends seemed impressed as we came out. They wanted, I think, to be impressed by this rampant, exotic display from their countrymen. There was pride in their

Spanishness coming through.

'The *macho* with the guitar was incredible,' said José Carlos, 'and the other *macho* was singing *cante jondo* – you know, how hard it is being a gypsy and things.'

'I thought the dancers were terrific,' said Miguel. 'What did you think, Mike?' he asked me.

I dived straight in.

'Oh, yes, *macho*. Those dancers... They ... they ... they really excited me all over,' I gabbled, as my desire to be a *macho* like them brought the usual level of exaggeration.

'*Macho*,' said José Carlos, 'we'll have to chat one up for you.'

'Oh, he's done that already,' Antonio assured him. 'There's a girl at the *hostal* called Rosa that he's got to know.'

Impressed looks from José and Miguel. A weak smile from me.

'Oh, I don't really know her. We just said a few words.'

'It's not the words that are important. It's the actions.' José laughed and clapped me, as he always did at such junctures, firmly on the back. 'I hope she's still there when we get back. That's what this week is about. Adventures.'

My only solace in trying to disentangle myself from the dismal web of half-truths (actually, they were lies) that I had woven was the sneaking suspicion that, for all their bluster, these Spanish *machos* probably had little more knowledge of girls than I had. I was sure that most Spanish girls, like the ones I had met in Gandia, were beautiful to look at but certainly much less available to touch than their sisters to the north.

'I'm hungry now,' said Miguel. 'Where shall we eat?'

'We found a great place yesterday that does the best fish soup for only forty pesetas,' said Antonio. 'Let's go back there.'

I winced and my stomach started revolving at the thought, but the others were in favour so we climbed into the car and went back there.

The gypsies had made me forget the parlous state of my insides but walking into the restaurant again with the odour of bodies and, I now thought, gently rotting fish, brought it savagely back into the foreground. They slurped and gobbled down the fish soup. I visited the rudimentary lavatories twice and managed to consume a plain omelette.

*

We returned to the *hostal* at about nine o'clock. I, as usual, just followed the others and took no part in any planning process – inasmuch as there was one.

José Carlos and Miguel had a room just across from ours and we flopped down on the beds in their room, talking about nothing much. José went along to the bathroom and then reappeared in great excitement.

'*Machos*, the girls from upstairs are there. I heard them talking. I think they're talking English.' He pointed upwards. 'Your friend Rosa, she must be there with them, *macho*. Ask them if they want to come down and have a chat with us.'

This idea met with general approval from the other two.

I gulped. I was going to be found out. The girl wasn't called Rosa, and it now looked like she probably wasn't even Spanish. I would look very silly.

They practically pushed me out of the room, and I walked hesitantly along the corridor. I looked back and there they were, their three heads poking round the door.

'Go on, *macho*,' José encouraged me. 'We'll have a great time with them.'

I smiled feebly and went up the staircase and out of sight. When I got to the next floor I stopped, my mind sluggish and unable to decide what to do next. Perhaps I would be able to brazen it out somehow or be able to make an excuse about the girls. Perhaps I could say that they were trainee nuns and didn't talk to boys, or they were in mourning for a dead parent and not feeling very playful. I knew that both of these were ridiculous suggestions and I drifted along the corridor to where I could hear the voices, now clearly distinguishable as American, were coming from. The door was open and there was an animated conversation going on about the weather.

'You said it was like California,' a girl's voice said.

'Well, it rains in California as well,' responded the other.

The first voice came back with an edge of anger.

'Not when I'm on vacation.' I could sympathise with this view.

I looked nervously into the room. There were the two female owners of the voices who were conversing, standing by the bottom of one of the beds in the room and looking in an accusing fashion at each other. They were both about twenty and dressed in the backpackers' uniform of jeans and T-shirt. Their hair, however, was much darker than 'Rosa's'.

'Rosa', I immediately noted, was lying on one of the beds with her back to me, her head propped up on one arm. She was wearing jeans and a denim jacket, and her long hair was as blonde as ever. She did not seem to be playing any part in the conversation about the weather. However, as I watched, at first unseen, she turned around to face them and, propped on her elbows, said in a very deep voice,

'Hey, you guys. Just cool it. The weather's the weather. OK? We can't change it. The sun'll shine tomorrow.'

I gave a little gasp, which drew their attention to me for the first time. 'Rosa', my so-called girlfriend, had an awful lot of facial hair for a girl. In fact the blonde wispy growth surely qualified as a beard. Yes, although androgynous from behind, 'Rosa' was in fact a very slim boy, probably about my age.

'Can we help you?' he said, looking directly at me.

I gave a little nervous giggle as the possible outcomes of this case of mistaken identity on my part raced through my brain. I didn't care if he was a boy or a girl. My insane boastings had only been brought on by my wish to impress my Spanish friends. Perhaps this was a way out.

'Hello there,' I started, sounding like an ageing Lothario in an old British comedy film. 'I'm sorry to butt in, but my friends downstairs thought it might be fun to get together.'

I was lucky on a number of counts. Firstly, Deke (the boy) and Sally and Lauren (the girls) thought this was a good idea, and so I was responsible for a pleasant evening with some beers that Miguel went out and bought. Secondly, the Americans' Spanish was as poor as my friends' English and so I was the only reliable channel for information between the two parties. This meant that I could fudge the whole issue of 'Rosa' who, so I said to the Spaniards, had to go off to stay with her aunt, as originally planned, and would only be reappearing after a week or more. I covered over the Americans' confusion at the mention of this unknown name by changing subject rapidly and making reference to the miscomprehension built in to cross-language conversations of the sort we were having.

Thirdly, with Deke very obviously a male in some sort of relationship with the two girls, an unspoken code of solidarity seemed to kick in for my Spanish friends. They now viewed the girls as fun companions but strictly out of bounds for anything else.

I felt an overwhelming sense of relief when, sometime after midnight, the three of them departed upstairs. My credibility as a true *macho* still seemed to be intact. I certainly wouldn't be pushing its boundaries any further on this trip. Fantasy girlfriends might be all right when kept to oneself. They were definitely not for sharing.

XVIII

We saw the Americans briefly the next day – in fact Miguel offered them a lift. I don't know how we would have all squeezed in the car but for a brief, guilt-ridden moment I wondered if they were considering dumping me for my duplicity. But the Americans declined the offer anyway. They were staying for a couple more days and my secret remained undiscovered.

We had a last, touching farewell with the old woman who appeared to have taken up residence again on her sofa in the little reception room off the courtyard.

'*Son buenos muchachos*,' – 'You're good boys,' – she sighed mournfully as we departed.

So, under leaden skies that still leached the colour from the landscape, we set off southwards round the edge of the Sierra Nevada towards the Mediterranean.

We stopped briefly in Motril, where we saw the sea. It was not like the sea at Gandia. This time it was green-grey and swirling frothily below us. We turned west along the coast and, after passing Nerja, Malaga, Torremolinos and Marbella, all dripping and sad, we eventually found a room for all four of us in Estepona.

After Estepona we made a brief stop the next day in Algeciras. It was as close as we could get to Gibraltar as the border was closed, so we gazed at the rock, wreathed in cloud, across the bay. I passed no comment on the political situation that had led to the closure. Franco wanted the rock back. My Spanish friends didn't really seem to care.

Further along I got my first glimpse of Africa. The coast of Morocco was visible – just – as more rain started to fall in harsh, uncompromising sheets. It was more like the view of the Scottish mainland from the Isle of Skye than the northern tip of the great dark, exotic continent.

Then, having swapped the Mediterranean for the Atlantic, we came to Cadiz. I was completely ignorant of its geography and surprised when we had to drive along a causeway to get to it. The Atlantic crashed against its walls from almost every direction. This was no calm, blue soothing sea. It was a wilder, voracious water that seemed to be ever massing for an attack, and Cadiz was almost completely surrounded – an ancient island with an umbilical cord stretching across the bay connecting it to Mother Spain.

Because of its constricted position it seemed, a bit like Venice, to be composed exclusively of old – often crumbling – buildings. There simply wasn't any more room left to build. It was, like the great Adriatic city, an old lady whose once splendid finery of baroque churches and ancient plazas was now looking decidedly tatty, but it was my favourite place that we visited that week. My opinion may have been swayed by the procession we saw that evening, after we had found somewhere to stay.

We had a meagre meal, as usual, with me plumping for an omelette again to pacify my topsy-turvy stomach. Afterwards, as it got dark, we joined the crowds wedged into the narrow streets as statues of Christ and the Virgin Mary were paraded along on vast stands. Christ was represented carrying the cross, his head bowed, and suffering etched on to his face. His mother, however, was gaudily decorated like some oriental potentate's consort, her face peering out through a cloak of brocade and lace. This was one of the processions in celebration of Holy Week that were taking place all over Andalusia to remember the events of that week long ago. I wasn't sure what God thought about seeing his only son and the woman he chose to bear him being dressed up like dolls. But I think he must have approved as, for the first time that week, it stopped raining completely and the sky cleared.

There was a murmur of anticipation from everyone and then the tremendous thump of bass drums filled the air as the statues drew near. They were positioned on ornately decorated stands. The one holding the Virgin Mary had a canopy over it – so she looked a bit like someone sitting up on a miniature four-poster. These stands were very heavy and were carried on the shoulders of members of the *cofradías*, religious brotherhoods whose membership was passed from one generation to another. The members of the *cofradías* wore strange, penitential robes. These were mainly white but with a splash of other – bright – colours.

On their heads they wore huge, pointed wizards' hats. Each hat had a cloth hanging down to obscure the face of the wearer, with little slits cut into them to see through. I made the immediate comparison, in terms of their look, with the Ku Klux Klan of America's Deep South. The Klan was more extreme, but there was a whiff of the Inquisition about these strange, anonymous penitents who were bearing Christ and his mother. Once again that advertising phrase – 'Spain is different' – surfaced in my mind.

But it was exciting – Christianity at its most muscular and entrancing. I was caught up in it and my heart thumped in time to the drums as the members of the *cofradías* and their burden made their way slowly along the crowded street.

As they drew near to us a little man, leaning far out from an open window on the first floor of one of the buildings further along, suddenly burst into a soaring, melodious type of incantation. To me it resembled the *cante jondo* singing that we had heard from the gypsies in Granada. I recognised that this spontaneous paean of praise, directed at the Virgin Mary, was a *saeta* – literally, an arrow – that fervent believers were wont to fire as they were swept along in the solemnity and emotion of the occasion. It lasted only for thirty seconds or so, but it was obviously a classic example of its kind as there was a loud burst of applause from the crowd, most of whom diverted their gaze from the procession to look at the little man, perilously close to falling out of his window.

I glanced at José, Antonio and Miguel. They too were transfixed, glassy-eyed as they drank in this previously unknown part of their heritage. José had even stopped talking. I was moved by the intensity of what we were watching, and hearing, but I imagined them somehow more connected with this age-old affirmation of belief than I could ever be.

The procession passed on and we started to move around as the crowd loosened and dispersed. We soon found ourselves a little way further on, leaning on the sea wall and gazing at the ocean crashing into it many feet below.

'That guy who sang...' said Miguel. 'Wow. It made the hairs stand up on my arms.'

'They call that a *saeta*, you know,' I told them. 'He launches it at the statue.'

'Well, an Englishman telling us all about it...' said José. 'You know so much, Mike.'

'I learnt about it in school,' I replied.

'I wish they'd taught us stuff like that,' said Antonio. 'It's really interesting to know, and these Andalusian guys are so much in tune with their world.'

I wasn't sure what he meant by this. I wasn't sure he knew, either, but their need to express admiration for what we had just seen was obvious as we continued chatting and looked out at the dark, swirling ocean. The Alhambra had failed to impress, perhaps due to the weather, but this robust assertion of suffering and eventual redemption had hit home as swiftly and accurately as the *saeta* flung from the window by the little man.

*

Gradually the weather was improving. We moved on along the coast the next day, and as we set off the sun appeared for the first time. The objective was to get to Seville by the end of day but, rather than go directly, we sauntered along a smaller road that took in some of the villages strung out beside the long Atlantic beaches.

We went through Rota and past the enormous airbase that Franco had allowed the Americans to establish and on to Chipiona – a small town renowned, so Antonio told me, for its oysters. My stomach was in no condition to consider shellfish of any kind – our eating habits were extremely irregular, and I was still surviving on omelettes – but Antonio was having none of it. He dragged me out on to the sea walls, on which the oysters were growing. With a stone he broke open the shells of a couple of them, still attached to the wall, and scooped out the contents.

'Come on, *macho*,' he said, holding out the slithery grey mass in his hand. 'They're lovely,' and he swallowed one.

José and Miguel had, very wisely, hung back and were not within earshot. For once, however, I determined not to act the *macho*.

'No, thank you,' I said. 'They upset my stomach.'

Antonio shrugged, pushed the other one into his mouth and swallowed it noisily.

We got back into the car and, as the now visible sun was setting, we entered Seville.

The first thing that we noticed was how busy the city was.

We had expected heavier traffic and lots of hustle and bustle. This was, after all, the largest city in Andalusia, and one of the largest in Spain. But it was now the Thursday of Holy Week – Maundy Thursday – and the population of hundreds of thousands had seemingly been joined by a similar number of tourists.

The most immediate effect for us of all this was that it took about an hour to find a parking place for the car. We circled the broad outer boulevards and then repeatedly ventured down the smaller side streets near the city centre, our progress slowed by the never-ending stream of pedestrians – couples or little knots of friends ambling along with no fixed destination in mind.

Our quest to find somewhere to park was not made easier by José who, ever the joker, kept winding down the window and shouting at unsuspecting Spanish matrons,

'Hey, *Señora*, does your boy like Tulipan?'

The others thought this amusing at first. I was completely nonplussed, not to say embarrassed. It was explained to me that Tulipan ('tulip' in English) was a popular brand of margarine and there was an aggressive marketing campaign to promote it going on at that time. One of the television adverts showed a comfortably built Spanish mother telling the camera how much her son enjoyed the spread from the tub with the tulip on the front.

The whole thing soon began to pall, however. José leant out one last time to shout his question at an old bow-legged woman dressed in black and was nearly decapitated by a motorcycle that was just overtaking us. Miguel hauled him back in and told him to be quiet.

Very soon after this the impatience of youth, mixed with the strong streak of individualism that lay at the heart of the Spanish psyche, meant that Miguel more or less abandoned the car in the middle of a side street. It was pressed at an angle against a high, whitewashed wall that had a palm tree peeping over its top. It looked like the outer wall of a private residence. Inside I imagined rooms grouped around a cool courtyard with comfortable bedrooms and succulent food.

We clambered out – Miguel with considerable difficulty, as his door was jammed right against the wall – and set off to look around. My major preoccupations, as ever, were food and accommodation. My companions had different ideas.

After about twenty minutes of roaming the streets near the cathedral we found ourselves in the Plaza de España. This striking nineteenth-century construction was a large plaza with a fountain at its centre and an artificial river running through it. All around one side was a vast semicircular colonnade with benches along its front. Each one was decorated with tiles and dedicated, in alphabetical order, to each of the provinces of Spain, from Albacete to Zaragoza.

Miguel, José and Antonio inevitably got talking to a group of girls there. I, both hungry and tired, played little part in the conversation but consoled myself with the thought that at least it wasn't raining. When it came to the girls guessing which province of Spain we each came from they said that I was from Soria. I was pleased that they thought I could be Spanish – I had hardly said a word, so did not give myself away – but a little taken aback that they had chosen a wild and remote upland region of central Spain, in fact the least populated province of all, whose inhabitants were known for their introverted, taciturn disposition. It was not how I saw myself but obviously how I appeared.

Their choice made José chortle repeatedly afterwards.

'*Macho*, they wouldn't have said Soria if they'd seen you in Gandia. You were more like a parrot that wouldn't be quiet there,' he said.

I thought that he was going to reminisce again about the evening when I had called Enrique a little rug and introduced them all to a unique toast but he stopped short, as the conversation at last turned to finding food and accommodation.

We were doubly out of luck. After an hour or so of asking at various establishments it became obvious that every *hostal* was absolutely full. We were in one of the most popular tourist destinations in Europe during its busiest few days of the year. There was nowhere to stay. We did not even try the better hotels, as they were too expensive for us. Anyway, the situation would clearly be the same there. The other blow was that, as it was now about ten o'clock and therefore prime dining time, every restaurant, certainly within our price range, was full, with people queuing at the doors.

Queuing was not something that appealed to my companions. They joked about our plight and then happily decided that the best thing to do was to continue walking around, grab some food from whatever source was available and then sleep in the car.

So it was that, at one thirty in the morning, starving and exhausted, I found myself squashed into the Seat, munching on the remains of a stale loaf, with the prospect of bedding down on the back seat with Antonio. The lack of proper food was again causing my stomach to somersault and, as the others laughed and joked around me, I felt utterly miserable.

For me the lack of a bed foretold of a long, sleepless night and then a grim, weary day ahead. For them it was a great opportunity for more fun and laughter without any thought of what would happen the next day at all. I resolved yet again to live in the carefree moment and not in an imagined and troublesome future, but even as I did so I knew how unlikely that would be.

I don't think I really slept at all. I managed to get my head down on to the back seat, but my legs were bent up against the door and I kept getting cramp. There were, furthermore, a number of passers-by and assorted revellers who continued to saunter noisily down the street right through the night, oblivious to the little group of sleepers squashed into the parked car.

None of it seemed to bother the others. José and Miguel snored gently in an upright position in front, and Antonio drifted off with his head propped up against his rolled-up jumper and his arms folded across his chest.

Sometime around five thirty in the morning they all seemed to rouse themselves. José rubbed his eyes and put his black-rimmed glasses back on, Antonio stretched his arms and yawned, narrowly avoiding hitting me on the side of the head in the process, and Miguel climbed over José and got out of the car altogether and proceeded to do a short routine of stretches and knee bends while holding on to the door handle.

'Hey, *machos*,' said José. 'That was great. I feel like new.' (He actually used the word '*rehecho*', which is more like 'made afresh'. Whatever the translation, I felt it highly inappropriate.)

'As good as eight hours in bed,' said Miguel, clambering back into the driver's seat.

I could not have disagreed more, but kept quiet. I was looking forward to getting back to Madrid, having a shower and something to eat and then falling asleep in my little bedroom with the tree outside.

But we still had a day to go, during which, I now discovered, we would be visiting Miguel's grandmother in the city of Ciudad Real.

This particular part of the trip had never been explained to me before. I uncharacteristically questioned José about why we were doing it. Apparently it had been part of the agreement that enabled Miguel to bring the car (which I had thought was his, but actually belonged to his mother). He had been less than dutiful in visiting the old lady recently and so had to agree to do so if he wanted to borrow the car for our trip.

In fact – and this had not been explained to me before, either – he had driven from Madrid to Ciudad Real the previous Sunday and stayed overnight with her. He had picked José up from the station early on Monday morning and driven on to Granada. The change of plan had meant that Miguel had had to drive much further to meet up with us than he had planned. Cordoba, our first choice of destination, was only about one hundred miles from Ciudad Real. Granada was nearly twice the distance. That, apparently, was why he seemed a little put out when we first met up at lunchtime on Monday.

So, after waiting for a bakery to open, we had our customary meagre breakfast of bread rolls and headed north for Ciudad Real, a small relatively unknown place (despite the fact that its name meant 'Royal City') marooned in the middle of the plain of La Mancha.

I imagined a larger version of Madridejos but was interested to be invited into a Spanish home, especially as it seemed that we were spending the night there. I also dared to hope that the venerable *señora* might be a good cook.

Although it was about two hundred miles away we had plenty of time for the journey. We had finished our breakfast soon after six, so we stopped off in Cordoba on the way.

I wanted to see it, as it had been our original intention to start our trip there anyway. It was only the unexpected, but welcome, lift from the pot-smoking Catalan wedding guests that had taken us off route in the first place. Furthermore the weather was gradually coming round to what I had been expecting all along – cloudless skies and warm sunshine.

So we had a lightning trip around the Mezquita, once one of the greatest mosques of the Islamic world but now firmly anchored in Christianity with Cordoba's cathedral built right in the middle of it, and walked across the old bridge that spanned the Guadalquivir River to gaze at the city from the far bank. It was only for a couple of hours but I could at least tell Madeleine that I had been there and, with the sun shining on it, it felt like the only Andalusian city that I had seen as it was meant to be seen – effulgent in the luminous southern light.

Then we turned north and started back across the reddish-brown plain of La Mancha – 'The mournful soul of Spain,' as Madeleine's boyfriend Manolo had described it. No more gypsies and *cante jondo* and graceful flamenco dancers. As if to emphasise the difference the temperature dropped by several degrees, and high streaks of cloud started to obscure the sun.

The conversation wandered around a variety of themes. There was more praise for the beauty and grace of Andalusian girls and, after a quick sideways glance at me, a question from Antonio as to where the lovely 'Rosa', my erstwhile brief love interest from Granada, might be. He said it in such a way as to make me think that he might just suspect something was not quite right with the whole tale.

I shrugged my shoulders in an unconcerned *macho* way and, not wanting to invite further speculation, I changed the subject.

'Do you know,' I said, 'that I know all the provinces on the car registration plates?'

Depending on where the car came from each car registration plate started with an abbreviation for the province in which it was registered. So Alicante number plates started with 'A', Albacete number plates started with 'AB', Almería plates with 'AL', and so on through the alphabet all the way to 'Z' for Zaragoza. Granada was 'GR', Seville 'S' and Cordoba 'CO'. (Those with 'C' in them were particularly difficult, as there were eight provinces starting with the letter 'C'.)

'How do you know that?' asked Miguel.

'I just do,' I replied truthfully. 'I just learn things like that.' This was indeed true. I had already learnt all the metro stations on lines 2 and 4, the ones I used to get to work, and was on my way to picking up the other three lines as well.

'What's "CR", then?' asked Miguel.

This was a bit tricky, due to the preponderance of cities and their provinces starting with 'C'. Nevertheless I answered straightaway.

'Ciudad Real, of course.'

Miguel nodded in approval.

'The *macho* knows his stuff.'

'What about "SS"?' asked José.

'That's San Sebastian,' I replied confidently, knowing that it was a city far to the north in the Basque country near the French border.

'He's good,' said Antonio.

'What about "TT", then?' said José.

I was confused. I didn't know that there was a 'TT'. In fact I was sure there wasn't one. Nevertheless, José had turned and was looking straight back at me from the front seat, his eyes, behind the black-rimmed glasses, betraying nothing.

'Err, Teruel,' I replied.

'No.'

'Tarragona?'

'No.'

I was quite annoyed.

'Well, what, then? There is no "TT".'

'Yes, there is,' he replied. 'It's Tan Tebastian,' and his face creased into a wide smile and then a giggle.

The others laughed and José asked,

'What about "TTT"?'

'I don't know,' I said, smiling as I anticipated a ridiculous response.

'Tan Tebastian Too,' he said, grinning like a maniac.

At least it helped the journey to go more quickly.

We arrived in Ciudad Real at last. It seemed small and rather unprepossessing, but in any case we were not sightseeing. We went straight to the house of Miguel's grandmother, which was in a narrow street whose antiquity seemed to indicate that it must be near the centre. Miguel parked the car, a little more carefully than he had in Seville, and we went through a very heavy old wooden door and up a flight of stairs.

On the first floor Miguel knocked at another, smaller door and we waited in silence. Shuffling feet could be heard on the other side and then the door was opened by an old lady dressed in the customary shapeless black dress. She was, however, wearing a patterned scarf with a black background but with swirls of red traced all over it. She smiled as she recognised her grandson and, uttering some words that I could not distinguish, indicated that we should all go in.

We all trooped past her, gangling and slightly awkward and, particularly in my case, not knowing what to say. Miguel led the way into a room best described as a parlour. There were a couple of upholstered chairs in front of an ancient-looking television and a big round table with a checked cloth covering it.

Miguel introduced us. The other two exchanged some form of pleasantry with her and then Miguel introduced me, his English friend. I shook hands with the lady, which I think came as a surprise to her, and asked after her health.

'Good day, *Señora*. How are you?' I said clearly and slowly with my best Spanish accent.

The old lady looked at Miguel.

'What did he say?' she asked.

'He said, "How are you?"' explained Miguel, speaking no more clearly than I had.

'Oh, I'm very well, thank you,' the old lady smiled back at me. She turned to Miguel. 'Tell your friend that I'm very well,' she instructed him.

'I think he heard you,' said Miguel, smiling.

'Oh, well, I suppose you boys are hungry,' she said.

I did not think it was my place to say,

'Yes, I'm starving,' but was hoping that one of the others would. But before they had a chance she went on,

'I've got something cooking for you, just in case. Sit down,' and she gestured to the table and the six chairs around it.

We all sat down around the table on the hard, upright chairs, eager as four puppies at feeding time. I noticed immediately how much warmer I felt sitting there and, as I stretched my legs underneath I understood why. My foot hit something solid and I realised that it was a brazier full of hot coals built into the table.

We had read about these devices in Spanish classes at school under the heading of what you can expect to find in a typical Spanish home. It had seemed very outlandish to us then and there had been jokes about tables bursting into flames and scorched backsides. In fact it was a very efficient method of heating – I got warmer from the bottom up and was soon feeling very comfortable indeed, in spite of the hardness of the wooden chair.

My mood improved even more when Grandma came back with cutlery and plates and then staggered in with an enormous casserole dish, which Miguel helped her to put on the table.

'I cooked a *cocido*,' she told us. 'Tell your friend I've cooked a *cocido*,' she told Miguel, nudging him. We all smiled appreciatively.

The *cocido* – yet another thing that I had read about in

My Reign in Spain

Spanish classes but had not yet experienced – was a type of stew based around cabbage and potatoes and beans combined with chicken and various unusual parts of a pig. By unusual I mean the bits that I, and probably most of my compatriots, had never considered eating. There were strong, garlicky sausages and fatty strips of pork belly in it but also a snout and trotters and something that looked like an ear. I didn't care much what it was. It smelt delicious and, when offered, I said,

'*Si, por favor*,' to a large portion. It was big, hearty fare and as I ate it I thought briefly of Milan and his commentaries on the lack of subtlety in Spanish cuisine. This was truly barbarian cooking at its best.

We had some wine as well, and soon the atmosphere got very jolly. The other three gave Grandma an edited version of our exploits and she nodded and smiled politely. Then it was my turn to attempt some conversation. So:

Me: 'This *cocido* is delicious, Señora.'

Grandma (smiling serenely): 'What did he say?'

Miguel: 'He said the *cocido* is delicious.'

Grandma (to me, slowly): 'I'm glad you like it.' (To Miguel): 'Tell him I'm glad he likes it.'

Miguel: 'We're all glad you like it.'

Grandma (to me, even more slowly): 'You've got a good appetite.' (To Miguel): 'Tell him he has a good appetite.'

Miguel: 'You've got a good appetite.'

Me (very indistinctly, due to my mouth being crammed full): 'It's the first time I've had *cocido*.'

Grandma: 'What did he say?'

Miguel: 'I don't know. I couldn't understand him.'

Grandma (relieved): 'Well, I'm glad you couldn't, because I can't understand a word he says.'

And so on until it was time to clear the dishes, indulge in a bit more *macho* banter and then bed down for the night – Antonio and I on a couple of makeshift couches that appeared from somewhere and Miguel and José Carlos in the spare bedroom along the corridor.

I dreamt wildly that night of pigs' trotters and whirling, flamenco-dancing gypsies and torrents of rain. I suppose it was because it was the first time since we had set out that I had gone to bed with a full and uncomplaining stomach.

XIX

We got back to Madrid the next day at about four o'clock. They dropped me off at the end of Calle de Canillas and I walked the hundred yards or so to no. 68.

The one-armed doorkeeper was there, sweeping with an old broom. The action seemed to emphasise his disability and I still expected him to fall over like an unbalanced wooden toy.

'*Muy buenas* – Good afternoon,' he said to me. 'Did you have a good trip?'

'Yes, thank you, *Señor*. I had a good time.'

'The weather wasn't the best this week.' He gestured out towards the street.

'No,' I replied. I wanted to say, 'You're telling me,' but didn't know how to in Spanish. So I simply said, 'But we still saw many interesting things.'

Upstairs all was quiet. As I entered the living room I noticed that the remains of the two chairs that had fallen victim to Anton's drunken outburst, which I thought Santiago had disposed of, were arranged in a little pile in one corner. Resting on top of them was a large sheet of card on which was written: *Anton Ivanov – RIP April 1974*. I looked at this strange monument and half-smiled at Santiago's sense of humour. I could not imagine, however, that Anton would find it very funny. He was certainly contrite, but would not want to be reminded of his transgressions. I felt a little uncomfortable about it and hoped that he was spending most of his time at the university, as usual, so that our paths would not cross much.

I shouted out a quick *Hola*, but it was obvious that no one was there and I had the apartment to myself.

I went along to my bedroom and looked out at the tree on the waste patch of ground. It seemed to have sprouted a lot of leaves in the week that I had been away. Perhaps it was all the rain. It made a great improvement to the ragged semi-developed urban landscape that I looked out on, and I could see the birds flying in and out of its branches. It was a small counterweight to the relentless march of Madrid that seemed to be going on all around us.

After unpacking I went out to get some food from the supermarket that was close by. When I came back with my two plastic bags of simple essentials I could hear Santiago in his room. I put the bags down and went along the corridor and put my head around his door.

'I'm back,' I said. 'Is everything OK?'

'Oh, yes,' he replied. 'Did you have a good time?'

I told him briefly some of our exploits. I missed out the bit about the pot-smoking Catalans and my fantasy transgender girlfriend and being tempted to eat oysters straight from the sea wall and some of the other stranger occurrences.

'Well, there have been changes here last week,' he told me. 'Anton has gone back to Bulgaria and Gutierrez has headed home to the Dominican Republic.'

'That was quick.' The news about Anton did not surprise me but Dr Gutierrez must have packed up and gone in some haste – and haste was not one of his everyday traits. 'Why did Gutierrez go?'

'Some family problems back there apparently – with his wife,' said Santiago.

Yet again, revelations about Gutierrez's life managed to stun me. I had not imagined that he had a wife. It would have been far too energetic a commitment for someone as lethargic and world-weary as him. But yes, he had a wife in the Dominican Republic. Why was she not with him in Spain? Why indeed had he come to Spain? I did not pursue it with Santiago, however, as I then remembered the little *in memoriam* tableau to Anton that he had erected.

'Did you put the chair pieces in the living room with the card?' I asked.

He smiled.

'Do you like that? I thought we could keep it there for a week or so to remind us of that afternoon. I think he was very lonely. That's why he went back so quickly. He told me that someone else was coming over from Bulgaria and asked if I wanted them to come here.'

'What did you say?' I asked somewhat apprehensively. I didn't want to share my temporary home with any more scientists home sick for the Balkans.

'Oh, I said no.' He smiled again, gleefully. 'Anyway, we have two of your compatriots moving in next week.'

'What do you mean?'

'I advertised again and a Spanish lady rang up from the university accommodation office to say that two English students were coming out next week for eight weeks and needed somewhere to stay, so they're coming here. I wrote down their names,' he added, picking up a piece of paper from the bedside cabinet. 'They are called Brian and Robin, from university in Manchester.'

I thought about this. On balance it was good news. They could not be more eccentric than the previous two occupants of the interconnecting bedrooms. On the other hand I would probably speak less Spanish with them around, but fellow Brits would be a reassuring presence after my first experiences of sharing a multinational apartment.

So, the next day, I spent a quiet Easter Sunday: no

chocolate eggs but another enormous beef chop, which I was now quite proficient at cooking, and my habitual stroll around the Retiro Park.

*

I had to return to work on Easter Monday. The Institute had only closed for one week and so I was straight back to two hours with Jaime Sancho. I managed to spin out the narrative of my trip to occupy a lot of the lesson and we concluded with him telling me about what he did. This was just as well, as I had not prepared anything – other than a rough lesson plan in my head.

I was, in fact, taking a much more cavalier attitude to lessons and positively prided myself on going into them without any serious preparation. This sometimes meant that I ran out of things to say and do with pupils much more quickly than I should have done, and there would be several surreptitious glances at my watch as most lessons progressed, as I waited for Mariuca or Elena to ring the bell that announced the lesson's end.

Wanting to see how quickly I could get to the Institute, I also left the apartment in the mornings as late as possible. If I was late the only person who would suffer would be Jaime, as he was my first pupil on all three days when I worked in the mornings. On the Wednesday after my return from Andalusia I only left the apartment at 9.15, which gave me fifteen minutes to complete the journey and start the class with him. I took the metro but despite the frequency and efficiency of the system, which was extremely reliable, I only arrived at Ópera station at 9.40. As I bounded up the steps I met Jaime on his way down. He had thought that I was not coming and had abandoned the class. I made a very weak excuse about a delay on the metro (something which I never experienced in all my time in Madrid – and I'm sure he never had, either) and we went back to the Institute.

I told Madeleine and Hilary and Chris and Sabin and Elena about my week in Andalusia. It was agreed by all that I had been unlucky with the weather.

'You'll have to go back again,' was Madeleine's advice. 'There are lots of public holidays coming up in May.'

This was true. Madrid, with its patron saint San Isidro celebrating his feast day on 15 May, was particularly well-supplied with national and local holidays. I had heard several of my pupils saying that, if the holiday fell on a Tuesday or a Thursday, the normal thing was to take off the intervening Monday or Friday as well in a practice known as '*hacer el puente*' ('making a bridge').

This sounded like a thoroughly decent principle to me. I was beginning to think that teaching English to foreigners, albeit very kind and friendly foreigners, just wasn't my vocation.

Elena promised to give me something to make up for my wet and hungry week in Andalusia. We frequently talked about the things that we really liked eating – it often dominated our conversations as I recounted either which restaurant I had eaten in or what I had attempted to cook at home. One of her favourite childhood treats had been something she referred to as *leche rica* – 'rich milk'. This apparently was obtained by getting a tin of condensed milk and boiling it for several hours.

The result was a thick, sweet and sticky goo that was, according to her, indescribably delicious to eat on bread or on its own. Such was its richness, however, that it could only be consumed in very small amounts. She promised to prepare a tin for me as a special treat but made me promise not to eat it all at one sitting, however much I was tempted.

'If not, your kidneys and liver…' and she put her hands

behind her in the small of her back and made an exploding sound.

'Oh, I promise,' I said. I had had enough trouble with my tummy without blowing up my liver and kidneys as well.

Brian and Robin arrived on the Thursday after Easter, the day after I had nearly failed to arrive in time for Jaime Sancho. I met them when I came in at about 9.30 that evening. They were with Santiago, who was explaining to them the meaning of his impromptu memorial to Anton.

Brian was the shorter of the two – probably an inch or so shorter than me. He was stocky with long, straight brown hair which he wore brushed over to one side of his head. He came from somewhere near Liverpool, which was obvious when he spoke. He had a light Merseyside accent that was reminiscent for me of the Beatles (who had only recently broken up). He sported the normal range of semi-scruffy student clothing but distinguished himself by his footwear. He only ever wore sandals, without socks, but seemed to have at least five or six pairs. Admittedly they suited the late April weather in Madrid, which was now decidedly warm, but I wondered if he had anything sturdier for January in Manchester.

Robin was much taller and thinner and several years older. He had, I gathered, gone back to a technical college to study for A levels after having started work at sixteen, and his route to university had required more dedication and determination than either Brian or I had needed to exhibit as we passed seamlessly from year to year through our middle-class schooling. Perhaps it was this that made him slightly less confident. He was certainly the quieter of the two.

They had come to Madrid to attend the university for a term as part of their degree course. The question of accommodation had only been settled at the last minute, however, and they had spent the first couple of nights in a hotel near Atocha.

'Full of tarts and guys with flick knives,' was Brian's verdict on the place.

'Yes, this seems a much nicer area,' said Robin.

'Oh, it's all right,' I said.

'So what are you doing here, Mike?' asked Brian.

'I teach English at a language institute,' I explained. 'I've been here since January and I'm doing it before I go to university to study Spanish.'

'Oh, where are you going?' asked Robin.

'To Oxford,' I said. 'The Queen's College.'

Brian's demeanour immediately changed.

'I don't know why you want to go there. I went for an interview.' He curled his lip slightly.

'What happened?' I said, anticipating the answer.

'They didn't know what they were talking about. I saw some silly old duffer at St Catherine's – St Catz (he deliberately exaggerated his pronunciation of its nickname). I told him I thought Lope de Vega's plays were all rubbish. Turns out he was a world expert on the guy. He didn't like me.'

I didn't think this was surprising. In terms of interview tactics it was perhaps a high-risk strategy.

'I didn't get in,' Brian then confirmed.

Unfortunately thereafter I always felt that my success where he had failed rankled with Brian and, although we were friendly to a degree, as anyone sharing a common expatriate experience is likely to be, it was Robin, who was calmer and less judgemental, who I found easier company.

They occupied the two interconnected bedrooms at the front that had been vacated by Dr Gutierrez and Anton. Brian had firmly established himself in the front one with the window. I imagine that Robin had good-naturedly gone along with whatever arrangement he had proposed.

So the household at no. 68 Calle de Canillas had changed

complexion – no longer leaning towards the Hispanic or even Slavic, but firmly under Anglo-Saxon occupation.

The broken-up bits of chair, and their placard devoted to Anton's memory, were disposed of the very next day.

XX

About this time it was announced in all the media – TV, radio and newspapers – that *El Caudillo* or The Leader, as Generalissimo Franco liked to be known, was seriously ill. He was eighty-one and had not been seen or heard in public for some time. Meanwhile, over the border in Portugal, a peaceful revolution had been taking place. The government, Fascist in all but name, had been overthrown by demonstrators who had brought the country to a standstill. The key event had been the army throwing in its lot with the protesters, and putting carnations in their rifle barrels as a gesture of solidarity.

This had caused a stir in Spain – largely, I have to say, unnoticed by me – and Franco's illness made the authorities edgier than ever. Furthermore, it was coming up to the first of May, a date full of left-wing associations. So as Franco's condition deteriorated the decision was taken to close the border. This eventually came to my attention via Elena on the day before the May Day holiday. I was slightly anxious, although I still had at least two months or more before the Institute closed for the summer. She did not think it very serious, however.

'They'll open it again as soon as they see that we are not all going to run out on to the street shouting tomorrow,' she said. 'Anyway, he's tough. He may go on for years yet.' She was as good as most other Spaniards I came across at hiding her feelings in this regard, so I wasn't sure whether there was hope or regret in her voice.

'By the way,' she continued, 'I have something for you.'

She reached under the desk and pulled out a small tin.

'I had some time at the weekend so I boiled this for you – it's the *leche rica*.'

'Thanks,' I said. 'I'll look forward to eating it – but not all at once.'

'Oh, no. Remember your liver,' she laughed.

I showed Hilary the tin later during another break.

'She's lucky it didn't blow up, boiling away for hours like that,' was her comment. 'Careful when you open it.'

I placed the tin gingerly at the side of my desk for the rest of the evening, unsure as to whether or not it would explode at any moment. I then had a nervous journey back on the metro that evening, looking, I am sure, very suspicious at a time of heightened security, shifting the tin and its supposedly volatile contents round and round in my pocket.

Elena was right, though. It was delicious. I opened it successfully at home, and inside was a rich brownish-coloured goo – more solid than liquid. I spread some on a piece of bread and enjoyed its sumptuous caramel flavour.

As I sat in the kitchen Brian came in.

'What's that?' he asked, on seeing me sitting on one of the kitchen chairs, licking my lips with a contented look on my face.

'It's something Elena at work gave me. Apparently it's condensed milk, which is boiled for about four hours, and it goes really thick and creamy.' I spread a little on a piece of bread and offered it to him.

'Try it.'

'Wow, that's good,' he agreed. 'She's a very kind lady to do that for you.'

'But apparently it's so rich that if you have too much it can harm your liver,' I warned him, 'or so she says.'

'It'd take a bit more than a tin of that to harm my liver,' said Brian.

'Well, that's all for now,' I said and put it in the fridge.

'Do you want to go out tomorrow, then?' Brian asked, affably. 'You don't have work, do you?'

This was true. It was the first of May and we had a day off. I was particularly looking forward to the month of May, anyway, with its procession of public holidays, so I said yes.

'We'll go into the centre and have a mooch about,' Brian continued.

'OK. I want to go to the bullring as well and see how you get tickets,' I said. 'What about Robin?'

'He says he's got some work to finish. It should have been in today, but they've given him a couple of extra days. An essay on Góngora, or something.' He laid extra emphasis on the first syllable of the poet's name, enunciating each syllable in a languid drawl, as if passing judgement on him and all who studied his works.

The next day was fine and bright. It was springtime, slipping into summer already. I pulled on a T-shirt and a pair of brownish-red flared jeans that I had bought just before leaving the UK. I was very pleased with them – they were stylish to the point of being trendy, which for a nineteen-year-old from the Fens was an achievement to be celebrated by wearing them as much as possible on days off.

Brian had his normal uniform of shirt and blue denim jeans worn with number four (or was it five?) pair of open-toed sandals. Proud though I was of my new jeans, they did not differentiate me particularly, and we both looked every inch the student.

We did not notice any real difference to anything as we went down to the metro. There were a couple of knots of policemen near the entrance, but this was fairly unremarkable. I wanted to go to the Las Ventas bullring in the city centre, where I had heard that tickets for the Sunday bullfights that took place during May and June could be bought. I was more than half-certain that I wanted to go to the bullfight. It was a part of Spain that I was curious to see, and I also wanted to test my own stomach and stamina with a ringside seat – although one that was set back a few rows from the spectacle just in case my resolve to watch it outstripped my ability to do so.

The trip to Ventas was in vain. As it was a public holiday the ticket office was shut. Brian commented that I should have checked beforehand, but did not seem too put out. He even said that he might accompany me to the bullfight when I finally did go. I wasn't entirely sure I wanted company – I was still a little uncertain about what my reaction would be and would prefer to find out alone.

At this stage I did remark that there seemed to be a lot of police around, some of them looking more surly than usual.

'Probably think there's going to be a riot,' said Brian, unconcerned. 'Doesn't seem to be much sign of one, though.'

This was true. Because it was a public holiday there were fewer people – and cars – than usual. But there was still a significant number of passers-by, and the noise of the traffic was only slightly diminished.

We went into a bar just along from the Retiro, had a couple of beers and played on the pinball machine. There was a song playing on the jukebox called 'Waterloo'. I had heard it several times before but wasn't sure what it was.

'It won the Eurovision Song Contest,' Brian told me.

As it was clearly in English I presumed it was by an English group.

'Nah,' he said. 'Some Swedish group called Abba. I don't suppose it'll ever catch on. Just a one-hit wonder.' With that he dismissed them and their song and concentrated on pressing the flipper buttons on the pinball.

Neither of us had anything to offer in the way of a plan as to what to do – perhaps the habits of my Spanish friends were rubbing off on me – so we stayed in the bar until about one o'clock and then set off to get the metro down to the old part of the city near the *plaza mayor*, with the intention of getting something to eat.

As we came out we saw immediately that there was an increased police presence. There were several Land Rovers parked along the street and small groups of policemen were gathered idly around them, smoking and talking. They were not in the grey uniform of the *grises*, or traffic police, who I was used to seeing everywhere as they tried to control the wayward Madrid traffic. These were more serious altogether, with weapons clearly in plentiful supply. Some wore peaked caps but several of them had hard crash helmets on their heads.

What was noticeable was that all of them were wearing mirrored sunglasses – the aviator type, with metal frames and elliptical lenses. It made them look as if they were all part of a weird tribe who had developed insect eyes.

I looked at them, nevertheless, more out of curiosity than anything else. There were people passing by and cars were still driving up and down the street. Everything seemed completely normal. Brian, likewise, did not seem to be put off by them in any way.

We turned into a side street, which we knew led back to the Retiro metro station, and walked along, chatting about nothing in particular.

'Have you ever been stopped by a policeman?' Brian asked.

'No,' I replied. 'I've never done anything that a policeman would be interested in, I don't think. What about you?'

Brian's answer was evasive.

'The police in Liverpool were always looking for an

excuse. Every time you come out of a pub in the city centre they'll be on the lookout for trouble.'

'There's not a lot of trouble in March,' I replied truthfully. 'My only brush with the law was when I was stopped once when I was riding my bike home from school years ago by a policeman after I didn't stop at a stop sign in the High Street. He told me off, but that was all.'

'Didn't confiscate the bike, then,' chortled Brian.

I laughed loudly.

'Ha ha, no. Didn't look like that guy over there, either.' I pointed up the road to where an officer in a helmet and jodhpurs was surveying the street from the opposite pavement. He was standing, hands on hips, next to a small police Land Rover that had a wire mesh over its windscreen.

'Looks like he's lost his horse,' was Brian's comment.

I laughed again, more out of politeness than anything else, and we continued walking. As we did so, however, the policeman crossed the road just ahead of us and, as I got closer, he beckoned me to him with a leather-gloved hand. My heartbeat suddenly increased and, for the first time, I realised that there was no one else in the little street at all – just the two of us and about ten policemen, who now started to look very intimidating rather than just curious.

'Can I see your identification?' he asked as I went up to him, although it was not a question.

I looked at him and swallowed hard. His voice was detached and emotionless. All I could see of his face was a nose and a mouth. His eyes were hidden behind the mirrored sunglasses and I could see my distorted reflection in them as I shifted from one foot to the other.

'I haven't got my passport with me,' I explained, 'but I have this.' I fished a student identity card out of the back pocket of my jeans. Santiago had got it for me a few weeks before as he said it would get me into the university swimming pool when the weather got warmer.

The policeman took it from me and, from the tilt in the angle of his head, seemed to look at it.

There was a long silence during which I felt my stomach begin to churn. I at last realised that this was not a jolly, helpful copper. This was an armed police officer from Europe's last remaining Fascist state – whose dictator lay dying – on duty on one of the most politically sensitive days of the year. I noticed his long leather boots, and the image of serried ranks of goose-stepping storm troopers flashed through my mind.

'Where are you from?' he asked me, surveying the street to his right at the same time, as if to emphasise how inconsequential I was.

'I'm from England,' I squeaked.

'And do you laugh at policemen in England?' he continued in the same uninterested monotone, still gazing somewhere over my shoulder.

I could see myself, my head absurdly large, in his green-tinted glasses. I gave a nervous laugh, which came out as another strangulated squeak.

'Oh, I wasn't laughing at the policemen. My friend,' and I jerked my thumb towards Brian who was, sensibly, hanging back a few paces, 'was making a joke about something else.'

There was another long and menacing pause, as if to further underline his complete control of the situation. I waited, listening to my heart thump.

'Why are you wearing red trousers on the first of May?' he said eventually.

I was truly stumped. I hadn't really considered their colour when I put them on. Perhaps he saw them as a provocation on May Day with its Socialist connotations. The people's flag was deepest red – but their trousers? I didn't know what to say. Perhaps it would be best just to say that I didn't know why I was wearing them – I hadn't ever thought of them as really red, anyway. There was a lot of brown in there as well.

'Err, my mother gave them to me on my last birthday,' I blurted out eventually. This was untrue. I had bought them myself, but it was around the time of my last birthday. So now I was lying to the police.

He gave a snort. I don't whether it was amusement, disdain or anger but he gave me back the student card and, still not looking at me, said,

'Go away, and don't laugh at policemen again.'

I took the card.

'*Si, Señor*,' I said in my most obliging voice, and slunk away.

'Phew,' I said to Brian. 'That was unpleasant. He thought that I had been laughing at him, and he said that my trousers were red. They're not really red. They're more brown.'

'My trousers would be brown if I'd been stopped by him,' said Brian as we walked briskly away. 'Fascist bastard.'

'Don't make me laugh again,' I told him. 'I'll be arrested next time.'

We seemed to have lost interest in going over to the *Plaza Mayor*. I just wanted to go back to the flat and hide for the rest of the day. I was angry and a little scared at what I had experienced. The safe and comfortable everyday world had been taken away for a few minutes and I had seen something much harsher and more unfeeling take its place. As we went back down the metro the safe and comfortable world reasserted itself, but I was now aware of what lay behind the curtain, ready to emerge, if ever it was pulled aside.

*

When we got back to the flat we told Robin and Santiago about our brush with the forces of authority. They were both sympathetic and intrigued.

'What did you say, then, to make him stop you?' asked Robin, looking up from his essay on Góngora, which was spread around him on the living room table.

'I didn't say anything. It was him,' I gestured to Brian. 'He made me laugh and they thought I was laughing at them.'

'These policemen are very repressive. They stop lots of people who are going about their business,' said Santiago, with an uncharacteristic hint of anger in his voice. 'If they think you are from Latin America they always stop you.'

'I thought they would be more sympathetic to fellow Spanish speakers,' I said. 'You all share a common language and history.'

As soon as I said this I thought of his previous flash of anger when I had suggested that he had Spanish blood in him before I moved in. I was right to regret my remark.

He curled his lip and reminded me,

'I am not Spanish. I'm pure Indian. I have nothing to do with the Spanish.'

Robin and Brian looked slightly taken aback at this glimpse of another – militant – Santiago.

'Well, why are you studying in Spain, then?' asked Robin, his confusion quite innocent.

'You must know your enemy from within,' snarled Santiago. 'Then,' and he banged his fist on the table, causing Robin's pen to jump slightly in the air, 'you can strike without them realising.' With that he strode dramatically out of the room.

'Blimey,' said Robin after a couple of seconds. 'We ought to call him Che.'

'Can't see him manning the barricades,' Brian opined.

I agreed. Santiago was mild-mannered to the point of indifference. Apart from these two flashes of anger I never heard him even raise his voice again. I kept a lookout for many months afterwards, after I left Spain, for mention of an outrage carried out by a bearded and bespectacled Ecuadorian, but his 'strike' against the enemy never came.

I went into the kitchen and opened the fridge. It was time to seek comfort in the delicious little tin of condensed milk that Elena had given me. There were a couple of slices of crispy bread left, and a dollop of the magical cream spread on them would help eradicate the memory of my brush with the forces of repression. I looked on the middle shelf, where I thought I had left it. It wasn't there. I moved a couple of jars and packets as I searched for it in the furthest recesses of the fridge. It had never been very full so it was obvious very quickly that my little tin wasn't there.

I strode back into the living room, already half-aware of what had happened.

'Have you seen my condensed milk spread?' I asked Brian and Robin. 'I left it in the fridge last night. Now I can't find it.'

'I had a little bit on a slice of bread last night,' said Robin. 'It was very nice.'

'I know it's very nice. That's why I want to eat some more of it.' I replied, and then looked pointedly at Brian.

To his credit – although it was probably undeniable anyway – Brian looked straight back at me and said,

'Oh, yeah. I finished it off last night.'

'What?' I cried, anger rising.' You ate the lot?'

'Well, it was only a small tin. I didn't know you were so attached to it. I'll get another one and boil it for you,' he promised.

'Oh, yes. I'll believe that when I see it. It was my tin. She made it for me.' I was angry and shocked at the way that he had so casually taken what was not his.

He obviously did not share my view as to the seriousness of his actions. He shrugged his shoulders, muttered,

'It was only a little tin,' and walked out of the room towards his bedroom.

'Sorry about that,' said Robin. 'I didn't know it was yours. He just told me to try it.'

'It's not your fault,' I seethed. 'He's just thoughtless about what he does.'

The next day I went into a stationer's and bought a pack of little coloured labels and dots. I stuck a blue label, a green one, a yellow one and a red one on the fridge and, with a marker pen I wrote a name next to each of them. I was blue, Santiago was green, and Brian and Robin were yellow and red respectively. Then I stuck little blue dots on everything in the fridge that I considered to be mine. It all looked very colourful but rather bizarre – like a light show in a deep freeze disco.

I explained the system to my sceptical flatmates. It was not a success and quickly broke down, due to a lack of supply of coloured dots and the fact that Brian in particular completely ignored it.

XXI

I told my friends at the Institute about my May Day experience when I went in the next day.

Hilary, Chris and Madeleine were sympathetic and thought it was a terrible thing to happen. I didn't tell Tim. He had more pupils than anyone else so rarely had time or, I suspect, the inclination to stay around the reception desk to chat, as the rest of us did.

Elena and Sabin were more equivocal in their reaction. They were clearly not unsympathetic but expressed no opinion as to whether there was any justification for what happened. Their reluctance to comment was not really out of fear, I think, but more as if they had no practice in marshalling their thoughts into a coherent view. So they said nothing.

Elena had a problem, anyway, which required our assistance and which was beginning to affect her behaviour. Her general demeanour was what one would call happy-go-lucky, but she was getting more and more nervous every time the phone rang. She was a potential victim of her own success and was worried that she would be unmasked as an impostor at any time.

The background to this story revolved around Elena's relationship with the Belle Vue School of English in Bournemouth.

Some time a month or two before she or, I suspect, Peter Garrett, had responded to an advertisement that the

Belle Vue School had sent out to English language teaching establishments such as the Instituto around Europe. It encouraged them to send their students to Bournemouth for a total immersion course in the English language. Peter Garrett may have sent the first person across to Bournemouth, but thereafter it was Elena who recommended the school to all and sundry in the Instituto – with some success. She had persuaded many Instituto pupils of the benefits of a total immersion course and, with little to do at reception while classes were taking place, had written to Tony and Val, the owners of the Belle Vue School, giving details of each person and booking them a place…

Except that she, who was unable to speak more than a couple of words of English, had not written the letters herself. She had composed something in Spanish and then asked Hilary or Chris or one of the others to write the letter for her. She had then signed the letter, either in a moment of sheer folly or to boost her credibility with the reader, like this: *Elena Sacedon, Director of Studies*. (I think Hilary or Chris had again provided the translation for this. Elena could be very persuasive.)

Tony and Val had written back, thanking her for the number of pupils that she was sending. They had, of course, written their letters in English, thinking that they were corresponding with a fluent English speaker who had the authority to act on behalf of the Instituto. We then had to translate the letters for Elena. So far, so good – it was no more than a bit of harmless fun with a dash of duplicity.

The latest letter that had arrived a day or two before, however, gave cause for concern. It said that Tony or Val would be phoning her soon as they wanted to discuss with her, in her capacity as director of studies, a commission system and an exclusive agreement to take all Instituto pupils who wanted to visit the UK as a means of improving their language skills. They had even sent a poster and some brochures that they asked her to put up around the Instituto.

Elena realised that she was getting in over her head. She had certainly not discussed her initiative with Peter Garrett, who was unaware of the close liaison that was being proposed for his establishment.

So every time the phone on the reception desk rang between four in the afternoon and ten in the evening Elena looked at it nervously before picking it up and saying very quietly, '*Dígame*,' – the normal phrase used for answering the phone.

I was sitting there between classes, one evening shortly after my May Day conversation with the policeman, when the phone rang. I was only half-aware at first that Elena was speaking to anyone but then she said in a slow, emphatic tone,

'*Un … momento … por … favor*,' put her hand over the handset and turned to me.

'Mike,' she hissed. 'I think it's the Belle Vue people. I think they are asking for me. She doesn't speak Spanish, I don't think. You'll have to tell her that I'm not here.' She thrust the handset towards me.

Uncertain what to say, I took the phone from her.

'Hello, can I help you?' seemed to be a good start.

'Oh, hello,' a woman's voice came back. 'It's Val Baker from the Belle Vue School in Bournemouth. I was hoping to talk to Elena Sacedon. My Spanish is not very good and I don't think the lady I was talking to understood me.'

'Oh, well … err,' I looked to Elena for guidance but she just shrugged. 'She's not here at the moment, I'm afraid.'

'Oh, well, when will she be back? We wanted to talk to her about the school and perhaps making a more formal arrangement. We're very happy that she is sending so many of her pupils across,' Val gushed down the phone.

'She may be away for some time, I'm afraid. She's … err … lost her voice, and the doctor has told her to stay at home for a few days.' I was stumbling hopelessly over my words. Surely Val would not believe me, would she?

'I see,' she came back in a surprised tone. 'Well, when do you suggest we phone back?'

'I would try next week. She's really quite poorly,' I lied, looking at Elena and raising my eyebrows as I said it. She looked blankly at me, not understanding a word.

'Well, give her our best, won't you? We'll speak next week.' And Val rang off.

I relayed to Elena what I had said and she could not help laughing.

'Perhaps I should lose my voice permanently,' she suggested. 'What are we going to do? I can't speak to her and I don't want her to contact Peter. He won't like me agreeing anything with her.'

We discussed it with Hilary and Chris and Madeleine. Hilary felt responsible, I think, because it was she, apparently, who had written the letters to Bournemouth for Elena in the first place.

'We shouldn't have done it,' she said. 'What a fiasco.'

'There's only one thing for it,' said Madeleine with mock solemnity. 'If Elena doesn't want to be exposed as a fraud she'll have to die.'

Elena giggled.

'That's a drastic solution. Anyway, what happens when pupils go across to Bournemouth and talk about me?'

'Mmm,' Madeleine mused. 'That's tricky. You can't die and then come back to life. Perhaps a long illness?'

'I'd just tell her the truth,' said Chris.

Elena looked at her sternly.

'I can't do that. I would look very silly.'

Chris shrugged. Looking silly did not seem to be

important to her. It obviously was to Elena.

'We'll just have to take it in turns next week when the phone rings,' said Hilary. 'We could always say that we've spoken to Elena and she doesn't think it's the right time to take the relationship further.'

We couldn't come up with anything better – or that would not further complicate the situation, at any rate – so Elena answered the phone quite happily for the rest of the week and thereafter went back to her quiet '*Dígame,*' and stayed ready to hand over the phone to one of us if it was Val Baker's voice at the other end.

She was also vigilant about the incoming post – it was one of her and Mariuca's jobs to sort and distribute it – in case the Bakers decided to write to her using her formal title of director of studies. So far they had not, but Mariuca particularly would be intrigued if a letter addressed in such a way were to arrive – and she was not the sort of person who could be taken into a confidence of this sort.

In the end it all petered out. Madeleine took one call from Val Baker, during which she said that Elena was on a business trip to Barcelona for a week– a rather over-elaborate excuse, I thought, when she could have said that she was not available that day – and then Val's marketing campaign seemed to lose steam.

There was a letter, which was successfully intercepted, asking when would be a convenient time to call, but after that Val gave up, much to Elena's relief. No more pupils were referred to the Belle Vue School, and Elena never again experienced the rush of blood to her head which had caused her to pass herself off as director of studies. I was both shocked at what apparently went on in this adult world and also rather disappointed, in a way. It had all the ingredients of a farce with impersonations and cover-up conversations, but it was a welcome distraction from my everyday labours.

The other person with problems that spilt over into the Instituto was Hilary. She also manipulated the truth to breaking point, and was nearly caught out by Peter Garrett.

To be fair, she had a lot on her mind. Her American neighbours, Waldo and Martha, seemed to be heading further down the path to drunken and dermatological oblivion.

She told me about it as we were on the metro, heading to the Cat Restaurant one lunchtime. The strain of dealing with them was pushing her towards irrational outbursts of near-hysterical laughter at the slightest thing.

We passed through a metro station called Goya, which was under the Calle de Goya, the street named after the famous Spanish painter. Of course, as with most railway systems, underground or above, all along the walls were large metal plates bearing the name of the station. It was also being redecorated, and Hilary caught sight of a man in overalls with a pot of paint and a brush standing on scaffolding daubing a fresh undercoat on to the walls with the name of the station, Goya, directly above him. The idea that this was a sign informing everybody that this little man with his paintbrush was the famous eighteenth-century artist was too much for her.

'Ooh, look,' she burbled, 'It's Goya,' and lapsed into a fit of throaty giggles.

I smiled politely and then gave a little laugh.

'Looks like he's doing a good job,' I said. 'But he'll need to make it a bit more interesting if it's going to stand comparison with his earlier works.'

'Oh,' Hilary gasped and patted her chest. 'I think everything's getting to me, you know. Jaime, you know - the private pupil - wants more lessons, and is talking about starting earlier or doing some in the evening.'

'You should be pleased. He obviously thinks you're good,' I told her.

'Yes, but it's just the early mornings and having to prepare all his lessons. I want to do it properly, and then there's Waldo and Martha. It's getting ridiculous.' She stopped as we arrived at our destination and headed up to the Cat Restaurant.

'The thing is,' she continued after we were seated and had ordered the *sopa de verduras*, 'Waldo and Martha seem to be almost wholly reliant on us now.'

'Oh, dear,' I said. 'What have they been up to?'

'Well, we paid the electricity bill… Do you remember? But now they come round almost every evening for something or other, and they want me to drive them to the American embassy.'

'To drive them?' I said. 'Why can't they go on the train or the bus?'

'They'd never get there,' said Hilary. 'They'd get lost. They can barely go to the shops on their own. Martha fell down the stairs yesterday.'

'Was she hurt, then?'

'No. Nigel said she bounced, but she's got a shocking black eye. Plus their skin problem seems to be getting worse, and Waldo's got something wrong with his knee. They need to see a doctor, but I'm not sure they could manage that, either. Just being with them makes me itch,' and Hilary started rubbing her arms and I felt my skin begin to itch and tingle as well.

'Why do they need to go to the embassy?' I asked.

'They want to go there to get their passports renewed and then they're going to try and fly back to the States – which would be a great relief for all. The thing is … Waldo has got this dodgy knee now and he doesn't think he can drive. He's not very good, apparently, with a clutch at the best of times – you know they have automatics mostly in America – but he says he's happy for me to drive them. He said that if I do drive them we can use the car at the weekends – which would be very nice.'

Hilary looked worried, but just then the soup arrived so we took a few seconds to sample it. It tasted reassuringly the same as always.

'Have you passed your test?' I asked her after a couple of slurps. I remembered her saying something about learning.

She shook her head.

'Not yet.'

'Well, can Nigel drive?'

She shook her head again.

'Never really had time to learn.'

'I don't think you should do it, then. You might get into trouble if the police stop you.' I was very aware now of the possibilities of this happening.

'Mmm.' Hilary lapsed into thought. 'Of course,' she said eventually, 'getting their passports sorted out and then getting them on a plane to the States, providing they can remember where they need to go, would get them out of our hair, and having a car at the weekend for trips out to the sierra would be nice. Oh, I don't know. I can't decide what to do.'

'What does Nigel say?'

'Oh, he just laughs and says let them stew – but I just can't let them go to rack and ruin without stepping in.' She looked pensive, so to lighten the mood I asked again how the private lessons with Jaime Sanchez de Toledo were going.

'Yes, they're fine. But, like I said, I need some more time to do them, really. If it's not early mornings then it'll have to be in the evening.'

'You'll have to fit it in with your lessons at the Instituto,' I warned.

'I know – but he's such a catch and the money's so good.'

Her expression changed and she looked dreamily into the middle distance, where two of the resident cats lay sprawled on a radiator on the far side of the bar. I began to suspect that it was not just the money that made her lessons with *Señorito*

Jaime so attractive.

So Hilary had several things on her mind – which may explain her irrational actions that, on two fronts, almost ended in disaster.

XXII

The first of Hilary's problems was how to fit in the extra lessons with her prize pupil. In the end she said he suggested – but I think demanded was probably the word – that they have an extra lesson on the following Monday at 4.30. This was highly inconvenient as, although she would not have to get up any earlier, 4.30 was the beginning of the afternoon, a time when everybody at the Instituto had classes on just about every day of the week. Monday was no exception.

Hilary, Chris, Madeleine and I discussed this one evening a few days beforehand. We went into Madeleine's classroom, which was empty at the time. It seemed improper to involve Elena in our machinations. She had only just recovered from the Belle Vue School of English debacle.

'What can I do?' asked Hilary. 'I don't want to miss out on the lesson – and he is insistent.'

'You could always ring in sick,' said Madeleine. 'It's been done before, you know, and none of us has a bad sick record. We always turn up, whatever.'

I was shocked. Already we had had deceptions with the Belle Vue School of English, Hilary was proposing to drive a car without a licence … and now people were suggesting ringing in sick when they were in good health. At least my fantasy girlfriend in Andalusia had only had the potential to rebound on me. This seemed likely to become a deception that could enmesh everyone.

Hilary stared at Madeleine for a few seconds.

'Mmm, yes,' she said slowly. 'That might work. Michael,' she turned to me and fixed me with a stern gaze, 'you've heard nothing.'

'OK,' I said readily, and I could feel my heart beat a little faster. I was convinced that I would buckle immediately under interrogation from Peter Garrett. The fact that I never saw him, apart from payday when I ran up the stairs to his office to receive my cheque, did not console me.

I did forget about Hilary's first problem for a while over the weekend, but when I came back in on Monday I was reminded of it all when I heard Mariuca take a call from someone – obviously Hilary – informing her that she was ill.

'Who was that?' I asked innocently as she put the phone down.

Mariuca pursed her lips and then smiled unctuously.

'Poor Hilary. She is not very well.' She sighed. 'There is so much terrible illness around at the moment.' She made it sound as if the Black Death was stalking us. 'I must try to phone her pupils. Perhaps one of you other teachers can take one or two of her classes.'

I had no wish to increase my workload but nevertheless nodded and, barely audibly, breathed, 'Perhaps.' I knew that I had the three nurses that evening and a new lady from the Banco Hispano Americano called Lola, and I was pretty sure that Nervous José would be booked in for the later session, so I felt confident that I could appear to want to be helpful without running the risk of actually having to do anything.

When Chris and Madeleine appeared between lessons at midday I said, pointedly,

'Hilary's not well. She phoned in.'

'Oh, what a shame.' Chris's eyebrows shot up expressively.

Anne came bustling out of her room as we spoke.

'What's wrong?' she asked.

'Hilary's not coming in today. She's ill,' said Madeleine.

'Oh, yes, I know,' said Anne. 'Mariuca told me,' and she gestured towards Mariuca, who was still perched on her stool behind the reception desk. In deference to her Anne started speaking in Spanish.

'Mariuca asked me to take Hilary's eight o'clock class, so I said OK. It works out all right as I have to stay for a nine o'clock one, anyway,' and she continued out through the door and down the corridor.

'Yes,' said Mariuca, now coming into the conversation, 'and Tim Hewitt will take the three gentlemen at seven o'clock – oh, and I persuaded Peter to come down and take her class from four until five thirty, so it was only the late class that I had to cancel as nobody was free to do it.'

I was most surprised at how busy Mariuca had been. She never actually gave the impression of doing anything. Clearly her efficiency was such that it went unnoticed.

So ... we would be treated to a visit from Peter Garrett at four o'clock. I made a mental note to try and make sure that my four o'clock class was in full swing with the sound of intense but enjoyable study drifting out towards reception as he passed through.

I had lunch that day with Madeleine. We went to a bar just down the road that she had discovered and grabbed a *plato combinado*. This was a set dish, the ingredients of which never changed, and which were illustrated by a cartoon-like drawing on the wall of the bar. There were four or five different *platos combinados* up there. Each was numbered, usefully if unimaginatively, one to five. I think I chose number three and Madeleine had number four – or perhaps it was the other way round. I know that one involved fried eggs and the other one Russian salad.

As a result of lunching only next door we were back at about quarter to four to find the Instituto empty – or so we thought. As was often the case, we went into the little office next to my classroom. It was immediately on the right as you entered the Instituto – just before my classroom – and was used from time to time by Mariuca or Elena when dealing with any correspondence.

There was a desk with a typewriter on it – presumably the one that had been used to write letters to the Belle Vue School of English by the 'Director of Studies', Elena, and some shelves with various files stacked up on them containing paperwork. There was also a phone, which Hilary and Madeleine had encouraged me to use to call home. I had never done so, of course. I was too nervous about the cost and the propriety of using office equipment for private purposes.

There were two or three other chairs in there, mainly because they didn't fit anywhere else, but the office was not in reality used much so it served as an unofficial staffroom – a place to sit and talk if the reception area was too crowded. It also served as the smoking room and Madeleine wanted a cigarette, which was why we went in there.

As we entered, talking about something inconsequential, there was a scrabbling sound and a small squeak and there in front of us, apparently trying to flatten herself against the far wall, was Hilary, looking terrified. As she saw us she let out a sigh and her features were transformed by the relief that she obviously felt.

'What are you doing here?' Madeleine asked in a stern, low voice. 'You're supposed to be sick.'

'I know,' said Hilary 'but I was on the metro going to Jaime's flat when I realised that I'd left his textbook in my room here.' She motioned to a thin volume lying on the desk. 'I came in to get it as I thought no one would be here and I was just about to leave when I heard you coming. I dashed in here to hide. Oh, God, what a mess to get myself into.'

'Well, never mind,' said Madeleine calmly. 'You've got it now, so you'd best get out quick. Be careful no-one sees you on the way down'

As she said this we heard the main door outside open and someone came in. Hilary looked horror-struck and shrank further into the wall as Madeleine coolly looked through a crack in the door. Totally confounded by the whole situation, I was motionless.

'It's Chris,' Madeleine hissed over her shoulder. 'Chris,' she said gesturing to her round the half-open door, 'come in here.'

'Hello, having a staff meeting?' said Chris as she came in, still in her coat. 'Hilary,' her voice rose in surprise, 'what are you doing in here?'

'Never mind,' said Madeleine, assuming complete control. 'She has to get out before anyone sees her.'

Chris looked blank.

'I'm sick,' said Hilary, reminding her. 'Not supposed to be here.'

'Oh, yes.' Chris gave a little giggle.

The main door opened again. Hilary gave a stifled groan. Madeleine motioned her to be quiet.

'It's Anne,' she said. Then to Chris, 'Go and take her into your room and talk to her there.'

Chris looked hesitant.

'Go on,' hissed Madeleine.

Chris went out and we heard her talking, loudly to Anne about one of the textbooks that they both used. Their voices trailed off as they went along to Anne's room.

Another collective sigh of relief had barely escaped from all of us when the main door opened again and then again. From the sound of it pupils were starting to arrive.

The door to the office opened slightly and Chris slid into the room.

'Where's Anne?' asked Madeleine.

'It's all right. She's in her room, getting ready. You'll have to stay here for a bit until classes start,' she said to Hilary.

Hilary looked glum.

'I'll be late for Jaime,' she said.

Madeleine, on duty at the door, let out a gasp.

'Oh, God,' she said. 'It's Garrett. He's come to do your four o'clock class.'

Hilary's reaction was similar to that of a hen discovering that there was a fox on the prowl. She moved one way against the wall and then the other and then looked around desperately as if there might be a concealed door that none of us had spotted.

'You'd better get under the desk, just in case,' said Madeleine, peering through the crack in the door.

'What? I don't think I can,' wailed Hilary.

'Shush,' said Chris. 'He'll hear you.'

I looked on unbelievingly as Hilary got down on her hands and knees and crawled under the desk. It was a very old desk, with sets of drawers built in to each side and, luckily for Hilary, what was known as a modesty board in front to hide the legs of whoever was sitting behind it from the unwelcome gaze of fellow workers or passers-by. Hilary pushed the desk chair to one side and curled up in the space reserved normally only for the legs of the desk's occupant. The modesty board made her invisible to anyone standing in front.

This, nevertheless, made some considerable noise and, just as she had squashed herself into the tiny compartment, like a stowaway in a tea crate, the door opened and Peter Garrett started to come in. It was Hilary's – and our – good fortune that he at first only stuck his head slowly round the door, which gave us a fraction of a second to compose ourselves.

Chris jumped quickly on to the desk and sat, legs swinging idly, with a look of ostentatious nonchalance on her face as she inspected her nails. It was hopeless overacting. I, meanwhile, was still frozen at the back of the room, glassy-eyed, a rabbit caught in the headlights of Peter's amiable gaze. I was desperately trying not to look at Hilary as she screwed up her face with the effort of resisting the temptation to move into a more comfortable position.

Madeleine, however, was magnificent. She had moved back into the room, to encourage Hilary to get under the table, but she now glided swiftly over to the door to greet Peter – and to almost totally block his view.

'So,' he said affably, trying to peer over her shoulder. 'This is where you all hide, is it?'

Madeleine stood as close to him as she could without looking confrontational.

'We're just preparing for the afternoon's lessons,' she said. 'You're going to cover for Hilary, aren't you?'

'I am, yes. Poor girl has picked up some bug or other. She's flat out, apparently,' he said sympathetically.

Seeing the contorted position that Hilary had had to assume under the desk, it struck me just how far from the truth this statement was.

'Her classroom's over here,' said Madeleine, ushering him out and across the reception area to Hilary's room.

I moved at last and with Chris we peered out round the door. Madeleine had taken Peter right into Hilary's room, and the pupils appeared to be following. Meanwhile I noticed that Juana, my dear nursing friend, was sitting in reception trying to gain my attention, and I realised that it was four o'clock already. So much for my plans to have an intensive study session in progress when Peter came down. I waved to Juana and motioned her into the classroom, watching as Madeleine came out of Hilary's room and closed the door behind her.

Madeleine strode confidently back into the office. I shut

the door after her.

We went round to the back of the desk. Hilary was still squashed into her hiding place.

'He's in your room, teaching,' Madeleine told her. 'We'll have to go as well now.' She indicated Chris and me.

'Can I come out?' asked Hilary mournfully. She was trying to move her head but there was no room.

'No,' Madeleine replied sternly. 'You'll need to wait a couple of minutes until we're all teaching. I think Tim's back in his room and your pupils are all in with Peter, but leave it a few minutes.'

'OK. Oh,' a further troubled look crossed Hilary's slightly distorted features. 'What about Elena?'

'You'll just have to hope she's late, as usual,' was Madeleine's advice. This was reasonable enough. Elena sometimes did not arrive much before four thirty.

We walked out of the office and into our classrooms. All three nurses were there, waiting, so I launched into our familiar routine, but I was distracted some minutes later by what I thought was a scrabbling sound coming from the room next door, as if there were mice behind the skirting board. Then there was a bang and a loud squeak.

'Yes,' I turned and laughed at the three nurses, 'it must be the mice.'

Hilary managed to get out unobserved. All classes were in progress behind closed doors and Elena was, thankfully, late that afternoon. The lesson with *Señorito* Jaime, the prize pupil, went well, but he did ask her why she held her head slightly to one side throughout. She told him she had slept in a draught and as a result had a stiff neck.

No more Monday afternoon classes were scheduled with him.

XXIII

None of us were there to see the development of Hilary's other problem so we only heard about it at second hand, but by her own admission she again only narrowly averted disaster.

I was somewhat distracted, anyway, at the time, as I had another bout of tummy trouble, brought on most probably by the less than hygienic conditions that sometimes prevailed in the kitchen at no. 68 Calle de Canillas.

Santiago was well-practised in looking after himself. His clothes were always neat and clean and he ate regular, nourishing meals. Although very gradually expanding, my skills still went no further really than a beef chop or a fried cheese sandwich.

There was also a period, following the unauthorised consumption of my *leche rica* tin of condensed milk and the failure of the coloured dot system of identification, when I felt unwilling to leave anything in the fridge. Instead, I accumulated a small pile of food under my bed.

This, or my possible inattention to the proper washing and drying of cutlery, brought on a stomach upset, which I did not seem able to throw off completely. It rumbled on – literally – for several days, diminishing and increasing in severity quite unpredictably. I still went into the Instituto and was half-expecting my female guardian angels to suggest a course of suppositories, but then one morning that week Mariuca handed me a card.

'Elena told me that you have a stomach problem,' she said. 'Poor you. It can't be very nice. You should go to see this doctor and he will make it better.'

I was quite taken aback by her care and consideration. As a former bride of Jesus I half-thought that Mariuca might view any bout of illness as something to be endured as God's punishment for previous sins. She smiled sweetly at me, her crimson lips upturned at the edges.

'Do you want me to make an appointment for you?'

I certainly did. I knew that I would have to pay but we were all insured through the Social Security system; my money would be reimbursed.

She made an appointment for me for the following morning, when I had no classes.

Meanwhile, that afternoon Hilary appeared, looking haggard. She had to go straight into her classroom for a couple of hours but we all had an opportunity at about six o'clock to gather at Elena's desk to hear what had been happening to her.

It was unclear whether there was a continuation of the prize pupil problem – it was only a couple of days since she had been forced to seek refuge under the desk – or if it was the other thorny issue of Waldo and Martha, the severely incapacitated neighbours. For me, whatever was happening, I was sure that it would prove to be a further lesson in the way the world worked, far beyond anything that I could, in my innocence, imagine. I looked forward to her revelations excitedly.

All was going well, she told us, with *Señorito* Jaime, the prize pupil. They were starting half an hour earlier three mornings a week in order to accommodate his zeal for more learning, and there was no danger of a repetition of the desk incident.

'No,' she said. 'It's Waldo and Martha. I've been driving

them around this morning. It was terrifying.'

'Driving them where?' asked Chris, astonished.

'Everywhere,' said Hilary.' All around Madrid. Waldo came round this morning about eleven o'clock just after I got back from Jaime and he was threatening to get the car out and go to the embassy and the hospital and everywhere, and he stank of drink.'

'What did Nigel say?' I asked. Although I had not met him I was sure Nigel would have got rid of them promptly.

'He wasn't there. He'd already gone to work. I was so worried about what they would do that I just said I would take them,' Hilary continued.

'I'd have told them to get lost,' said Chris bluntly.

'It's not that easy. They're a sweet old couple and they've got no one else at all, as far as I can see. What was I supposed to do? Just leave them to it?' She looked at us, appealing for our understanding.

'Oh, no. You couldn't do that,' I said, to placate her. It all seemed so far-fetched that it was quite funny in a way to me. Hilary answering the door to this decrepit, gin-sodden old pair who were scratching madly at themselves all the while as they threatened to take to the road in a car that they couldn't drive.

'So I started to drive them to the American embassy – except we couldn't find it. Do you know how mad the traffic is around the Cibeles roundabout?'

We all did. This was a major junction in the centre of Madrid – a roundabout with a giant classical fountain at its centre. Traffic poured in from different routes to this one point and revolved around it in a seething mass of honking horns and bumper-to-bumper manoeuvrings. It was amazing that vehicles managed to avoid each other and that it was not permanently gridlocked. The behaviour of most motorists who drove round it seemed to me like that of a group of mischievous ten-year-olds on fairground dodgems whose only intention was to cause fear and panic in others while, at the last moment, escaping unscathed themselves.

'You drove round Cibeles?' Madeleine asked incredulously.

'Yes, and then I tried to find the American embassy and I drove the wrong way up a one-way street.' Hilary grimaced as she remembered it. 'I just couldn't get the hang of the gears, either. I kept putting it into fourth when I meant to go into second.'

'What did Waldo and Martha say?' I asked, imagining them clutching on to any available surface.

'They just kept laughing,' said Hilary. 'When I missed the gears Waldo just giggled and said,' and here she attempted an American accent in a strangulated voice, '"That's the way to do it, honey. If they don't work just grind 'em down till they do. That's what I say."'

Elena, who had now caught on to the general sense of the conversation, clapped her hand over her mouth and raised her eyes in horror.

'Hilary,' she said, continuing in Spanish, 'You could be killed.'

'I know, but it gets worse,' said Hilary in a voice on the edge of hysteria. She seemed caught up in the need to relay to us the ever-increasing horrors of her day.

'We knew where the embassy was, but I couldn't see how to drive there. I kept getting muddled up in the one-way system so I stopped in a side street and was going to ask one of the *grises* – you know, the traffic police – how to get there.'

'You actually went up to a policeman?' asked Chris, incredulity reaching a new peak. 'Even though you had no driving licence?'

'I know, I know, but I thought if I got out and asked one of them a little way away from the car just where the embassy was I could then ask him about the one-way system. That bit actually worked. He was around the corner so he didn't see the car. For all he knew I was on foot but planning to go there later. But then,' and here she paused and gave a ragged sigh, 'I went back around the corner to the car and Waldo was sitting in the driving seat. He said they were fed up with it all and were going to drive home.'

'Oh my God,' said Madeleine. 'I hope you pulled him out.'

'Well, no, actually,' said Hilary. 'I tried to reason with him but he refused to budge – so I just got into the passenger seat and off we went.'

More astonishment from all of us. From her description of him it appeared that Waldo only retained the faintest grasp on reality. In his alcohol-induced haze, with flaking skin and an out-of-action knee, I am sure none of us would have gone within a hundred yards of a car driven by him.

'It was terrible,' Hilary continued. 'Every time we got to a traffic light he stopped whether it was red or green and scratched both his legs.' She shuddered. 'I'm still all itchy at the thought of it. Then, because of his wonky knee, the only way he could operate the clutch was to use his hands to move his leg up and down on it, so he took his hands off the steering wheel. Even that was too hard sometimes. We drove the length of the Gran Via in second gear.'

We were all stunned into silence, imagining their noisy, fume-filled progress down one of Madrid's principal streets.

'Then Martha started singing "Way down upon the Swanee River" in the back seat, and Waldo joined in. I wanted to die.'

'You're lucky you didn't,' said Chris. 'Did he drive you home?'

'No. We got as far as Moncloa, somehow. I kept directing him and pulling the steering wheel round, and then, at some traffic lights he just sort of fell asleep.'

'I'd have just left him there,' said Chris.

'Well, no, I couldn't do that,' said Hilary. 'I felt responsible somehow, so I managed to get him across into the passenger seat and drove back – mainly in second gear,' she added with a wan smile.

We were all quietly visualising in our own way this nightmare journey which, miraculously, had concluded without serious injury. The idea of an inexperienced learner driver negotiating the Madrid traffic, while coping with two drunkards singing songs from the Deep South and constantly scratching themselves, was almost beyond imagining. I did briefly get a mental picture of Hilary in the car, looking like the horror-struck man in Munch's *The Scream* painting, kangaroo-jumping around Cibeles with the two Americans, their faces pressed up against the windows, shouting and waving bottles at the other motorists. I had to shake my head rapidly to get rid of it.

'So,' said Hilary. 'That was that.' And she gave a rather timid smile, as if seriously seeking our approval for what had happened.

'Well, yes and no. You can't do it again,' said Madeleine firmly. 'Promise you won't.'

'Oh, no, of course not,' said Hilary. She smiled again, weakly. 'But it would be nice to have their car at the weekends – even if it is all full of skin flakes.'

'No,' said Chris and Madeleine in unison.

'No more trips in the car,' I said, feeling faintly itchy myself.

We all had to go back in to our lessons soon afterwards, but it was agreed that something had to be done. In the end it was Madeleine again who took the lead. She phoned Nigel and we all assembled in a bar after classes that evening to formulate a plan. Sabin came along as well and was sorry to hear about the 'tight spot', as he called it, that Hilary had found herself in earlier.

The meeting took place with plenty of Ribeiro wine

to facilitate the proceedings. I temporarily forgot about my stomach problem as I enthusiastically embraced the team approach to finding a solution, and Hilary was uncharacteristically quiet. She was embarrassed, I think, about the rashness of her actions and her big-hearted sensitivity to the plight of her American neighbours, which had put them all at risk.

The upshot was that Nigel would phone the embassy and try to get them to take responsibility for Waldo and Martha. They were clearly American citizens and Waldo was an ex-serviceman, so there was some hope that the problem could be handed to the American authorities. Hilary, meanwhile, was instructed not to open the door to them and, under no circumstances, to get into the car.

As we left the bar, very late, Hilary thanked us all for our support. I wasn't sure I had given any, but we all made appropriate comments like,

'It's nothing,' and, 'That's what friends are for.' Possibly as a result of the numerous glasses of Ribeiro wine that she had drunk, and definitely as a result of her travails over the previous few days, Hilary burst into a flood of grateful tears.

XXIV

Because I had imbibed copious amounts of wine at the previous evening's after-work planning session about the Waldo and Martha problem my stomach was very upset during the night. It was fortuitous, therefore, that I had my appointment with the doctor that Mariuca had recommended the following morning.

I was anxious to find a cure, both because it was unpleasant and because I was now planning a weekend trip down to Cordoba.

This trip was on Brian's advice. Before coming to Madrid he had spent a week or so in Andalusia – presumably just after my soggy sojourn there – and had stayed in Cordoba in a private residence that rented out rooms around its ancient courtyard. Brian had apparently got on very well with the proprietor, who had said that he must come back for the Festival of the Patios, which was held each year in mid May. Unfortunately Brian's university stay in Madrid precluded him from doing this but he passed me a card with the name and address of the *residencia* on it and recommended that I go.

Madeleine confirmed that the Festival of the Patios was well worth a trip. Every year private residences, public buildings, religious establishments and ancient palaces – all of which contained at least one shaded patio or courtyard – vied with each other to see who could put on the most colourful and decorative display of plants and flowers. If I caught the overnight train on Friday I could spend all day Saturday and most of Sunday there.

So, anxious for a cure for my stomach problem, I entered the surgery of Dr Saenz Herrera, as recommended by Mariuca.

The doctor did all the normal things that I expected. He asked me what my symptoms were, felt the surface of my tummy and peered down my throat. He took out a pad and, for one moment, I thought he was going to prescribe suppositories. I was relieved when he told me that he was prescribing antibiotics – to be taken orally, he added.

'Thank you very much,' I said, about to leave.

'Oh,' he continued almost as a throwaway remark, 'and you must eat only white fish, boiled rice, grated apple and natural yoghurt for four days. Everything white – and drink only boiled water.'

'Ah, OK,' I responded vaguely, not fully taking in what he had said. It was only when I got outside that I mused on the restricted nature of the diet. Apple and yoghurt did not present a problem – but fish and boiled rice… I wasn't sure how to prepare those. I certainly didn't remember them featuring on the menu of any restaurant that I had visited. It looked like I had several demanding and, from a gastronomical viewpoint, unsatisfactory days ahead of me.

I couldn't find a grater in the flat so I went out and bought one. I started taking the antibiotics as soon as possible and also bought a large pot of yoghurt and a bag of apples. The yoghurt stayed in the fridge. Even I, with only a rudimentary knowledge of kitchen hygiene, realised it needed to be kept cool and it was fairly unappetising anyway, but the apples and grater went under my bed – just in case one of my flatmates should be stricken with a yearning for a nice grated apple in the night.

The fish and rice presented more of a difficulty. On my

way home in the evening I bought some frozen fish and a bag of rice but had no idea what to do with them. There was no one in the flat to ask. Santiago was, unusually, out for the evening, and Brian and Robin weren't there either. So I had a go at preparing it myself.

There were some instructions on the rice packet but they were a little vague about quantities, so I boiled a saucepan of water and poured the contents into it. Within fifteen minutes I had a saucepan overflowing with partially cooked sticky rice, enough to feed a very large and hungry family. It was, due to its parboiled state, inedible. So it went in the bin and I set to cleaning the glutinous mess off the surface of the cooker, where it had congealed like the spawn of some hideous amphibian.

After doing all that I could not face attempting to cook the fish so I went down to my bedroom with the pot of yoghurt and grated an apple into it. I went to bed very hungry.

The next day I went into the Instituto and managed to get through the morning on a couple of ungrated apples. I then sat in my classroom and consumed a pot of yoghurt at lunchtime. Chris was of the opinion that I should have some soup or something light, but I determined to stick with the advice of Dr Saenz Herrera. When Elena came in later in the afternoon and I told her about my trip to the doctor and my debilitated state she asked me for his card. When I gave it to her she laughed and said to Chris, who was standing next to me in the reception area:

'Mariuca sent him to a *puericultor*.'

I had no idea what a *puericultor* was. I had presumed it was another name for a doctor.

'This is a doctor who treats children. Peter's children go to him when they are sick,' she said. 'You don't need to see him.' So Mariuca had sent me to a paediatrician whose cure was presumably designed for the delicate stomach of a five-year-old.

'When is your next class?' she asked me.

'Not until six,' I replied. She looked at the clock. It was ten past five.

'Come with me,' she said, and got down off her stool. She took my hand and we went downstairs and across the road to the little cafe where we often had coffee or hot chocolate.

'A black tea,' she said in a loud voice to the waiter, 'and two *Magdalenas*.'

We sat down at the table and the waiter brought the order over. There was a cup with a teabag in it and two plain round fairy cakes.

'You can't live on yoghurt and apples,' she said. 'You're not five years old.' She emptied a sachet of sugar into the tea. 'Drink this, and eat the *Magdalenas*. They won't do you any harm. Then tonight get a lean beef chop and fry it for about ten minutes slowly on each side in a little olive oil, but,' and she laid emphasis on every word that followed, 'make sure the pan and the plate and the knife and fork are clean. That's why you've got an upset stomach, I'm sure. I know what men are like in a kitchen.'

'OK.' I didn't argue. It was reassuring to be told what to do especially when the advice was so much more palatable, literally, than that given to me by the paediatrician.

I fell on the *Magdalenas* like a wolf on a lamb and had eaten them in a trice. I slurped the tea – even without milk it tasted good – and then asked,

'Can I have another *Magdalena*, please?' like an infant at the tea table.'

'Just one more, then,' she laughed. 'You mustn't overdo it.'

So I had one more *Magdalena*. They were only plain little sponge cakes but they seemed like ambrosia to me. I had only lasted thirty-six hours on my plain, all-white diet – admittedly I'd missed out on the fish and the rice, but I can't think that eating them would have given me any pleasure. Now I had discovered the *Magdalenas* and I felt the strength return to my limbs.

Elena was right. I bought a chop and a little flagon of olive oil, scoured the frying pan and a plate, and then cooked the chop slowly. I polished the knife and fork until they gleamed, ate the chop and went to bed pleasantly full with an uncomplaining stomach.

*

There was good news the next day. I had a class with Dolores, the formidable spinster lady who did not need lessons but who came anyway to distract herself from her humdrum life. She told me that her painter friend, whose name was Eduardo, had returned to Madrid and he was keen to start private classes with me as soon as possible.

I replied that I was available as soon as he wished to start. It would have to fit in with my timetable at the Instituto. I was not prepared to get involved in a Hilary-type deception – ringing in sick, and then hiding in cupboards or wearing disguises – but there were several lengthy gaps on most evenings. His studio was only in the Calle Arenal, which was no more than two minutes' walk away, so I could start as soon as he wanted to.

Dolores promised to relay the message and the next day after my five o'clock class Elena gave me a handwritten note from Dolores, saying that her friend would like to start that evening at eight o'clock – a time that I had indicated I was available. She had written his name and address as well in her large, firm handwriting.

So, a mere two hours later, I was ringing the bell of an apartment three floors above the busy Calle Arenal. The door opened with a click and I sprinted upstairs to the studio.

My Reign in Spain

Eduardo the painter was waiting for me by the door of his studio. He was somewhere between forty and sixty in age – I was still very hazy about anyone who looked older than thirty – with dark, slicked-back hair and a broad face with prominent nose and lips. He was wearing a bright red shirt and black trousers, and I was immediately reminded of the flamenco singer that we had seen in the Sacromonte caves in Granada. He grasped me firmly by the hand and ushered me into the studio.

'How very exciting to meet you,' he said to me. 'I hope you will teach me to speak excellent English.'

'Oh, of course,' I replied in my most confident voice. After all, I had nearly perfected the Giddings method of teaching English to foreigners now. It all revolved around how quickly we could move Martin and Jane away from the birds and the park bench.

We went into a large, cluttered room with windows running all along one side. It was unusually light for a Spanish interior, where the sun is more often shut out than let in, and it was full of old, heavy furniture and hundreds of paintings.

In one corner was the place where Eduardo obviously worked. I could see the back of an easel with a large canvas propped up on it and there was the paraphernalia of an artist all around it – tubes of paints and palettes, rags stained with a thousand shades from burnt umber through vermilion to Prussian blue and smaller pieces of canvas and paper with daubs and sketches on them.

Stacked against the walls were canvasses of all sizes – some finished, some apparently not – mainly portraits, from what I could see. One of the most eye-catching was a reclining nude, placed prominently on top of a pile of others and executed in large, rough fleshy-pink brush strokes. Her figure was ample and curvaceous, with more than a passing resemblance to the well-rounded classical nudes of the seventeenth and eighteenth centuries. There was a look of permanence in the way it was positioned above and slightly in front of the other canvasses. I was taken aback, however, when I saw the face of this recumbent creature. It bore, I thought, an uncanny resemblance to Dolores. I could not imagine her agreeing to pose like that , but I was immediately curious.

He led the way across to a pair of upholstered, solid wood chairs at the opposite end of the room from the easel and indicated that I should sit down.

'So,' he said. 'Let us begin.'

He knew one or two words already, and I soon had him saying phrases such as,

'My name is Eduardo,' 'I am an artist,' and 'I live in Madrid.' He seemed to catch on very quickly and, because my eyes were being drawn every so often to the reclining nude, I thought for a moment of teaching him to say,

'I paint Dolores in the nude,' but dismissed it instantly.

We agreed that I would obtain for him the first volume of Martin and Jane's exploits for our next lesson and he handed over two one hundred peseta notes, which I put straight into my pocket. He wanted another lesson later in the week, so after a quick look at my timetable we agreed to meet on Friday at six o'clock.

As he was showing me to the door I glanced again at the portrait of the nude.

'What a beautiful painting,' I commented. 'Is the model a friend?'

'Ah,' he sighed. 'I painted this a long time ago. But you know the lady, I think?'

I feigned ignorance. I thought it better not to recognise the subject before being told.

He continued.

'I painted Dolores over twenty years ago, but she could

not have the portrait. Her parents were unwilling to accept it. In fact they were furious when they found out. So I keep it here.'

'She has changed very little in twenty years,' I said. In fact the more I studied her face the more it looked quite recent.

'Oh,' he laughed. 'No, no. I change the face from time to time – but not the body.'

I felt slightly uneasy as I took this in. Here was Dolores with a forty-year-old face and a twenty-year-old body. What on earth would the painting look like if she lived to be seventy or eighty?

'What does she think?' I asked him.

'Oh, she has not seen it. She does not come here. Her parents never permitted it. I meet her only at the bridge club.' He spoke the last sentence wistfully, the sadness almost tangible. Had he loved her and, by painting her in a state of undress, incurred the wrath of her parents, meaning that they could never be together? Had his painting in fact condemned her to a spinster's life? And was he himself condemned to live only with her image as she grew older, altering the only part of her that he now ever saw?

I was silent for a moment, puzzled and touched by the unspoken sense of loss that hung around him and the picture.

'Do not tell her you have seen the portrait,' he said as he accompanied me out into the hallway. 'She has forgotten about it, I think. I am looking forward to our lesson on Friday,' and with that he shut the door and was gone.

I walked slowly down the stairs, rubbing both the one hundred peseta notes in my pocket between my fingers. Life seemed very strange at that moment. There were endless possibilities still before me as the world called me onwards, but I had reckoned without the endless disappointments.

XXV

My next lesson with Dolores was not for a couple of days, so I managed to recover from the state of melancholy that my much-anticipated private lesson had brought on. When I eventually did see her she asked how the lesson had been. I said that it had gone well and that we would be having another one that week as well. I also said how interesting Eduardo's studio was.

She stared at me as she so often did from under her heavy eyelids and bushy eyebrows and for a brief second I thought I saw a flicker of emotion, but then she said,

'What is the topic for today?' in her gravelly voice and soon we were on to the pros and cons of public transport – the topic for the day.

It was a difficult lesson, nevertheless, if only for the fact that I kept superimposing the portrait of the voluptuous nude on to Dolores's tweedy twinset-clad body.

Eduardo, it turned out at our next lesson, was a native of Cordoba, so when I told him of my proposed jaunt to the Festival of the Patios he was very much in favour of it.

'I wish I could accompany you,' he said. 'But I have many commissions here,' and he waved his hand airily around the studio.

Madeleine, a sometime resident of Cordoba, also had plans – a proposed trip to Huelva in the far south-west to meet Manolo's family. She was very nervous at the prospect.

'They're very aristocratic, you know,' she told me, just

loudly enough for Hilary and Chris to hear. 'His father's family name is Diez, which is very ancient.'

'You'll have to be on your best behaviour, then,' I joked.

'Yes. I think they have their own bodega for sherry, you know. I hope I can keep up with the drinking.'

Having seen Madeleine at the Tankstelle, I couldn't believe that this would be a problem for her. I caught a glimpse of raised eyebrows and rolled eyes from Hilary and Chris in the background.

'By the way,' she said, 'I've contacted my friend Isabela about meeting up when you go down to Cordoba next weekend. There's a large cafe called the Imperial in the centre. I'll draw you a map. You're to meet her there next Saturday evening at eight o'clock. She and her friends will show you the sights.'

As the end of the week approached I made a reservation on the overnight train to Cordoba. I also made sure I had the card that Brian had given me with the address of the private residence that he had stayed at. I had asked Madeleine if she thought it was all right to stay there and she said it sounded a great way to meet the locals and soak up the festive atmosphere.

I would be gone for two days, with one night spent on the train, so I only planned to take a change of clothes. My rucksack would be far too big, so I borrowed a small bag from Santiago. It was black with a clasp on it – similar to the Gladstone bag once carried by doctors – and just the right size for my needs.

My previous experience of Andalusia had left me very wary, however. There was one item that was essential if the trip was to be successful. I purchased a small, tightly rolled black umbrella . I did not intend getting soaking wet again.

I went into the Instituto on the Friday with my little valise, ready to go straight to Atocha station that night to catch the train. I was wearing my raincoat as well. I still did not trust the weather in the south.

I passed a lot of the morning with Jaime Sancho, as usual, talking about his schoolwork and introducing him to the limited uses of the subjunctive in English. ('If I were to go to Andalusia I would need an umbrella,'; 'I will do extra English homework if it be necessary, to pass my Advanced Cambridge Diploma'.) There were then a variety of students after lunch, and the afternoon dragged as I waited for my final class to end at eight o'clock. I normally had Nervous José last thing on a Friday but we had agreed that, as I wanted to leave a little earlier, we would do an extra hour the following week.

So I came out of my room at eight, bag in hand and ready to take the night train to Cordoba. I was a little apprehensive at the new acquaintances I would be making: the private proprietor of the house with the courtyard where I would be seeking lodging, and Isabela and co., Madeleine's friends, who would be waiting to welcome me on the following evening.

The others were assembling at reception as their classes left as well.

'I'm off,' I announced to Elena and Madeleine and Chris.

'Have a great time,' said Madeleine, 'and give my love to Isabela.'

'I will.'

Hilary's door opened and she came out. I stood there, my little black bag in my hand with the umbrella poking out of it and my raincoat slung over my arm.

'Cor blimey,' said Hilary in her best cockney accent. 'It's Mary Poppins.'

I left, slightly red-faced but not really put out, to general merriment and good wishes for a successful trip.

*

The night train to Cordoba was as slow as the night train that we had taken to Valencia two months earlier. On the map the route did not look quite as circuitous but the speed was, if anything, even slower. The other difference was that it was much more crowded. I had to sit up all night in a compartment with a young couple with a small child, an elderly man and his wife and a middle-aged man who did manage to sleep for much of the journey, propped up in the corner and snoring gently.

The young child, a girl, was the centre of interest for much of the time. I gathered, from the conversation between her mother and the elderly wife, that she had a slight cleft palate, which they hoped could be operated on soon,

'Before the heat sets in,' as her mother put it reinforcing my conviction that we had not seen Andalusia at its best during the Easter week celebrations.

It seemed that the child's unfortunate affliction was only visible if her mouth was forced open. This her mother proceeded to do, at the behest of the inquisitive elderly wife, and it prompted the obvious reaction from the child. She started to howl with indignation and quite possibly pain, and continued to do so off and on for many hours. As I was seated in the middle of this little group of travellers I consequently got very little sleep. It was quite a relief when the train rolled into Cordoba at seven in the morning and I stepped off into the fast-approaching dawn.

The first thing I noticed, which hadn't for some reason been obvious on the train, was that it was very warm. Although only just getting light this was real shirtsleeves weather. I glanced at the raincoat slung over my arm and the umbrella poking out of the bag. Perhaps I wasn't going to need them after all.

I had some breakfast in the cafe at the station, taking my time, as it was still so early. My intention was to go to the tourist office when it opened and get a plan of Cordoba. This, I had been told, would show the main areas where patios were on show. The patios were not individually indicated, however. It was a case of walking around and peeping through open doorways to discover what was inside.

I also planned on revisiting the Mezquita and having a longer, more leisurely look than we had managed at Easter during our brief stop-off. At some stage I would go to the private residence that Brian had stayed in and check that they had a room for me, but that could only be done later in the day.

After making two cups of coffee and a pile of *churros* last as long as I could I paid and went out into the street. It was light now. The sun had risen and I could feel its warmth as it struck me gently on one side of my face. I began a leisurely but self-conscious stroll along the busy pavement towards the city centre. I imagined everyone staring at me with my raincoat on my arm and the umbrella prominently displayed, every inch the inappropriately dressed foreigner, as the sun climbed higher in the cloudless blue sky. I wasn't sure if the film of *Mary Poppins* had ever reached this far into Spain, but even without the image of the wind-blown nanny to compare me to I was certain that I must look a curiosity. The soggy days of Easter week, a month before, were probably the last time that an umbrella or raincoat had been seen in Cordoba.

Eventually the tourist office opened and I procured a map, which showed the main areas to visit. In truth it was not difficult to find them as I walked around the narrow streets in the old quarter near the Mezquita. It was simply a question of looking for the open doors and gateways, some large and splendid, others no more than small holes in the white walls.

As the morning progressed their location became ever more obvious, anyway, as the number of visitors grew and

I followed groups into small, cool enclosures whose walls were festooned with brilliant cascades of red and purple and white pelargoniums. Some had their main display at ground level in large earthenware or ceramic pots that spilt over with plants and flowers whose names I did not know, but whose firework display of colours I marvelled at.

In other, wider courtyards, where the sun struck one side brilliantly there was room for climbers – bright, delicate ipomoeas scrambling through the woody stems of trumpet vines, creating a vivid contrast of blue and orange that grew more profusely near the top as the flowers strained to reach the sun.

An artistic eye had been at work in each of these floral spaces. There was colour – in some cases in an almost overeffusive abundance – but there was room for the plain white walls as contrast, and carefully placed statuary to lead the eye where the gardener had dictated as well. There was also water, and this time it did seem like the 'precious commodity' of the Alhambra guidebook that I had read about under the dripping trees in Granada.

Pools and little fountains splished and splashed in even the smallest courtyard and fulfilled their role as counterpoint to the heat of the sun. In every place I looked the seemingly random was almost always in fact artfully arranged to harmonise and support, and I understood why the Moors of Granada had been so sad to lose their stronghold all those centuries ago and why the Spaniards of the north had been so keen to reclaim their ancient lands in the south.

There was an incentive, anyway, to put on a good show. The patio owners were competing for the prestige of a prize, which would recognise the perfection of their creation.

I was captivated and spent the whole morning walking around under an increasingly hot sun. There was an expression that I came across that weekend – '*El sol pega*'

('The sun is sticking') – and I understood it as lunchtime approached. It felt as if the sun's rays hit my face and then, only very slowly, like a heavy, viscous liquid, slid off towards the ground, to be replaced immediately by the next sticky layer. There was respite in the shade, but the sun had a physical force that possessed the streets as I walked along. (I found out later that the Guadalquivir river valley between Seville and Cordoba is the hottest spot in Spain, and possibly in all of Europe. It is shielded from the balmy influence of the Mediterranean by ranges of low mountains, and is known as *El sartén de España* ('The frying pan of Spain').)

The tourist office had indicated for me with an 'x' the location of the *residencia* where I hoped to find accommodation. I toyed with the idea of going there as midday came and went. I was less conscious of my umbrella and raincoat now, and confident that I was not really turning heads, but nevertheless I would have welcomed the chance to get rid of them.

I did wonder if they would be ready for someone seeking a room so early in the day but, on turning the corner of a narrow street, I found myself in a small square surrounded by houses that were obviously serious contenders for the prizes on offer. On one side, urging my sore feet to make my way over to them, were a group of small tables, deep in shade outside a neat little bar, which was itself covered in bright pots of multihued blooms and trelliswork adorned with climbers.

I gave in and sat down at one of the tables. There was a menu chalked up on a blackboard next to the doorway, so when someone came out to the table I ordered a plate of *albondigas* – small spicy meatballs – and a beer. When these arrived I consumed both food and drink greedily and ordered another beer. As a result of this, and a night spent sitting upright on the train, I passed a sleepy couple of hours at the table dozing occasionally and contemplating a huge purple bougainvillea that was climbing a wall on the opposite side of the little plaza and which became hazier as the torpor of the afternoon set in. A few other people came and went, but such was the level of inactivity at this time of day that nobody bothered me and the bar staff made no attempt to move me on.

Eventually I did rouse myself and paid the bill. I looked at the tourist office map and made my way towards the private residence where, I was now hoping, there would be room for me. It had not really occurred to me that it might be full. I felt already, thanks to Brian's description of his welcome there, that a place had somehow been reserved for me, but as I entered the narrow street I began to hope that the situation would not be the same as we had experienced a few weeks previously in Seville.

I need not have worried. I found the house halfway along the street. There was a wooden door, flung open, in the white wall. The owners were obviously candidates for one of the patio prizes as the small, cool courtyard inside was full of pots and little beds all fizzing with colour. On one side there was a colonnade with a long balcony above. At the end of the colonnade, almost hidden from view, I could see the start of a staircase that obviously gave access to the balcony above and the upper rooms on that side.

In the far corner was a table with a group of five or six people gathered round it who were preparing to eat. Although it was now past four o'clock I had arrived in the middle of lunch. At the head of the table was a man who bore a striking resemblance to Eduardo, my private pupil. He had the same dark, slicked-back hair, a broad, smiling face with a prominent nose and lips and large expressive hands. As I walked nervously into this idyllic spot he saw me, got up from the table and came across.

'Good day, *Señor*,' he said, showing two rows of gleaming white teeth behind his smile. 'How can I help you?'

I took out the card – his card – that Brian had given me and explained that Brian had stayed there a few weeks before. Did they have a room for me tonight?

'Ah, *Señor* Brian,' he said. The look of recognition on his face seemed genuine. 'What a charming man. He was very nice. We had a good time.'

So Brian had made a good impression. Perhaps I had judged him too harshly.

'Of course you may have a room,' he said, indicating that I should come further in. He clapped his hands and addressed two women who were sitting at the table, one middle-aged and the other much younger.

'*Sábanas limpias*,' he shouted. 'Clean sheets.'

I took this as a very good sign, for some reason. There were obviously high standards of hygiene here.

Both women got up and bustled through a doorway at the back, presumably to fetch the said sheets.

(I remembered, just then, Madeleine telling me how easy it was to do the washing in Cordoba at most times of the year.

'You just wash the sheets and anything else you need when you go home at lunchtime and hang them out. By the time you're ready to leave after lunch they're dry. You can even rinse through a blouse, hang it out and then iron it before afternoon classes.')

'Come with me,' said the man. 'This is your room.' He led me across the courtyard to a door off the colonnade and, after opening it, showed me a small, spotlessly clean room with a bed, as yet not made up, a table with a lamp on it and a tiny washbasin. The walls were all painted blinding white. It was a cool, cosy hideaway from the hard-beating sun.

'You're next to *Señor* Ramon,' he said, indicating the room next door.

I nodded appreciatively.

'We are just having lunch,' he said. 'We're a little late, but it's fiesta time. Last night we were all here having dinner at two in the morning. Two in the morning,' he repeated, as if to emphasise the ridiculously late hour. 'Would you like to come and join us now?'

I went across with him to the table and was soon eating a bowl of cold, oily *gazpacho* and helping myself from a plate of fried anchovies. There was a cold, sharp red wine which I also took full advantage of and, for the second time that afternoon my lunch seemed to pass in a pleasantly somnolent haze.

Señor Ramon was sitting next to me. He was an old man (which for me meant past forty or fifty) with short, cropped grey hair and a cackling laugh, which came out frequently as he and the host chattered away incomprehensibly. Their accents together were so pronounced, their sentences so difficult to follow that, due perhaps to my feeling of sleepy well-being, I did not even attempt to try and understand what they were talking about. I had absolutely no idea who Ramon was or why he was there, and I couldn't raise the energy to try to find out.

Again I eventually roused myself when they all got up from the table and I went back to the little room where the bed was now made up with the spotless white sheets. I washed my face and set out for the Imperial Bar. As it was only seven o'clock I intended going by way of the Mezquita. The social festivities with Madeleine's friends would be preceded by more contemplation of the spiritual. I had not been to Mass for several weeks, and a visit to the Mezquita would somehow make up for this in my mind.

As a result I was slightly late at the Imperial. It was a large, modern cafe and very crowded. In spite of the number of people and the fact that I had left my precautionary wet weather gear in my room, I felt my normal self-consciousness as I stood at the bar, beer in hand. It was a perfectly reasonable place for a young man to be, but I imagined every eye turned critically towards me, wondering what inadequacy caused me to be sad and alone.

I was nevertheless expecting to be approached at any time. There were a number of people circulating, obviously meeting friends, and gradually finding them at one or other of the tables or groups that were scattered all around. I saw a tall, very pretty young woman looking from side to side as she made her way through the cafe. She looked pointedly at me and I looked back. I managed a faint smile and shifted position and did all I could to show that I was alone and obviously waiting, but she turned her head and walked away. Clearly this was not Isabela.

Time passed. It was eight thirty. I knew of course that Spaniards were not the most punctual of timekeepers, especially the younger generation, but as the clock slipped forward another quarter of an hour I began to feel very disappointed. I did not want to spend the evening on my own and the prospect of going back to the room just yet was not appealing. I was staring at nothing, thinking gloomy thoughts, when I noticed that the girl was back, still patrolling the room but now accompanied by a young man. They had obviously not found whoever they were looking for.

With a huge intake of breath and a resolution that came from somewhere deep inside me I pushed past a couple of groups of people and went up to them.

'Are you Isabela, Madeleine's friend?' I asked her, hoping desperately that she was.

She looked at me, surprised, and I thought that I had made a terrible mistake. Would the boyfriend be the jealous, hot-blooded *macho* who would take my approach as an assault on his honour?

Apparently not. The girl broke into a broad smile.

'Yes, I am,' she said, 'but Madeleine told us that you were a girl.' She indicated the boyfriend. 'This is Pablo, my friend. Also a friend of Madeleine.'

There had been some confusion over my name, it seemed. Madeleine's pronunciation of Michael had somehow caused an 'a' to be added to it, and the assumption had then been made that I was a girl.

We had a good evening, nevertheless. We had a drink in the Imperial and then ambled through the warm, crowded streets to a small restaurant that they knew. There was one moment when I registered mild alarm. Young men and women in Cordoba referred to each other as *pavo* or *pava*, meaning a peacock or peahen. Pablo, who probably felt that our little group was unbalanced, was all in favour of *ligando una pava* for me ('chatting up a peahen'). I was too tired, and far too lacking in confidence, to attempt anything of the sort, and I managed to divert the conversation down another route before any suitable target was identified.

I said goodnight to them sometime after midnight. I asked if they thought staying at the *residencia* was safe. It seemed a curious question to them, I was sure, but I had one or two concerns about the cropped-haired *Señor* Ramon. He reminded me, I realised, of Magwitch the convict in *Great Expectations*, as portrayed in a recent television adaptation of the Dickens novel. They assured me that all would be well. There were many such private residences that took in visitors at this time of year. No grisly murders had ever been known and there was no convict reported as being on the loose.

So I trudged back the short distance to the *residencia*. The wooden door in the wall was open and I could hear conversation as I entered. Keeping up their tradition of dining only in the small hours, the same group of people were assembled around the table in the far corner. The host, whose name I never did find out, greeted me and invited me to join them. I wearily nodded my assent but went back to my room with the idea of leaving my wallet and guide map, which bulged uncomfortably out of the back pocket of my jeans.

The next thing I was aware of was sunlight striking my face through a small window covered by an ornate metal grille high up in the wall opposite the bed. I did not at first understand. I was lying under one of the clean sheets dressed still in my jeans and T-shirt but minus my socks. I sat up, shook my head and looked at my watch. It said the time was a quarter to nine. I appeared to have lost about eight hours.

I got out of bed, splashed water on my face and then brushed my teeth. I took off the T-shirt, took the spare one from my bag and retrieved my socks, which were neatly rolled up in my shoes under the bed.

There was a knock at the door. As I opened it I discovered the host outside with a large cup of milky coffee in his hand. In the background I could see the two ladies, clearly mother and daughter, laying a large cloth on the table in the corner. All of them seemed to exude both contentment and energy and I wondered if they ever slept.

'Ah, *Señor*. You are awake. I was bringing you some coffee to wake you up. I know that the English like it with milk,' he said.

'Oh, thank you,' I replied taking the cup from him.

'Last night,' he went on with a grin on his face. 'You were very tired.'

Considering I had sat up for eight hours on a train the previous night, had spent all day trudging round in the heat carrying an umbrella, a bag and a raincoat, and had then eaten two lunches and a dinner accompanied by generous amounts of beer and wine until one in the morning, this was hardly surprising.

I nodded in agreement.

'Yes. I was.'

'When you did not come out of your room for dinner my wife and *Señor* Ramon came over to look for you,' he explained. 'You were asleep on the bed.' He looked over towards the bed and I followed his gaze as if I expected to see myself there, asleep. '*Señor* Ramon put you to bed,' he finished.

'Oh.' I was lost for words.

'You were lying on your side so he just took off your socks and covered you over,' he said.

'That was— That was very kind of him,' I stuttered, taking the coffee cup as he held it out to me.

'*Señor* Ramon is a very kind man,' said the host. 'When you are ready we have some rolls and *Magdalenas* for breakfast,' and he turned round and left me standing in the middle of the room, coffee cup in hand.

After a couple of minutes I found myself rather touched by the image of *Señor* Ramon and the host's wife taking care of me in that way. They could have just left me but they quietly tucked me up as you would a child, although I was a complete stranger. I was annoyed that I had felt distrustful in any way towards Ramon, and his convict haircut. They were kind, genuine people and I felt grateful to them.

XXVI

I left Cordoba soon after midday and, in a less crowded compartment, slept for most of the journey back to Madrid. We pulled into Atocha station at about nine o'clock and I went straight back to no. 68 Calle de Canillas.

The next day I was able to report on my successful trip to Cordoba, both to Brian who I saw briefly in the morning before I left for work, and to Madeleine during a break between classes in the afternoon.

Madeleine was looking very tired when I saw her. The lightning trip to Huelva to meet Manolo's family had taken its toll. Not only was it a long journey – and they had travelled both ways overnight – but the entire Diez clan seemed to share Manolo's ability to function perfectly well on very little sleep and plenty of alcohol.

'I met his parents and his sister and her husband,' Madeleine told Elena and me. 'We seemed to be drinking sherry all day, then at dinner they brought out the wine and we were up until about two o'clock in the morning talking.' She sighed. 'I've got an hour, so I'm going over the road to get something to eat. I'm starving. Are you free, Michael?'

I said that unfortunately I wasn't.

'A late lunch for you?' said Hilary, who had come out of her room as Madeleine was speaking.

'More like a very late breakfast,' said Madeleine, lighting a cigarette and exhaling slowly and noisily.

More raised eyebrows from Hilary and Elena.

My Reign in Spain

Madeleine was soon back to normal, however. She told me the next day that José and Maite, the couple we had met in Gandia, were coming up to Madrid for a long weekend on Friday. There was a plan afoot to show them the sights on Saturday evening, so could I come along?

Of course I could. Although no longer skulking in a cold, dingy bedsit at weekends my social calendar was never unmanageably full.

So the next Friday evening saw me meeting up with a group of my friends and acquaintances, not at the Tankstelle but at a large cafe along the Avenida José Antonio Primo de Rivera. This was one of the principal streets in Madrid and was more generally known as the Gran Via. (It had, incredibly, been on Hilary's itinerary with Waldo and Martha during her frantic tour of the city in second gear a few weeks earlier.)

I was with a crowd of people – Madeleine and Manolo, Miguel and another friend of his called Miguel Angel, Susan from the British Council, whom I had met once or twice in the Tankstelle, and Enrique's brother Antonio. There were others as well, most of whom I could name but had rarely spoken to. We all ordered drinks and the conversation, of course, soon got very lively. I had a particularly interesting talk with Miguel's friend, Miguel Angel about the correct functioning of the kidneys.

The reason for this was because he had leant slightly forward in his chair, which was next to mine, and rubbed the small of his back soon after we had arrived. When I had asked if his back was hurting he replied,

'*No, me duelen los riñones.*' ('My kidneys are hurting.')

I had barely understood where the kidneys were located until a month or so before. I had then been alerted to the potentially explosive dangers of exposing them to too much of Elena's *leche rica* but had not had the opportunity to see how far in this direction I could push mine, due to Brian's nocturnal greed. Now it seemed that it was a fact of everyday Spanish life that even young, healthy individuals (Miguel Angel looked fine to me) could find their kidneys under assault as a matter of course. I reached around and prodded myself in the small of the back. Everything seemed all right, but I would keep the situation under review.

'But it doesn't matter,' he then said. 'I'll drink plenty of water and wash them through.'

'OK,' I said, looking at the beer glass in front of me. Perhaps it would wise to order a bottle of water as well to flush out my own internal plumbing.

Just then a small cheer went up as José Carlos and Enrique walked in. Behind them were José and Maite still, I noted, holding hands. I thought Maite, in particular, looked very tired, but she was smiling as she gazed at José.

'Here's the happy pair,' said José Carlos. 'Let's get you a drink first of all.'

José had a beer and Maite ordered a Coca-Cola. The conversation continued, but when their drinks arrived José Carlos stood up, raised his beer glass into the air and proposed a toast.

'To José and Maite … May they have a long and happy time together – and still be our best friends when we come down to Gandia.'

I joined in the applause but gave Madeleine a look that well expressed my confusion as to what was happening.

Manolo caught my glance.

'They've just got married,' he explained. 'So they're spending a few days in Madrid – as a honeymoon.'

I was taken aback by this. Although they were clearly a year or two older than me the thought of a permanent girlfriend, let alone a wife, seemed so remotely far in the future that I could barely imagine it. Yet here they were before me. They had agreed to spend the rest of their lives together. How could they be so sure? It all suddenly seemed far too adult for me.

From downstairs the sound of music came drifting up – not a soulful Spanish ballad or a rhythmic flamenco song. It was 'Waterloo' by Abba, obviously enjoying the last of its popularity before sinking into the obscurity that Brian had predicted. Someone suggested that we go down there and dance (this apparently was the purpose of the basement), so we all took our drinks and bundled downstairs. Others were there as well, shuffling and gyrating in time – some more convincingly than others – to the music.

I joined in, as did most of my companions. José Carlos immediately started doing a comic dance routine, and even Miguel Angel managed to drag himself on to the dance floor and jig up and down despite the fragile state of his internal organs. Enrique stood at the side, however, watching us and talking to José and Maite. He again seemed to be regarding us benignly as a father would his children. He was missing Maica, I supposed. He seemed nearly as adult as José and Maite.

I stopped dancing when the music finished and went over to where they were standing. Another song came on, very loudly, and I stopped trying to make conversation over it. I was mishearing everything they said and they were straining to make out my imperfect Spanish, hampered as it was by a strong foreign accent and the consumption of several beers on an empty stomach.

On the dance floor Antonio was dancing with Susan. She was quite short and he had to bend down to talk to her, particularly as the music was so loud. As I watched he said something that made her laugh, and then seemed to demonstrate some sort of dance move which involved her turning away from him and then falling slightly backwards so that he could catch her. They did this once, successfully, and he congratulated her with mock applause, which made her laugh even more. The next time she turned and fell back, however, he made sure that he caught her rather later than the first time so that she grabbed hold of him for support as he pulled her up. Almost instantly, completely in line with Antonio's strategy, they were kissing – and continued to do so for the rest of the song, oblivious to anyone else in the room.

I had had no idea what was in his mind until that moment but was then instantly in awe of the way that he had laid his trap and sprung it on his willing victim. I immediately wanted to be like him, to have the confidence to impress and seduce, to have a girl dissolve into my arms in that way. For a moment or two I thought that perhaps I could do it – even tonight if I could find someone – but then my conviction and belief melted away and I looked at José Carlos, still laughing and joking on the far side of the room. That was a much easier route to follow, with less danger of rejection.

Beside me Enrique was looking at his brother and his conquest, still firmly in each other's arms. His face seemed to show a strange mixture of disapproval, admiration and envy.

After a couple of dances most of us sat down at one of the unoccupied tables. José and Maite, still close to each other, were at one end with José Carlos. I was at the other end with Manolo and Madeleine again on one side and Antonio and Susan on the other. Suddenly there was a commotion and we all looked up the table to José and Maite. She had her head forward, almost on the table and he was fussing over her, the concerned husband. Even José Carlos looked serious.

'What's up?' I asked Madeleine.

'I don't think Maite feels very well,' she said. And as she said it Maite got up, with José supporting her. She did look very pale, but managed a smile.

'Thank you, everyone,' said José. 'We are going to go now.

Maite's very tired.'

Everyone crowded around them for an instant and then slowly they made their way over to the stairs.

'I wonder what's wrong with her,' I said, watching the two of them as they went.

Madeleine looked at me almost with a sense of reproach on her face.

'Can't you guess?' she said.

I looked blank.

'She's pregnant,' said Madeleine.

Again I was taken aback. I had not even imagined that that might be the reason for her fatigue, or for what I now saw was a very hastily arranged wedding and short honeymoon. The adult world of confident actions and limited possibilities, a spectre at my feast, was intruding more and more into the evening.

I did briefly compare José and Maite's situation to Moya, at the Instituto, and her rugby-playing boyfriend. There seemed to be no pressure with them to get married as a result of her pregnancy. Perhaps there was a difference of attitudes in cosmopolitan Madrid to those that existed down by the sea at Gandia. Perhaps it was Moya's foreignness that shielded her from the expectations of this still parochial, conservative society – but these thoughts left me very soon as we continued dancing and, eventually, had something to eat.

We emerged on to the Gran Via at about two o'clock in the morning. The air was chilly even though it was nearing the end of May, but the streets were packed with people promenading up and down arm in arm or sitting in the cafés. Some braved the night chill, others were inside. We joined them in wandering aimlessly for a while, chatting and joking, moving along the pavement together or in pairs. I glanced at my watch and realised that the last metro for home had left.

'How are we going to get home?' I asked Manolo. 'The last metro has gone.'

'Well, we can walk, then,' he said. 'It's not far.'

So, very slowly, we all made our way north-eastwards towards La Prosperidad. I wondered at first how tired I would be and how long it would take. None of the others seemed at all concerned. Miguel Angel walked beside me for a while – the rigours of the dance floor did not seem to have affected him or his kidneys, and gradually I stopped asking,

'How far?' and 'How long?'

For the rest of our night-time amble through suburban Madrid I just enjoyed the walk and the company.

I eventually climbed the stairs at no. 68 Calle de Canillas at five thirty in the morning and fell asleep on my bed to the sound of the birds awakening in the tree outside.

XXVII

A strange buzzing noise seemed to fill my head. I was in that state of dreamy semiconsciousness, neither awake nor asleep. Images of the night before – José and Maite holding hands, Antonio and Susan locked in an embrace – had been playing out in front of me. Although the images spun this way and that I was just about in control of where they were going. They were recollections and not dreams. But the insistent buzzing was intruding from somewhere outside, beyond my power to turn it off.

I became fully awake, pulled myself up and leant on my elbows. The buzzing sound was coming from outside my window. I got out of bed and looked at my watch. It was ten fifteen. I crossed the room to pull back the shutters and see what was going on.

Outside there was a group of three men, cutting down the tree. One of them was armed with a chainsaw and was up in the canopy. He was sawing off some of the smaller branches and the other two were on the ground, busying themselves with picking up the debris as the tree came down.

As I stood watching there was a knock on the door. It was Santiago.

'I thought that the noise would wake you,' he said as he came in. He surveyed the scene outside for a moment and then uttered a sigh.

'What a terrible thing to do to a living organism. What brutality. They have need of more trees here. They should not be chopping them down.'

I agreed. What a sorry sight. As we watched the tree was mutilated, its branches sheared off forever, until only a network of larger stumps, denuded of leaves, were left. The sadness of the birds, perched on adjacent buildings and watching the destruction of their home, was almost tangible.

A lorry came along, and the splintered remains were loaded on to it. Then the man with the chainsaw swung down on the rope that had been holding him aloft and set to work on the trunk. After what seemed like only seconds he turned his chainsaw off. There was a terrible creaking sound and the tree crashed to the ground, sending dust and shards of wood flying in all directions.

'One hundred years to grow and two minutes to destroy,' said Santiago.

'Why are they doing it on a Sunday?' I asked.

'They want to get started on building the next apartment block, I suppose,' said Santiago. 'There is money in it for them, I have no doubt. Even a Spaniard will get out of bed on a Sunday if there is money in it,' he added, a touch scornfully.

He went out of the room and I sat on the bed, saddened by the loss of my tree – it was my tree – and glad that I probably wouldn't still be here when a four-storey apartment block obscured the view.

That afternoon, to console myself about the loss of my tree, I went to the cinema.

My nerve-grating introduction to cinema-going in Spain with *Family Life* on my very first evening had, surprisingly, not put me off. I had seen *El Golpe*, starring Paul Newman and Robert Redford, (known as *The Sting* when it was made), and several other American imports. There didn't seem to be any Spanish films worth seeing, though, and I was, for some reason, drawn to a rather moth-eaten cinema at the bottom of Calle de Fuencarral which was showing, in rotation, *The*

Ten Commandments, *Ben-Hur* and *Spartacus* – all epics, both of the biblical and the sword and sandal variety.

The reason for my attraction to this wide, heroic sweep of ancient history was difficult to determine. Perhaps it was so that my own life and the loneliness that I sometimes still experienced could somehow be put into perspective by the great events, the sacrifices and the perfect love that Moses, Ben-Hur and Spartacus lived through. I always felt the prick of tears when Spartacus's men stood up, one by one, to proclaim, 'No, I am Spartacus,' rather than let him be taken for crucifixion by the spiteful Roman general. The moment when Ben-Hur offered water to Christ as he stumbled on his way to Calvary, mirroring an earlier moment in the film when a young Christ had offered the enslaved Ben-Hur a cup as he was taken to join a chain gang in a quarry, had the same effect. This was, for me at least, human experience writ large and meaningful and put on the screen using every trick and effect that 1950s Hollywood had at its disposal, and it drew me back to the fleapit where it was showing two or three times. Others might see it as corny. I saw it as real.

So a mid-afternoon viewing of one or other of these helped the day to pass and raised my thoughts to the beauty of selfless love and sacrifice, which stayed with me for at least a few minutes after I came out into the hot, bone dry Madrid afternoon.

Brian and Robin shared little of my interest in the fate of the tree when I told them about it that evening. They were both making plans for what to do after their term in Madrid came to an end.

Robin was going home, but Brian wanted to spend longer in Spain and had managed to find a job, via a university contact, working for the summer in a hotel in Galicia in the far north-west. They would both be departing soon and Santiago would yet again be faced with finding more suitable flatmates to occupy the interconnecting bedrooms.

One other notable event for me as May turned into June was attending a bullfight at the Ventas bullring. I went again to the ticket office, this time checking in advance that it was open, and bought a ticket for the following weekend. Everyone at the Institute told me that it would be better to pay extra and make sure I was sitting in the shade rather getting the cheaper ticket in the sun.

'I've known people go to the bullfight and sit in the sun and then faint clean away,' Madeleine told me. 'It's worth the extra for a *sombra* seat.'

'Are you sure you're ready to see the bull killed in front of you?' asked Hilary. 'I'd get a seat a good few rows back.'

'Have you never been?' I asked her.

'Oh, no, it's not for me,' she said, shaking her head as if possessed of some knowledge that I did not have.

So I went along to the bullring, worried in equal parts about my ability to stomach the predetermined life-and-death struggle that would be played out in front of me and whether or not I would succumb either to sunstroke or a fainting fit as a result. My attitude to a parachute jump would have been the same. If others can do it then so must I – but I wasn't sure if I was looking forward to it.

My seat was far enough back to avoid seeing all the detail of the kill but near enough to appreciate the spectacle of it. I looked intently at what was happening in the sandy bullring to begin with but also kept an eye on the sun as it edged its way around the tiered arena, turning the shady seats into sunny ones. I had paid extra for the shady seat. I would be very annoyed if I ended up hemmed in on each side by spectators able to withstand the heat better than I could as the sun, now as hot as the sun in Cordoba, 'stuck' to me.

In fact after the first two of the six bulls had been dispatched, and the crowd, always capricious, had applauded by way of their approval, I began to think more of the sun and less of the bullfight. It was interesting to watch the picadors and their ancient nags prime the bull and tire it with their well-placed lances. Their job – and that of the *banderilleros*, who, unlike the picadors, were on foot – was to stab the bull in its massively powerful neck. Then, when the matador approached with his cape, the bull, now weakened in the neck, kept its head lowered and the matador could begin the series of sweeping passes with his crimson cape before plunging his sword down between the bull's shoulders.

Inevitably I suppose it all seemed a bit one-sided, but I was surprised at how unaffected I felt when the sword went in and the majestic bull, covered in its own blood, fell to its knees and expired noisily. In fact bulls three to six got little support from me. I was disappointed that I found it all rather tedious and didn't experience the surge of adrenalin and admiration for the *arte taurina* that people such as Hemingway, that great American *macho*, had described.

In the end the sun disappeared over the back of the bullring before it reached me and, as bull number six coughed blood from its mouth and nostrils and collapsed, the sun set in a ragged extravaganza of red and yellow that seemed to reflect the blood and sand of the arena.

I came out into the bustling dusk strangely unmoved. It had all seemed a bit mechanical, as if the bulls and their various tormentors had been wound up at the beginning and gradually wound down through the performance until they all just stopped as the bull died. I had not been bitten by the bullfighting bug, but neither was I converted to a supporter of the bulls and their right to life.

It was my only visit, ever, to the bullring.

*

There were other acquaintances who came and went as each hot day gave way to another. Some of them just shimmered in and out with the heat and I, at times feeling no more than an innocent bystander to my own life, accepted them without question and let them go just as easily.

Ruben and Luis were two brothers from Cuenca, a small city that lay between Madrid and Valencia. They were engineering students with Manolo, and he had found them a flat to share in the same building as the one he shared with Madeleine.

I was introduced to them at the Tankstelle one evening and they invited me round to their flat. This was quite an unusual occurrence. Spaniards met their friends in the street as a rule but I accepted willingly, keen as always for somewhere to go and someone to be with. When I got there they were frying peppers in a large pan in the kitchen. It was obvious that their culinary skills were severely limited, which probably explained why they seemed to me to have such large heads and thin bodies. So I rolled my sleeves up and joined them in the kitchen, where we dined on burnt green peppers and fried cheese sandwiches – all washed down with a bottle or two of exceedingly rough tinto.

Julie was a secretary with a large British company that had a sizeable subsidiary in Madrid. She was a couple of years older than me and, coincidentally, came from Peterborough, just like Tim Hewitt. This was therefore only nineteen miles from March, where the background to my previous life continued – but without me in it. She was a vague acquaintance of Santiago, I think, though just how was never revealed to me, and I never asked.

We went to the university swimming pool together sometimes – I with my student card, which Santiago had managed to obtain for me, and she with a photo card that said *International Scholar* on it, which someone at her office had given her. It was an obvious fake but it got her through the turnstile, so it served its purpose.

We swam – me very badly, she much more proficiently – and sunbathed on the crowded terraces. I was keen to go back to March with a suntan just to emphasise the otherness of my life now to the pale inhabitants of the Fens. There was never any question of physical attraction for either of us.. She was quite pretty and easy to talk to – but it was more company than anything else that I was looking for, and she treated me as a girl would a trusted younger brother.

I went one weekday to the swimming pool on my own. Julie was at work and I did not have any classes until four o'clock. I must have been taking my tanning mission seriously that day as I lay out in the sun most of the morning and well into lunchtime. The result was that I entered the Instituto at about a quarter to four with a bright red face and a twitch to my gait that was activated every time my shirt rubbed against my sunburnt chest.

My first lesson that day was with a lady from Banco Hispano Americano called Lola. She was probably in her mid-thirties and unmarried with dark shoulder-length hair, the middle tresses of which she gathered into a bunch as a topknot that sat somewhat awkwardly on the top of her head. She was very thin with a long neck and was very similar to Nervous José in terms of temperament.

Her highly strung nature did not, however, manifest itself in a stutter, or an inability to complete sentences. Instead she had a pronounced tendency to shout and to talk very fast as she moved her head in short, jerky movements. The overall impression was one of a hen, startled by a fox, trying to scare it away with high-intensity clucking. (Such was my lack of discretion by this stage that I even referred to her as *La Gallina* – The Hen – to Elena, who thought it very funny.)

Lola looked at me oddly as soon as she entered the room

and cocked her head to one side as if to get a different view.

'You are very red,' she said flatly.

I had hoped to gloss over the fact that my attempts at sun-kissed had ended up as sunburnt but she gave a sudden, loud staccato burst of laughter and told me,

'You look like a cockerel that has been in the oven but is not yet cooked.'

I had no rejoinder to this. It was on the tip of my tongue to reveal my pet name for her – the term had only a week or two to run and my commitment to educating the bourgeoisie of Madrid had worn paper-thin – but I managed to hold back and we resumed our lesson at the point where Martin and Jane were packing their suitcases before departing on holiday.

I did tell her, in our discussions that, before they were married – which I very much hope they were, although it was never specified – Martin had a stag night and Jane had a hen party. I mischievously then asked Lola if she had ever been to a hen party to which she replied (in Spanish),

'My sister was married last year and we were all hens for one night.'

I had to exercise all my powers of self-control at that point to suppress the image of Lola and others like her all scratching the ground in their high heels and pecking at whatever they uncovered.

Dolores came in later that evening as well. My private lessons with Eduardo the painter had been continuing every week. His enthusiasm had waned somewhat, and there was no demand now for a second lesson on Fridays. I was disappointed at the drop in income – but glad of the reduced need for preparation. He was now making such slow progress anyway that my original lesson plans, such as they were, were being spread over several hours rather than the sixty minutes that I had at first allowed for them. The painting of

Dolores was always there, untouched for the moment, with the youthful body and the strangely out of place face, like some odd variation on the portrait of Dorian Gray. He did not mention it again, so neither did I.

Dolores made no reference to my red face. She just stared at me very hard for a minute or so, made a noise like a muted growl and then said,

'Let us continue, then.'

I wasn't quite sure what the lesson was a continuation of but it passed uneventfully, apart from me twitching if I moved my reddened arms and shoulders too much.

XXVIII

Just as casual acquaintances came and went, so a more established relationship was now coming to an end. Brian and Robin were leaving – Brian to his hotel job in Galicia and Robin back home to the UK – and Santiago was left with the task of finding replacements to share my temporary (and his semi-permanent) home.

The two of them left one day when I was at work. I said goodbye to them before I left in the morning. Brian gave me his address in Galicia 'just in case', and I swapped home addresses with Robin, and when I came back that evening they had gone. I didn't really notice it at first. They had often been out in the evening when I came in, but after several days of just Santiago and me it did seem rather strange.

Santiago, meanwhile, was busy looking for somebody else to move in. I knew nothing of the financial arrangements of the flat other than that I had to pay my rent, in cash, on the first day of the month. Madeleine told me, however, that having two empty rooms would be hurting Santiago financially. She said that he probably paid the owner of the flat a fixed amount every month that he had to recoup from fellow flatmates. She also told me, much to my amazement, that as he effectively managed the property for the owner (whose identity I never thought to ask about) he probably paid no rent himself. At first I thought that this was unfair, but as Santiago worked hard that week on his search for two more residents I began to appreciate that his role as

My Reign in Spain

intermediary with the landlord was tougher than it seemed.

It was not a good time to find suitable candidates. The university and other higher educational establishments were winding down as summer settled firmly on Madrid. No one in Santiago's target population was starting anything. In fact people were already beginning to disperse. So he was very happy when two Guatemalans, Pablo and Ernesto, answered the advertisement he placed every day in *ABC*.

'We have two new people coming,' he informed me. 'They are businessmen from Guatemala called Pablo and Ernesto.'

'I don't think I've ever met anyone from Guatemala before,' I told him. I wasn't even sure exactly where it was.

'Well, they'll be here next week,' he said. 'You'll be able to meet them then.'

'What sort of businessmen are they?' I enquired.

'Oh, something to do with import and export,' Santiago said airily.

I told Elena about my new flatmates.

'Guatemala,' she said, raising her eyebrows. 'Import and export,' she continued raising them ever higher.

'Will they be all right?' I asked, a little nervous at her attitude.

'I'm sure they are. But don't get too friendly with them,' she added enigmatically.

Bemused by her response, I nevertheless forgot about it temporarily, as Tim came out of his classroom and asked if I would like to go to lunch with him and Milan on the following Saturday.

An outing with the two of them was now a very rare occurrence. The Monday to Friday trek to the Tibet, preceded by the throat-scouring aperitif, was something I did not now need or want. I had established other, cheaper lunchtime options and I tended to eat with Hilary or Madeleine. On Tuesdays and Thursdays when I was free until four I ate at the flat or even – if I decided to go to the university swimming pool before work – alone just across the road from the Instituto, where I would have a *plato combinado*. The confusion and nervousness that I had first felt about entering establishments on my own had diminished as I realised that my custom was as welcome as anyone else's.

However, when Tim asked me if I was busy on Saturday I replied, truthfully, that I was not.

'Milan was asking about how you were the other day and I said you were often busy now during the week, so he suggested Saturday lunch at the Tibet – his treat. There's some Polish guy he wants to bring along as well,' Tim explained.

'OK.' I was intrigued. My exposure so far to the Slavic nations had either shown them to be cynical and embittered (Milan) or randomly drunken and violent (Anton). I looked forward to meeting someone with whom I might more recognisably empathise.

We arranged to meet in the normal bar for an aperitif on the following Saturday. I was quite looking forward to seeing Milan in some ways. I had not been out to lunch with him for many weeks and, as Tim was either dashing into, or out of, a lesson I did not often have the opportunity to talk to him either.

When I got there they were both standing at the bar in the same spot as always. Milan had shed his layers of tweed for a very smart pair of light brown trousers and a checked sports jacket. There was also a straw-coloured panama hat resting on the bar next to him. It all gave him an air approaching jauntiness as he turned to me on my entrance to the bar.

'Ah,' he said, smiling benignly, and extending his arms as if about to give a papal blessing. 'Here is Michael, our Oxford undergraduate.'

I smiled and shook his hand. Tim was standing on one side of him but, on the other, was a tall, heavyset young man, several years older than me, with a florid complexion and a thick neck. He had light brown hair that grew in loose curls over his ears and down to his collar.

'This is Paul,' said Milan.

'Hello, Paul,' I said, and shook his hand.

'Hello,' he said, in a voice that registered total disinterest, and then turned to Milan. 'As I was saying,' he went on, 'the Polish nation has always had a tragic history. That's why I feel that more should be done for them and I think you, as a senior member of the Madrid Slavic community, should be consulted.' His accent sounded very Home Counties. Perhaps he was from Poland via somewhere like Tunbridge Wells.

Tim confirmed Paul's origins to me as we walked along to the Tibet, having finished our aperitif with customary swiftness.

'Apparently Milan met him at some do at the university,' he explained. 'His father is Polish and his mother English and he was brought up in London. I'm not sure he's ever been to Poland.'

'They certainly seem to be getting on well,' I observed as the two of them strolled on ahead of us.

'Yes, Milan's always a sucker for the Slav connection,' said Tim. 'I think Paul's already borrowed some money from him for some Polish charity or society or something that he wants to set up.' Even I, naive as I was, could pick up the cynical tone in his voice.

We had reached the Tibet by this time, so we followed Milan and Paul in as they talked and laughed together. During the meal Paul continued to flatter Milan about his senior status among the expatriate community and his standing at the university. He appeared to want Milan to be the figurehead for some charity that he was trying to establish but every time Tim or I tried to interject and find out more about it he simply changed the subject and turned back to

Milan, always emphasising their common Slav background.

They started comparing simple words in Polish and Serb, Paul almost squealing with delight as Milan pointed out some apparent similarities. Neither of them paid any attention to me and I decided that I did not like Paul at all. I chatted sporadically with Tim about the Institute, wondering as I did so why Milan had bothered to invite me. Apart from the advantage of it being a free meal, I found the whole thing very dull.

When the bill came Milan took it, reached inside his jacket and pulled out a money clip, from which he extracted a thousand peseta note.

'Thank you very much, Milan,' I said. 'That was very enjoyable.'

Milan glanced at me for almost the first time since he had greeted me in the bar.

'Oh, it's all right. I am always very glad to see you,' he said – and he winked at me.

I was somewhat taken aback. Before I could show any other reaction he had turned round to Paul to continue their conversation.

It was a warm day so we strolled back slowly along the street and went into a small public garden just near the entrance to the metro. I thought we were going to sit down on one of the benches but Paul then announced that he had to go.

'I've got a female friend arriving very soon,' he said. 'I'd better go and clear up a bit. You know,' his hand swept the air dramatically, 'fling a bit of perfume around, that sort of thing.' He gave a loud and very false-sounding laugh.

'Of course,' said Milan. 'Women are very fussy about these things.'

'But you know what,' said Paul, appearing to alight on an idea. 'You must come round and visit me. We can play chess together. The only thing is I'm on the fourth floor – and there's no lift.'

'Oh, that would be difficult, then,' said Milan, smiling. 'I am not very good with stairs.'

'You'll have to have a breather on every landing,' suggested Tim.

'I know,' said Paul, with an engineered grin on his face, 'I'll have a decanter of brandy put at the top of every flight of stairs – just to revive you.' The grin turned into another false, staccato laugh.

'That would be good,' said Milan.

'Or perhaps some slivovitz,' suggested Paul. He looked at his watch. 'Oh, I must go. Good to see you,' he said to Milan. 'I'll look you up next week.' He turned about, completely ignoring Tim and me, and headed off towards the metro.

Milan stared after him as he went. Neither Tim nor I said anything as Milan continued to look. Eventually he turned to us.

'What did you think of him?' he asked us.

I said nothing but Tim told Milan,

'I don't really know. He's a bit of a joker. I'm not sure I'd trust him. He never really gave a straight answer to anything we asked – and he was really trying to flatter you.'

'That's because he is a – what's the word?' Milan brow creased as he searched for what he meant. 'Ah, yes,' he smiled. 'That's because he's a wanker.'

Tim and I looked at him disbelievingly. Not only was I surprised by the breadth of his knowledge of colloquial English but also by this clear indication that Milan had a very different opinion of Paul to the one that Tim and I had both expected.

'Well, yes, I suppose he was,' said Tim eventually, with a smirk on his face. I continued to say nothing, totally bemused by the whole situation.

'But why did you buy him lunch and bother with him at all?' asked Tim,

'Oh, it was amusing,' said Milan. He winked at me again, 'and I don't get much amusement nowadays. But I shan't give him any money for a Polish charity, and if he calls me I will be too busy to see him. You see,' he said, addressing me and putting his hand on my shoulder, 'it is much better to be quiet, and honest with people, like you are, and to let your achievements speak for themselves. He,' he jerked his head towards the metro entrance, 'would never be able to get into Oxford. All talk, but no brains. I just wanted you to see what you are not so you can appreciate what you are. Please stay like that,' he added.

I was flattered by his comments and grandfatherly interest. Milan had his foibles and peculiarities, which his particular experiences had produced, but he was clearly a shrewd judge of character and actually not at all taken in by Paul's blandishments – Slavic connections notwithstanding. It was Milan who had clearly taken in the young Anglo-Polish chancer and enjoyed playing him along.

We walked to the metro and Milan bought a copy of the *Corriere della Sera* at a news stand by the entrance. I was impressed again, this time by the cosmopolitan outlook, and linguistic ability, that this showed.

Tim was walking on to somewhere else so did not come down into the metro, and Milan and I were travelling in opposite directions so descended different staircases. As I got on to the platform his train drew into the one opposite and I saw him get on and sit down. He unfolded the newspaper and, with that slight, characteristic scowl on his face, started to read it. That was the last time that I saw him, sitting poring intently over the headlines from Italy as the train lurched out of the station.

XXIX

When I got back to the flat Santiago was in the living room. He had some news for me.

'It's Pablo and Ernesto,' he said.

I must have looked confused because he added,

'The *Guatemaltecos*.'

'Oh, yes,' I said. 'Aren't they coming?'

'Oh, yes. They've already come. They put all their luggage in their bedrooms.'

'They're here, are they?' I said, looking around the living room as if expecting to find them hiding behind the door.

'They're here, but they've gone out again,' said Santiago, and he frowned. 'They asked me where the best place was to look for prostitutes.'

Again, this was far outside my realm of experience and I did not know what to reply. I had little idea of what a prostitute looked like, let alone where to find one.

'I do not think I made a wise choice,' he said, shaking his head as he left the room.

That night I met Madeleine and some other friends at the Tankstelle. It was an unusually crowded day in my social calendar. I rarely had both a lunchtime and an evening engagement.

It was a very productive visit as well. Enrique was there, celebrating the end of term and the fact that he was heading down to Gandía for a couple of weeks. His parents would not be using the apartment until later in the summer so he could, surreptitiously, move in for the rest of June and enjoy his proximity to Maica. My completely innocent remark about what fond memories I had of the place produced an invitation from him for me to go down there the following weekend.

This was a result that I had truly not foreseen, but I readily accepted. Nobody else was able to go – the others had not yet finished their studies for that term, apparently – but I was still very happy at the prospect of another visit to the place where I had had so much fun before.

Madeleine and Manolo also mentioned to me that, when term ended for Manolo at the university and for Madeleine at the Instituto, they would be going down to Huelva for some time. They would be happy, if I wanted to stay on in Madrid, to let me have their flat, where I could stay free of charge.

This also sounded good. There were only another two weeks to go at the Instituto, and I had been thinking more and more about what to do. Eduardo the painter would be stopping his lessons in a couple of weeks as well and July in Madrid was not the time to search out more private pupils, but an immediate return to my former life in the Fens was somehow not the option for a well-travelled cosmopolitan such as me. I wanted to see my parents but I felt the need to stay away in my exotic overseas life for a while longer before an interim stopover in March on my way to the next lap in Oxford.

So that week I had my trip to Gandia to look forward to and some thinking about what to do when my job – and the salary that went with it – finished.

The *Guatemaltecos* did not reappear until Wednesday. I had almost forgotten about them, but then I got home at about nine o'clock and was introduced to them by Santiago. They were all in the kitchen as I came in and, as I had to pass by on the way to my room, I put my head round the door.

'Come in,' said Santiago, giving me no choice as he yanked the sleeve of my shirt.

There were two men in the kitchen with him. He introduced Pablo, a short, stocky man with thinning light brown hair and a little moustache that curled up at the ends. He was wearing a smart pair of cotton trousers and a pale lilac-coloured shirt with the sleeves rolled up. There was a strong smell of aftershave coming from him which, I think, overlay a less pleasant odour underneath. Then there was Ernesto, as long and thin as Pablo was short and broad, with almost no hair on top of his head and a strange look from eyes that seemed too close-set.

'Hello,' I said to both, shaking their hands. Pablo's grip was firm but his palm was warm and clammy. Ernesto grinned and offered me the limpest handshake I had had for some time. They looked like a slightly smarter Latin American variation of Laurel and Hardy.

'It's nice to meet you at last,' I told them. 'Santiago tells me that you have been out for a while.'

'We have been out for three days,' said Pablo, by way of clarification. 'We found some beautiful ladies,' he went on. 'I called mine Pussy Cat because every time we, you know,' – and here he thrust his hips forward several times in a gesture that was unmistakable – 'she made a noise like a little cat.'

Ernesto gave a short, cackling laugh. Santiago and I were silent, simply exchanging glances that nevertheless betrayed our distaste.

Pablo went on, oblivious to our reaction.

'*Puta*, I haven't eaten anything for three days. I'm starving. What is there?' he asked, addressing no one in particular.

He got up from the table where he had been sitting, went over to the fridge and took two eggs out of it. Since the breakdown of the coloured dot system it had become impossible to discern who the owner of certain foods like eggs was, but I'm sure he hadn't bought them. There was a frying pan already on the stove and he poured in some oil and lit the gas ring. He cracked the eggs into the pan as we watched. Some fat splashed out and on to his hand.

'*Puta*,' he said again, sucking the affected area of his hand. 'I'm no good at cooking. I'll probably starve to death. It needs a woman. I must get my Pussy Cat to do it.'

The taciturn Ernesto gave yet another raucous laugh as Santiago's expression changed to one of alarm.

'She cannot come here,' he warned. 'No prostitutes here.'

Pablo looked hurt.

'She's my friend,' he said. Another cackle from the almost silent Ernesto. Then Pablo pulled a large bar of chocolate out of his pocket and broke off a sizeable piece. It was very soft – half-melted, due to the hot weather and, presumably, the proximity to his body. He crammed it into his mouth, offered a similar portion to Ernesto, who took it greedily, and then waved the bar at me.

'Do you want some?' he asked.

I declined politely, as did Santiago.

There was a smell of burning from the stove top. Pablo looked round. He had finished the starters, and it looked as if the main course was ready.

'*Puta*, these eggs are nearly done. How do I get them out?' he asked Ernesto.

His companion joined him at the stove and, with a spatula, lobbed the eggs on to a plate. The two of them sat down at the table and started to eat them with a couple of forks.

'We cannot stay long,' explained Pablo, 'More business to see to,' and he winked and grinned, his teeth yellow and brown with egg yolk and chocolate. Ernesto gave another lewd cackle.

'Do you want to come with us?' he added.

Santiago pursed his lips and inhaled forcefully.

'Oh, no. I have never done that kind of thing,' he said.

Pablo regarded him with a look approaching pity and then turned his gaze questioningly to me. I just shook my head violently.

'Well, you are missing a good thing,' Pablo told us and continued scoffing the eggs.

Santiago and I left them to it and walked along to his room.

'What business are they in – apart from the prostitutes?' I asked him sitting on the desk chair opposite his bed.

'I don't know,' he said. 'They have plenty of money and have paid me for a month – but I don't like them. I do not want them bringing their friends here.'

'Oh, no,' I said. 'That wouldn't be nice. I don't like them either.'

'We'll see,' said Santiago, 'but I cannot see why they want to live up here anyway.'

'What does *puta* mean?' I asked.

'A *puta* is the sort of woman that they have been with. A whore,' he said. 'But it is a swear word in Latin America. He says it all the time when he is surprised or angry.'

'Well, I'm locking my door,' I told him, and I shivered slightly

The front door banged and it was clear that they had left. I went back into the kitchen to cook myself some supper and clear up their dirty plates and chocolate wrappers.

XXX

I did not see the *Guatemaltecos* on Thursday. They were presumably still out with their 'friends'. Anyway, my thoughts were taken up with my return to Gandia.

I had agreed to meet Enrique in a bar in Gandia on Friday evening. I was able to travel on Friday as there was yet another public holiday in the capital, and the Instituto was closed for the day. One thing that was concerning me however was money – or the lack of it. I had one more payday only – then no more cash. If I was to stay for a few weeks more I would need to conserve what I could.

Staying at Enrique's apartment would entail no expenditure, but getting there would. Other than travelling on a slow overnight train again – and I had no inclination to do this – I would have to pay out a considerable amount on a train or coach ticket to travel during the day on Friday.

The alternative to the day or night train/coach options, which I regarded with no enthusiasm at all, was to hitch-hike. I would have all day on Friday to do it – unlike our previous trip to Gandia, when we had set out at about four in the afternoon. If I got down to the N3 at the Avenida del Mediterráneo in reasonable time in the morning there was a chance I might get a lift. A lone traveller might also stand more chance than a pair. Hours spent at the side of the road with my thumb stuck out was not a prospect I relished – but the economics were compelling.

So I found myself yet again by the roadside the following

morning at about nine o'clock, hoping that I would have more luck than we had had on the previous trip to Gandia. I had the little Gladstone bag and, hoping for more time on the beach, had packed my swimming trunks. I was wearing a light jacket and a pair of newly washed and ironed jeans in the hope of making myself look at least mildly respectable and lift-worthy.

The traffic roared past, picking up speed as urban restrictions gave way to the open road. My first few attempts at indicating that I wanted a ride were, to be honest, ineffective. It always took me time to work up to sticking my thumb out wholeheartedly. To begin with it looked as if I was giving a surreptitious wave or that I simply had a nervous tic in my arm.

But I soon lost my inhibitions and my more fulsome technique quickly yielded results. I got a lift in a small, dilapidated lorry that was carrying what looked like heaps of old bedding behind it. The driver said almost nothing to me once we had ascertained that I was going to Valencia and he could take me a considerable distance before he turned off to go to Cuenca, a small city about halfway to the Mediterranean but off the main road. Apart from this brief conversation at the beginning the only other words that were exchanged were when he offered me a cigarette and I politely declined.

So by midday I found myself in yet another tiny wayside village, just as I had with Antonio in Madridejos. I had obtained the first lift quite easily, so for a time my spirits remained high. Surely another battered lorry or van would stop soon and pick me up. There was, to be sure, less traffic on this road than the one down to Andalusia, and it was a public holiday, but for the first hour I watched as every vehicle approached around the bend, willing them to stop.

It didn't work. By three o'clock I was still there by the dusty roadside, my jacket now slung over my arm, pondering my next move. There was a small cafe further back along the road that a raging thirst had forced me to visit. I had not had a drink since before I set out and it was extremely hot. I had seen a bus timetable outside the cafe. It informed me that, on *ferias* – public holidays – such as today, there was a bus at five o'clock to Cuenca. This was not at all where I wanted to go but I had never visited the city – and I had been told it was well worth a visit. At the very worst I could divert there for a day or so.

As I looked up the road for the next vehicle I saw a figure approaching. From the slight stoop in his gait it looked like an old man. As he came nearer I could see that he was wearing a beret on his head, a ragged jacket and a pair of tattered greyish trousers held up with a thick leather belt. He was walking slowly, clumping along in boots that looked too big for him, and every time he heard a vehicle he turned towards it and stuck out his thumb.

I was both surprised and outraged. I had never actually seen another hitch-hiker during my various journeys but it was clear that this old man – and as he came nearer I could see that he *was* old – was a rival. How dare he! This was my patch of road, and if it was difficult enough for one hiker to get a lift it would clearly be impossible for two.

He came right up to where I was standing and grinned at me, showing a couple of grimy teeth and a lot of gaps.

'*Buenos d*ías,' he said. 'Where are you going?'

'To Valencia,' I told him.

'Been here long?'

'Oh, just a short time,' I lied. My pride wouldn't allow me to tell him that I had been unable to get a lift for three hours. 'Where are you going?'

'Oh, just to Motilla,' he said. 'It's only about twenty kilometres.'

My Reign in Spain

A car came round the bend behind us. The old man stuck his thumb out aggressively towards it. The driver ignored him and accelerated away.

'I've been hitching since this morning,' he went on. 'Not a lot of luck. Perhaps we can get a ride together.'

I looked him up and down. He was grubby and very dishevelled. It didn't surprise me that no one wanted to stop for him. I was sure that, with him for company, nobody would stop for me either. It was a potentially disastrous situation, and my prospects of getting to Gandia were receding as every vehicle whizzed past us. I had somehow to indicate that we were not connected, and that giving me a lift did not mean that he had to be included.

It crossed my mind that I could easily take him on in a physical contest. Perhaps that was it. I could wrestle him to the ground and threaten him with terrible consequences if he didn't just go away, or at least walk another kilometre on past me so that any potential lifts came across me first.

'It's hot, isn't it?' he said, as he frightened away another motorist who had come hurtling round the bend.

I grunted in reply, trying to accentuate what I hoped was my less than welcoming demeanour.

'I'm going to drink some water,' he announced and stomped off back towards the cafe, his boots crunching on the pebbly roadside verge.

As he disappeared into the building I renewed my efforts with great vigour. It would only be a few minutes at most before he re-emerged to spoil things. After several more minutes with no success a string of cars came around the bend, following a large lorry that was going very slowly.

I ran my hand through my hair to smooth it down, put on a broad smile and displayed my thumb prominently. The lorry driver ignored me, as did the first couple of cars. They seemed more intent on looking for an opportunity to overtake.

Further back along the road I saw the old man emerge from the cafe, wiping his mouth with his sleeve. My heart sank. It looked like the five o'clock bus to Cuenca for me. Another light-coloured saloon came round the bend and slowed down as it saw the procession behind the lorry ahead. I stuck out my thumb in a half-hearted manner, concentrating more on the old man than securing a lift. The car slowed even more and, just past me, pulled over to the side of the road. The driver reached across and wound down the passenger side window. I looked back and saw that the old man had seen him stop too. He was walking as fast as his oversized boots would allow and was raising his arm to get my attention. I ran over to the car, pulled the door open and jumped in.

The driver was a middle-aged man with large horn-rimmed glasses.

'I'm going to Valencia,' I told him.

'Me too,' he replied, looking in his rear-view mirror. 'Do you know that old man? He seems to be waving to you.'

I didn't look round.

'Oh, no,' I said. 'He's nothing to do with me. I'm completely alone.'

'OK,' he said, and we moved off.

I heaved a sigh of relief as we left the old man behind. I was on my way to Valencia and all was well.

As this welcome thought went through my mind I glanced at the driver. Apart from the horn-rimmed glasses I had not really taken in anything about him. I had been too busy getting away from my would-be travelling companion. Now I concentrated on him and gave a little involuntary gasp. He had a patterned short-sleeved shirt on that was unbuttoned almost to the waist. This was a little unsettling, but nothing to be alarmed at. However, what caused a rush of anxiety that resulted in my gasp was the fact that the zip on his fawn-coloured trousers was wide open.

Ever since the incident at Toledo railway station I had been aware that there may be a certain type of person who would be attracted to a fair-haired *majo* foreigner whom I did not want to meet. I suddenly wished that I was back at the roadside with the dishevelled old man and had not jumped into the car of a dangerous exhibitionist pervert who was now driving me away at high speed to a grisly fate. I realised that I had furthermore told him that I was completely alone. No one would miss me or know what had happened.

He looked at me. I stared back and then hurriedly shifted my gaze forward.

'Oh, sorry,' he said, pulling the zip back up almost to the top. 'I was very hot, and as there was no one in the car I decided to cool down.'

I gave a nervous, giggly laugh. I still wasn't sure. Perhaps it was a ruse to make me feel at ease, but he seemed perfectly normal and my anxiety level receded a little.

As we proceeded towards Valencia I gradually relaxed. My overheated benefactor told me that he was travelling down from León, way up in the north-west, and it had been a long, solitary drive so he was glad of the company. He had a small factory that made tin cans and he was talking to a group of Valencian orange producers about supplying them with cans for fresh orange juice. He jerked his thumb over towards the back seat as he told me this and I could see, on a cardboard tray, an array of about ten different sized cans with different labels on them. It seemed he was a genuine businessman rather than a sex fiend patrolling the roads looking for his next victim.

So I got to Valencia, and thence on the bus to Gandia just as the sun went down. I got a taxi out to the beach and, after waiting for him for about half an hour in the bar as agreed,

Enrique eventually turned up. I wasn't too concerned about his initial absence, anyway. I had asked in the bar if anyone knew him – they all seemed to – and if he had been in, and they assured me that he was somewhere close by and would be back soon.

I was impressed by him again. This time it was the wide circle of friends he had, the way that they spoke about him. By the time he arrived I was deep in conversation with one of them about the problems of Northern Ireland, which nevertheless seemed a million miles away.

'Mike, *macho*,' he greeted me with the customary slap on the back and then a handshake. 'Nice to see you. No problem getting here?'

'No, none.' I didn't think it worth recounting my adventures on the road. 'How are you? Where's Maica?'

A shadow crossed his face.

'She cannot be with me tonight,' he said sadly in his bass rumble. 'She has some family obligations for the weekend.'

'Oh, that's a shame,' I replied. I had been looking forward to seeing her – but my disappointment was clearly of a lower order than Enrique's.

In Maica's absence Enrique's behaviour could have gone either of two ways. He could have resorted to the boisterous, boyish humour that I saw him indulge in with José Carlos on our previous visit in March when Maica had had to go home, or he could have been the disappointed lover, sulking and downcast.

Unfortunately he chose the latter option. We returned to the flat early and he excused himself, saying that he wanted to go to bed, so I went into the spare room and did likewise.

The next day reinforced the idea that had already taken root in my mind: it's better not to revisit places where you have had a spontaneously good time. It's not possible to recreate the experience, and it's never as good the second time around. In true Romantic tradition, and underlining Enrique's role as the lovelorn hero, the weather mirrored his mood. We got up the next morning to be greeted by a steady, drizzling rain.

I was particularly indignant at this. Mid June in the Mediterranean and it was raining. This should not be allowed.

The contrast with my previous visit continued through the day as we wandered rather aimlessly from the flat to a number of beachfront bars drinking coffees and beers, exchanging pleasantries with his friends and then sitting on patios gazing at the rain dribbling off the brightly coloured awnings. Eventually, towards evening, the curtain of rain cleared away and the sun started to shine just as it was dipping down behind the hills a couple of miles back from the shoreline.

Enrique told me that there was a group of his Gandia friends who were planning to go for a meal up in the hills where the sun was now setting and he had said that we would be joining them – if that was all right with me. I replied that it certainly was. An evening with a group of people was bound to be more jolly than one spent entirely with him in his present mood.

We went back to the flat to get ready and as we tiptoed in I saw something fall from his trouser pocket. I bent down to pick it up. It was a little leather case containing his identity card – the sort that all Spaniards were supposed to carry with them at all times. I glanced at his photo – it was recognisably him – before I handed it back, but then I also caught a glimpse of his date of birth. It said *12 octubre 1955*.

I was thunderstruck. He was only eighteen years old. The well-regarded, strong and romantic lover, whose noble heart (and stomach) was sick with love for a beautiful girl, was younger than me.

It was impossible for me to look up to anyone who

had spent less time in the world than I had. The qualities I admired in him could only be forged with the passage of time and experience that my young and inchoate spirit had yet to be subjected to. Surely Enrique's youthfulness – he was still more of a teenager than me – disqualified him from those feelings I had attributed to him. And yet he seemed to have had them.

It was all happening too quickly. I wasn't ready for the suddenness of the approach of adulthood overtaking eighteen-year-olds, and clearly now hovering in my background threatening to overtake me at any time too.

He took the card from me.

'Thanks, *macho*,' he said, putting it back in his pocket. 'I would be in trouble without that.'

I was very quiet for the next couple of hours but then we met up with his group of friends, who were all strangers to me, and I began again to entertain a new audience with outlandish tales and deliberately jumbled language. This was made easier as they were mainly speaking the Valencian dialect, an offshoot of Catalan, which I could just about understand but not speak.

There were no girls so the tone was different but, as we sat in the restaurant up in the cool, rounded hills, I enjoyed their attempts to teach me all the worst words for male and female body parts and, talking Valencian gibberish, I entertained them until the rabbits that we had ordered arrived.

I was very hungry, and ate the poor little creatures with relish. The only Valencian words that stuck with me were *conil* (rabbit) and (I'm ashamed to say) *els collons* – most easily translated as 'bollocks' – a variation, I suppose, on the better-known *cojones*.

As the meal progressed I limited myself almost totally to repeating those two words as if they were a mantra against the grown-up, tightly bounded world that Enrique now represented for me.

After that the memories grew much vaguer as the wine kept coming. I did remember having a conversation with my neighbour at the table who was a young doctor, back in his native region after completing his studies in Madrid. I dropped the 'rabbit's bollocks' element from the conversation at that point, as it crossed my mind to ask him about the perils to which one's kidneys appeared to be subjected in Spain.

However, he was soon telling me about the daily contact that he had with my compatriots during the summer months. British tourists, as eager as me to return home with a tan, lay out in the sun for hours on end and then came to his surgery with something approaching third-degree burns. Apparently he had prescribed a cream a month or so ago to soothe their blistered bodies but an even greater horror awaited them (and him) when it was found that the cream was particularly attractive to mosquitoes. His surgery was then overrun with wailing tourists with red, flaking skin all covered in hundreds of sore, itching bites that threatened to turn septic.

He thought this was very funny and I, perhaps because he had politely laughed at my outlandish behaviour, felt obliged to laugh with him – although the scene struck me as anything but funny. I could almost hear a sigh from Milan in my ear and a comment about 'barbarity'.

Eventually we all got into a couple of cars and drove to a small village where there was a fiesta in progress. I don't know what I said or did, apart from hugging the mayor in front of everyone (I could remember his patriotic red and yellow sash), trying unsuccessfully to get on a donkey and then throwing up in a dried-out riverbed.

Enrique and I ended up in a car being driven back to Gandia very slowly by one of his friends, who appeared to be using the white line in the middle of the road as a guide.

This friend then stopped the car suddenly, opened the door and threw up with a violent heave. I became suddenly and horribly lucid at that point and shuddered, hoping that we would get back in one piece to the apartment as he sat back in the driver's seat, put the car into first gear and let out the clutch once more.

We did somehow get back without further mishap and I fell into a troubled sleep, with the spare room spinning around me.

So my second trip to Gandia was an altogether cruder, rougher experience than the first one. The next morning, a Sunday, with a raging hangover, I decided to cut it short by going back to Madrid. I couldn't face a day spent at the side of the road with my thumb stuck out so, after a brief thank you to Enrique, I went back to Valencia and bought a ticket for the slow train that was leaving that afternoon.

As I sat looking out of the carriage window at the lush Valencian landscape passing slowly by I reflected on how so many things are less exciting when experienced for the second time. Enrique was no longer the romantic embodiment of manly virtue that I had held him to be before. Gandia and its shimmering seashore had lost some of its magic … and nights out with groups of strangers, trying to turn them into instant friends by acting the fool, did not always work, and certainly did not make you feel better about yourself the next day.

XXXI

Friendships and acquaintances, the structures and the people that had sustained me for the previous six months, started to fall apart, and melted away under the burning Madrid sun.

I was entering the last few weeks at the Instituto. Jaime Sancho had already announced before I went to Gandia that he was going to stay at his parents' house on the Mediterranean for a month, so I had seen the last of him. It gave me a much later start in the mornings but I felt sad at the loss of my first, and it must be said, most diligent pupil. He had always turned up despite my obvious lack of preparation, which at times meant I was scrabbling around for something to converse about.

The three nurses had changed their travel plans radically. London and its park benches were no longer their destination. Juana had persuaded them to take a trip to San Francisco towards the end of August. Maria had not been altogether keen on this option when it was first mooted. She seemed to think that it was betraying me in some way if they changed their plans, although I assured them that I thought it was a good idea.

'Will they be able to understand us there?' she asked me.

'Oh, yes,' I assured her. 'They'll understand you just the same as they would understand you in London.' This seemed a rather mean-spirited comment to make in the light of their failure to really grasp any of the fundamentals of the English language, so I immediately continued,

'It's a great place. You'll have a fantastic time.'

'Have you been there, then?' she asked, looking me as straight in the eye as she could manage.

'Err, no, but I know a lot of people who have and they all had a good time.' I found her stare so unnerving that I simply could not lie.

One pair of acquaintances who were still in my life, however, was Pablo and Ernesto, the *Guatemaltecos*. Try as I might, I felt neither comfortable nor safe when they were in the flat. Admittedly, this was fairly infrequent. They spent a lot of time with their other 'friends', most notably in Pablo's case his friend 'Pussy Cat', so I rarely saw them. The one room they never now used, anyway, was the kitchen. Their entire repertoire of meals apparently had been exhausted by frying a couple of eggs and eating a bar of chocolate.

Santiago seemed to be warming to them slightly more. There was one particularly unnerving conversation I heard them having one evening when they compared atrocities perpetrated by the various military regimes that they had lived under in their native countries.

Santiago seemed to start it off by saying,

'In Ecuador we do not always work as hard as we should. The government does not do enough to make sure that we work. And on the coast, at least, it is so hot that everyone just goes to sleep all day.'

Pablo replied,

'Well, *Guate* (his abbreviation for his homeland) is the land of eternal springtime. The climate is wonderful for working but we don't always work, as we never have very good governments. They have done some horrible things to people. They arrest people and take them to the police station for nothing.'

Not to be outdone, Santiago responded,

'Well, in Ecuador the government and police have

sometimes tortured people.'

'*Puta*. That happens all the time in *Guate*,' scoffed Pablo. 'We have special jails where they take you.'

'Have they ever used electric currents on people?' asked Santiago, clearly about to make a boast concerning Ecuadorian proficiency in this area.

'*Puta*, yes.' Pablo dismissed such rudimentary measures with a wave of his hand. 'One of my friends was taken there and they took down his trousers, made him put his balls on the table and smashed one of them with a hammer.'

'Well, in Ecuador—' began Santiago, but I heard no more as I beat a hasty retreat back to my bedroom, feeling totally unnerved and with a curious, nagging pain in my lower abdomen. I had presumably come out in sympathy with Pablo's friend.

Santiago's scorn for the Spanish police was based, I felt, on an unequal comparison with the law enforcers in his own country. Although wary of them after my May Day encounter I had never heard of the Spanish police being directly accused of torture.

My discomfort with my flatmates, coupled with a wish to stay for a while longer in Spain with very little money, meant that I decided to take Madeleine and Manolo up on their offer, which they had recently made, to occupy their flat for free while they were down in Huelva.

I told Santiago of my decision to move out and he accepted it with rather more equanimity than I could have wished for. Rarely one to show emotion, he said he was sad that I was going, which I liked, but in fact told me within two days that he had found an Argentinian student named Hector to take my place. This would be a great opportunity, then, I imagined, for them all to sit around swapping stories of stomach-churning goriness about the violent excesses of government law enforcement methods.

Madeleine and Manolo were leaving the following week. I compared dates with them and Santiago and it was agreed that I would move direct from Calle de Canillas to their flat, which was not far away. Hector could then move straight into my room. As a result of this seamless transfer of tenants from flat to flat Santiago was not out of pocket and, after I had asked him twice, he handed me back my deposit – in all probability the cash that Hector had just given him. This meant that I now had a little more money to sustain me for a couple of weeks. I had already bought a ticket home for the end of July, but with three weeks still to go the extra cash was welcome.

So Madeleine and Manolo slipped out of my life. I had a farewell drink with them and they handed me one of the sets of keys to their apartment.

I had farewell drinks with Chris and Sabin as well. They were going back to Yorkshire for a couple of weeks and then going to try their luck in London. Sabin, ever patient and cheerful, was nevertheless fed up (or browned off, to be more accurate) with being a househusband and needed to find a job. Being an Anglophile, he wanted to go to Britain. They had enjoyed Madrid but it was, he told me over a few glasses of Ribeiro, only a phase in their lives and it was time to hit the road.

Hilary and Nigel saw Madrid as a more permanent home, apparently. Their apartment overlooking the sierra was where they wanted to stay. It was, Hilary told me over yet another farewell drink, all the more attractive now that Waldo and Martha were on their way home.

The scheme to persuade the American embassy to take responsibility for these two most needy of their compatriots had obviously worked. After a couple of taxi trips to the consular division, accompanied by Nigel, passports had been issued, relatives in the US had been tracked down and arrangements had been made to fly them home. They had even, as Hilary had wished, bequeathed to her their much-mistreated car with the ground-down gears.

I again expressed reservations about the wisdom of driving without a licence, but she assured me that they were both taking lessons over the summer. In fact it was clear that being the first to obtain a full driving licence had become an extremely competitive matter between the two of them.

That only really left Elena to say goodbye to. She invited me round to lunch at her flat, the one she shared with Judy, who taught alongside Peter Garrett on the floor above. Judy was not there – I only ever saw her about four or five times – but Elena invited Federico, her boyfriend.

Federico was much older than I had expected – probably about the same age as Peter Garrett – and clearly a very successful man. Exactly how he made his livelihood was never explained to me, but when I met him at Elena's apartment he was dressed in an expensive suit with a blindingly white shirt and carefully knotted red silk tie. He had crinkly grey hair, which was lightly smoothed down against his head, and an altogether patrician air about him.

We ate some very tasty, and very expensive, cooked meats that Elena had often told me about from one of Madrid's best delicatessens, some delicious wine that even I could tell was first-class and some little lamb chops and vegetables that Elena produced in a trice from the small kitchen that I could see through an open door. I wished Milan could have been there, in this beautifully furnished flat, eating well-prepared delicately flavoured food and sipping vintage wine. Barbaric it was not.

Federico asked me what I was doing now that the Instituto was closing for the summer.

'I'll have to go home, I suppose,' I said. 'I don't really want to, though.'

'*Hombre*, don't go, then,' was his advice.

'Well, I've booked a ticket for the end of July, but until then I'm not doing anything.'

'See a bit more of Spain,' said Federico. 'Have you been up to the north-west?'

'No,' I said. 'I hadn't really thought of that.'

'Right… Well, we must put together a little itinerary for you. It's a good time of year to go up there,' he told me.

Elena agreed with him and we decided that I should go out to Salamanca to the west of Madrid to start with. It was a very interesting city with two cathedrals, an ancient university and probably the finest *plaza mayor* in Spain. From there I could make my way up to Santiago de Compostela, a centre of pilgrimage and of great historic significance that was tucked into the far north-western corner of the country. They both recommended travelling by bus if possible, as a quicker and cheaper option than the train.

I gave Elena a big hug and Federico my manliest handshake at the end of the meal, said thank you and farewell … and, having decided to get the bus the following day, went back to Madeleine and Manolo's empty flat.

XXXII

As I got up the next day I realised that I was quite alone. The Instituto had closed for the summer, and everyone I had known there was now gone from my life. Yes, I had exchanged addresses and phone numbers, but more as a matter of course than in the expectation of seeing people again. They, these characters in my life, had all passed in front of me, entering from one side and now exiting on the other, probably never to be seen again, as my time – my triumphant time – in Spain gradually wound down. I do not even remember saying goodbye to Tim or Anne. They all just dissolved into the background as I strode off to the bus station with my rucksack on my back.

Although going by bus to Salamanca was quicker, I am sure, than the slow train, it still seemed to take an age. Eventually, though, I was there and I found a room in a cheap *hostal*. It was really only a partitioned-off space in a long corridor full of other such spaces. The partitioning did not quite reach up to the ceiling or down to the floor, so there was no feeling of privacy.

After dinner in a small restaurant in a side street I went back and lay on the bed, feeling quite as lonely as I had done when I had arrived at the Rincón in January, despite the obvious proximity of other guests. For the first time I started to feel glad that I had booked a ticket home for the end of the month. This exotic, other life was not perhaps as exciting as I had thought it would be.

Salamanca itself was a slightly larger version of those other cities – Toledo, Ávila, Segovia – that I had explored on day trips from Madrid months before. It had an achingly beautiful *plaza mayor* with cool stone colonnades and extravagant wrought-iron balconies through which, I am sure, dark-eyed young girls with mantillas perched on their heads used to look out provocatively from behind delicate fans. There were two cathedrals, which were both stunning, and a clutch of ancient buildings that belonged to the venerable old university along with narrow, inviting streets to amble through.

So the next day I walked slowly around, stopped for beers and a *bocadillo* and sat on various benches and watched the *paseo*, the evening stroll that families undertook in most southern European countries. Family groups, from grandmothers to the youngest child, strolled past, slowly greeting each other. This ritual, from which I was clearly excluded, seemed to emphasise my loneliness, and I decided that I had better move on.

The north-west was my ultimate goal, but the next day I only got part of the way there. I was dependent now on provincial trains and buses that did not radiate out from Madrid. They were less frequent and invariably even slower than the ones that I had been using. North from Salamanca there was only a single-track railway, along which a few trains a day made their way to a small walled city called Zamora. This was in the right direction but still some way from the north-western region of Galicia, where I was headed.

I caught a train to Zamora the following morning. It was a little railcar unit, which swayed from side to side as it chugged along through plantations of scrubby oak trees. These bore the acorns that herds of grey pigs would eat later that year before they themselves were transformed into the fabulous *jamón serrano* – a great delicacy, which I could never afford.

My Reign in Spain

In Zamora, which was smaller than Salamanca and with a feeling of real remoteness, I booked into a *casa de huéspedes*, a Spanish variation on bed and breakfast. It was someone's home, and they rented out a couple of bedrooms for visitors such as me. My hosts were a charming young couple with a baby daughter, and they gave me clear guidance on what to see and where to go. The main thing to do, anyway, was obvious. Zamora was surrounded by ancient walls, which were still remarkably well-preserved, and it was possible to walk around them and gaze down at the rooftops beneath and the strange Byzantine dome of the cathedral.

It was very hot as I made my circumnavigation, and I came down from the walls thirsty and tired. For some reason the notion that a cup of tea refreshes best in the heat – this notion was gleaned from my grandmother, I think – occurred to me.

I had not been a great tea drinker in Spain. It was not a very common drink apart from herbal teas designed to aid the digestion, which, unsurprisingly, had been much favoured by Milan. But I now decided that that was what I needed.

A piece of advice that Hilary had given me at some stage also inexplicably came to mind at that moment. Having asked for many cups of tea, and received many variations on the English cuppa, she had found that the worst transgression commonly made by the average Spanish bartender was to serve the tea quite correctly in a small metal teapot, but with a little jug of hot milk on the side. This, when mixed in the cup with the piping hot tea, was quite undrinkable. So she always specified,

'*Té con leche fria.*' (Tea with *cold* milk.)

Hot and dusty, I entered a small bar. It was little more than a hole in the wall, really. The bartender was busy talking rapidly and incomprehensibly to a weather-beaten old man who was sipping a glass of brandy at the bar. He broke off from his rapid-fire conversation for a second when I asked for a *Té con leche fria*, looked at me curiously, and then filled a small metal teapot with cold milk straight from the fridge and put a teabag in it. He placed it on the bar along with a cup, a saucer and a spoon and two lumps of sugar and went back to his conversation.

Unable to bring myself to point out the correct way to make tea in this tiny bar in a remote Spanish backwater, I sat down and poured the milk into the cup and drank it. There was the faintest swirl of brown in it where some tea had leached out of the bag but otherwise I had a cup of milk that was slightly chilled and with a strange heat-treated taste. It did nothing to quench my thirst.

Unabashed, I lingered a while as if to prove to myself and the barman how thirst-quenching it was. Then, after paying, I strode off towards the small maze of streets that formed the city centre. There was a larger-looking bar in the main square which, as it was now early evening, was starting to get busier. There were at least five people assembled there. I failed to notice that none of them were drinking beer and went up to the bar.

'A cold beer,' I said to the barman as he came over to me.

He looked at me in the same fashion that the previous bartender had and, with a slight shrug of his shoulders, turned around and went down to the other end of the bar. I thought at first that he was ignoring me, which heightened my feeling of being completely alone in this remote town, and then I realised that he was bending down under the bar, looking for something. I also observed at the same time that there was no beer tap on the bar, as I had seen in nearly every other bar I had ever been to. My request for a beer was clearly as unusual as my need for a cup of tea had been.

Eventually he came back from the far end of the bar with

a bottle in his hand. It looked beer-shaped and there was some sort of label on it that referred to beer. He took the cap of the top and it frothed half-heartedly, as if the effort was almost too much.

I poured the beer into a glass and sipped it slowly, expecting immediate relief from thirst. It was certainly quite cool if not cold, but the taste was foul. There was malt and gas and a fermented tang, which combined to produce a stomach-heaving awfulness that I just couldn't manage to keep down. The first gulp rose in my throat, and for a moment I thought that it was coming all the way back. Luckily it did not, but I abandoned any attempt to drink it.

'*Me cobra por favor*?' I asked. 'Will you get me the bill?'

The barman looked surprised, again, that I had apparently downed the beer so swiftly and stared at me as I left, which made me feel even more self-conscious. It seemed that Zamora was a very inhospitable place, with its bars and cafés dedicated to ensuring that I remained thirsty. It did not occur to me that, in remote inland Spain, tea (with or without milk) and beer were not the staples that locals would look to when thirsty. They had been a bad choice when coffee and wine were available.

I could not bear the thought of attempting to get a meal. I scurried back to the B & B, expecting to spend a long hungry night in my room. This solo travelling was not a lot of fun after the first day or so.

I let myself in with the key that the couple had given me when I had arrived and went into my room. I was lying on the bed and staring at the ceiling, thinking that I liked March, Cambridgeshire much more than Zamora, when there was a tap on the door. When I opened it I found the young wife there with her daughter in her arms.

'We wondered if you had eaten yet, *Señor*,' she said to me.

'Err, no. Not yet. I haven't decided what I will do this

evening,' I replied, as if I was spoilt for options.

'Would you like to eat with us? You looked very unhappy when you came in,' she said.

I was taken aback for a moment, but quickly replied, 'Yes, please.'

I was touched by their concern, and Zamora suddenly became a much kinder place. We had a delicious home-cooked meal, I drank several tumblerfuls of water and glasses of wine and, after offering profuse thanks, went to bed and slept soundly.

The next day, after a substantial breakfast by Spanish standards, they waved me off to the station, where I knew that a train for Galicia left at nine o'clock. It had come up through the night from Seville and was bound for A Coruña. This was not exactly where I wanted to be but, with a change at Orense I could pick up a train for Vigo, a city with a picturesque location on the Atlantic, where I had decided to go.

I spent another day gazing out of the train window as the colours of the landscape gradually became greener. I had time in Orense for lunch before going back to the station to catch the train to Vigo. It set off in the late afternoon, trundling along at the same speed as all the other trains that I ever caught. It had come up from Madrid, I think, and was very busy. I got a seat next to a fat Spanish matron and didn't move, for fear of losing it if I stood up.

As we progressed slowly along I overheard a conversation between two men, one who seemed to know the area and the other who did not.

'That's the Minho River,' said the local. 'It's the frontier. Over the other side – that's Portugal.'

I looked through and around a couple of people standing by the window and caught sight of the river below us. On the other side was Portugal, where the revolution had recently happened. I had thought about going there but it seemed too dangerous to me. I imagined gangs of revolutionaries roaming the streets looking for hapless foreigners to string up as an example to all who tried to interfere with the people's struggle. There was bound to be serious social dislocation – something I wasn't ready to face.

(In fact Hector, my Argentinian replacement at no. 68 Calle de Canillas, told me after I got back to Madrid that he had entered Spain from Portugal and had spent several delightful days in Lisbon where there was an almost holiday-like feeling in the air.)

As the train veered away from the river, and the revolutionary turmoil that I was sure lay on the other side, I had a new worry. It was getting very late. The train showed no signs of speeding up and I could see myself arriving in Vigo in the middle of the night with nowhere to stay. I looked at my watch every quarter of an hour and told myself that it couldn't be much further now. After a couple of nervous time checks I looked out through the gathering dusk and saw the Atlantic for the first time. I knew that Vigo was on the coast – it was one of the reasons why I had chosen to go there – and it was only about thirty miles up from the Portuguese border, so even on this train there could not be far to go.

Eventually, at around ten o'clock, we pulled into the station, a lofty, glass-roofed terminus. I jumped down off the train and, after briefly orientating myself, set off towards what was clearly the city centre.

Anxious to find somewhere as quickly as possible I booked into a hotel on one of the main *avenidas* of the city. It boasted two stars and I was informed that I could have half board for only a few more pesetas than bed and breakfast would cost me. The thought of not having to traipse the streets looking for somewhere to eat every evening was quite attractive, and so I readily agreed and booked for four nights.

It was a small, neat hotel, tall but not wide, very clean and bright, with winding stairs and a smell of fresh paint. The only drawback was that they had given me a room looking into the enclosed, central well of the building. Even in these blustery Atlantic climes it was incredibly hot, with no breath of air circulating. As I flung off the covers and lay on the bed that night I remembered Elena's advice when I had been flat-hunting about always having a room that looks to the outside.

My days in Vigo were better than those at the beginning of the trip. The weather was sunny, but the sun was more Cornwall than Cordoba, and it was a relief not to have to go out every evening to search for my supper on my own. I still felt a little self-conscious as I sat in the dining room every evening being served tasty soups and garlicky fish stews, but I nevertheless lingered there a little longer than I needed to rather than go up the winding staircase to my room on my own.

I went to a beach at the end of a well-served bus route and sat on the sand, gazing out to sea. I felt happier about being alone than I had since the Instituto had shut its doors for the summer. I realised that in fact no one was staring at me, but all were busy with their own sunbathing and frolicking in the water. My mind went back to that Sunday morning in January on the park bench opposite the Palacio de Oriente and the time I spent on the hillside overlooking the Escorial palace when my resolve to stay and enjoy my future had reasserted itself after doubt and disillusion had started to creep in. My time in Spain, my short lived and unremarkable reign, gave me nevertheless a sense of my own resourcefulness and determination. I could live, and be, on my own buoyed by the expectation of what my future would hold.

On the final day of my trip, I got the train to the great pilgrimage centre of Santiago de Compostela. This was at the damp, mossy heart of Galicia, the site where St James the Apostle's body was apparently brought and where it was buried at a place designated by a miraculous star. (Legend had it that Compostela was derived from the Latin *Campus Stellae* – the field of the star). I remembered reading that at one time it had been third only to Jerusalem and Rome as a place to visit for those who sought to accrue merit in God's sight and spend less time waiting in Purgatory.

Although the sun shone when I was there I knew that it rained a lot in Galicia. This was evident from the stones of the massive cathedral that lay at the heart of the city. Its magnificently decorated facade was stained green in places. It looked to me as if it was in the very initial stages of being reclaimed by the moist, fertile heart of greenness that lay all around beyond the city's boundaries – the beginnings of a temperate equivalent to those Maya temples hidden in the creeping, humid jungles of Central America.

It was strange that here, at the focal point of Spain's devotion to Christianity, there was an unmistakable whiff of the wood sprite and the damp, pagan rituals that celebrated an unstoppably fecund natural world. The whole building exuded an air of gentle, improvised decay and, although it was at the other end of Spain, the place that it most resembled for me was Cadiz, marooned in the Atlantic at the end of its peninsula, hundreds of miles to the south.

There was a hint of nationalism here as well. Galicia had its own language and culture, similar to Portuguese, and although it was not a candidate for full nationhood, there were signs of an underground movement coming to the surface. I saw, daubed on a wall near the city centre: *Galego nas escolas* (Galician in schools).

Franco, although from nearby A Coruña, would tolerate no such thing. I had been so caught up in the Spain of flamenco and matadors and arid, baking plains that I had been unaware of this misty, Celtic corner of the country and its long and separate history. Here was a culture and a way of life that was recognisably Spanish but which contained a lurking sense of druidic otherness as well.

As it was July there was a formidable contingent of foreign tourists milling around the Praza do Obradoiro, the main square. I joined a troupe of them as they entered the cathedral and tried to eavesdrop on the explanations that their guide was giving them. Unfortunately, rather than the Americans that I had taken them for, I seemed to be trailing a group of Scandinavians of some sort and the sing-song, guttural mix of language was far beyond my ability to follow.

So I just walked down the nave, taking in the elaborate decoration and the gaudiness of the statuary. I was waiting for a moment of revelation, here in one of the most ancient of Christianity's sites, but there was no epiphany in this powerhouse of sanctity and devotion. It was for me, as for almost everyone else, a great and curious sight, but I was still a tourist and not a pilgrim.

Even the *botafumeiro*, a giant censor suspended on a chain from the vault of the cathedral and filled with incense, failed to impress. It was situated at the heart of the building and designed to be swung from side to side on its massive chain at special times as the faithful congregated to express their devotion. For me, again, it was curious and splendid but not a shortcut to communing with the Almighty.

I walked around, somehow disappointed with what I saw. My expectations had been unrealistic or over-romanticised, but I was only lightly let down. I came out into the sunlight and immediately felt hungry. My bodily needs had swiftly overcome the spiritual.

On the train back to Vigo we stopped at a small station that I had not noticed on the outward journey. I stared at the sign and wondered why it looked familiar. Then it dawned on me. It was the name of the village that Brian had given me when he left the flat. It was the location of the hotel where he was working.

Knowing that I should probably have visited, if not that day then the next, I shrank back in my seat, as if fearing that he might be on the platform. But I reasoned that a visit was impossible, as I would be returning to Madrid the next day. But I knew that my reasoning was a sham. I could easily have stayed an extra day.

I had found out that the cheapest ticket back to Madrid was, predictably, on the slow night train that left at about ten o'clock in the evening. I went down to the station the following morning and enquired whether it was necessary to book a seat. I was well aware of how crowded the train I had caught four days previously had been, and standing for twelve or more hours overnight as we wended our way slowly through the night across north-western Spain was something I wanted to avoid at all costs.

'Should I reserve a seat?' I asked the ticket clerk as I bought my ticket.

He snorted derisively.

'It's normally empty. You'll probably be the only one on it.'

So no seat reservation was required, and I had the prospect of my own private train – or at least coach – back to Madrid.

I checked out of the hotel later in the morning and mooched around town with my rucksack on my back for the rest of the day. I sat in a couple of bars, lingering over a beer, and went into a park for about two hours and sat on every bench, smiling as I looked at the birds and thought of Martin and Jane.

The part of my life that they represented was now over. I didn't think I wanted to teach English as a foreign language again, so not only had I finished school, I mused, I had undertaken and completed a career as well – and I was still only just nineteen and a half.

After a *plato combinado* in a bar near the railway station I eventually went to catch the train. The booking clerk was right. The station was deserted, as far as I could see.

The coaches for the night train to Madrid rolled in and I got on. There were a couple of railway staff talking on the platform, which gave it a semblance of normality. Without them it would have been like boarding a ghost train in a horror movie with no people and just an eerie sense of foreboding.

I chose a compartment near the middle of the train, put my rucksack down beside me and settled in. If it was going to be as empty as predicted I could make this entire compartment my home for the next twelve to fifteen hours.

We did not leave for another hour or so, and two or three people did pass by in the corridor outside. But they were, I supposed, going through to their own individual compartments or, given the length of the train, coaches.

Eventually we jolted into motion. An inspector came and looked at my ticket and, reassured that there was at least some trustworthy human presence on the train, I curled up and fell fast asleep.

XXXIII

As the end of July approached I realised I would be leaving Spain as I had arrived - on my own. There would be no farewell party with streamers and tears. My departure would be as unremarked as my arrival.

In the early days, in my room at the Rincón, I had sometimes thought that I might meet the girl of my dreams – a girl who didn't exist. I would spend six romantic, magical months with her, perhaps leaving her on the platform at Chamartín, or bringing her back with me to be a part of my life forever. I knew now though that I was too self-conscious and busy with the preoccupations that came with such self-awareness to become involved with anyone.

I was also, I had learnt, not at all ready for all the adult confidence and apparent bravado that came with a relationship. I was not really a *macho* and probably never would be but, not wanting to bother with it now, I mentally placed it all in a position on the distant horizon far enough away to not require attention.

Besides, I thought, as I strolled the streets of Madrid for the last few days, popped in for one more showing of *Ben-Hur*, and visited the Cat Restaurant alone, I had an exciting future in Oxford to think about. My life was progressing along the high ground, moving from one glorious vista to another, so I did not need the complications of intimacy interrupting the view.

My meanderings through torpid afternoons, now

scorching hot in the sticky summer sun, brought to mind all the people I had met, some of whom I had walked those same streets with, but who had now dispersed, never to reassemble in front of me in exactly the same way again. Mostly, however, my thoughts were directed forward – real anticipation at seeing my parents again and at acting the well-travelled returnee in March, and the start of another chapter in the city of dreaming spires. I was already investing my time there with a magical quality that, at some level inside me, I knew it would be hard for it to deliver.

One thing I settled down to do in earnest was to read the novels, plays and poetry on the Oxford reading list that had been sent on to me by my parents. There was one particular novel, *La Ciudad y los Perros*, by a modern Peruvian novelist, Mario Vargas Llosa, that caused me great difficulty. The language was colloquial and South American, and it had me reaching for the dictionary every two or three sentences. I began to realise that there was a lot of hard work ahead. Excelling in the memory tests that were A levels did not necessarily mean that I was well-equipped for the analytical rigours of an Oxford degree course.

One morning just before I was due to leave a young man greeted me as I was on my way to the supermarket.

'*Lindo día*,' he said, referring to the balminess of the day, still fresh before the afternoon heat took hold.

I looked at him for a second and then realised that it was Hector, my Argentinian replacement at no. 68 Calle de Canillas. I'd met him on the day that I had moved out a couple of weeks before. I was impressed by his memory and the fact that I must have made some sort of impact on him.

'Yes,' I replied, hesitantly. 'How is everyone at the flat?'

'There's only Santiago and me now,' he said. 'The *Guatemaltecos* disappeared. Just took their things and went last week. Come round tonight and see us. Santiago would like that.'

I took him up on his suggestion and went round that evening. The one-armed caretaker was there, still sweeping with his broom, although I could see no speck of dust anywhere in the entrance hall.

'*Muy buenas, Señor,*' he greeted me as ever, half-raising his broom in salutation.

'*Muy buenas, Señor,*' I answered back, feeling I should say something else but not knowing what.

The flat looked just the same. Santiago shook my hand when I went in and he made Hector and me a cup of coffee.

We sat round the table in the living room. I noticed that he had replaced the two chairs that Anton had broken. They did not exactly match the others, but he had placed one at each end of the table to retain the symmetry.

'It's a pity you cannot come back,' said Santiago.

'I thought you were getting on well with the *Guatemaltecos,*' I said, half-hoping to provoke them.

I succeeded. Hector gave a snort.

'They got on well with us but we did not get on with them.'

'I did not like their habits,' admitted Santiago. 'They always left everywhere in a terrible mess and they drank all the milk.'

He made them sound like a pair of mischievous cats – quite apt, I thought, bearing in mind Pablo's enthusiasm for his friend 'Pussy Cat'.

'Anyway, they've gone now, so we will have to find someone else,' he concluded.

We talked about Anton and Brian and Robin, and then Santiago showed me a postcard from Doctor Gutierrez. He wrote that he had settled the problem with his wife in the Dominican Republic (he didn't specify the nature of the problem or the manner of its resolution), and that he was going to try to get into the US. I wasn't sure how much they needed disillusioned heart surgeons, but Santiago was sure that a man of his standing would have no problem.

'In America doctors can earn a lot of money,' he suggested.

'Yes,' I thought, 'but they do need to get out of bed in the morning to do it.'

Perhaps the prospect of an endless stream of wealthy patients with weak hearts would infuse Gutierrez with enough energy to stay the course, professionally speaking, and make a name for himself in Texas or California or Florida. I somehow doubted it, though.

'When are you leaving?' asked Hector.

'On Friday,' I replied, 'at midday.'

'We'll come and see you off, then,' he said.

Santiago nodded in agreement.

'Yes, we will make sure you get on the right train.'

I was sure I would have no problem identifying my train, but I was touched nevertheless.

'Thank you,' I said. 'I would like that,' which was true.

We finished the evening with beers for Hector and me and another coffee for Santiago. I told them about my ramble around north-western Spain and Hector told me how I should have visited Portugal when I had the chance. The terrors I had foreseen awaiting the solitary traveller there were, of course, all imaginary.

I walked back to Madeleine and Manolo's flat. I smiled as I thought about our quiet conversation and their gentle musings. It had been the nearest I would get to a leaving party.

For the next couple of days I packed my bags intermittently – the two battered suitcases and the rucksack that I had lugged through France and Spain six months before. Everything fitted in: my original wardrobe, a few new items of clothing that I had bought and a selection of little presents for people that I had accumulated on my day trips and longer journeys.

On the final morning I looked around the sparsely furnished flat to make sure that I hadn't missed anything. The table and chairs, the bed, the cupboards and sets of drawers were all flimsy, unsubstantial items of furniture appropriate to the transitory lifestyle of the flat's tenants, who would continue to come and go in the future. There were no hidden recesses or heavy wooden supports for things to roll under and be wedged behind. A quick glance told me that I had everything I needed.

I put my set of keys on the table, as I had agreed with Madeleine and Manolo, and went out on to the landing pulling the door firmly shut behind me.

Downstairs, after a couple of minutes' wait, a taxi drew up with Santiago and Hector in it. We loaded my luggage in the back and headed off to Chamartín station. As we got under way I realised that this was only my second ever trip in a Madrid taxi. My first one had been with Michael Garrett all those months before. I remembered my naive expectation that I would be going to the Garrett residence to stay and my confusion when Michael Garrett apparently had to read out his own address, and my realisation that in the adult world people didn't take care of you in quite the same way. You were expected to take care of yourself.

So my first and last impressions of the Madrid cityscape, the bookends of my experience, were seen through the grubby rear windows of one of its taxis.

We did not say much on the way to the station and very little more as we went down the platform at Chamartín. I was pleased that they were with me but stuck for conversation. I was already leaving Madrid before even boarding the train.

About halfway along the platform we found the coach and then the compartment with the seat that I had booked. There was no one else in it yet.

'Only one other person booked in here,' said Hector,

looking at the little stubs of paper tucked into metal holders above the seats. 'You should have plenty of room.'

'If I were travelling I would just go to sleep, I think,' said Santiago. 'It makes the journey go quicker.'

'Well, I've got plenty to read,' I said, taking *La Ciudad y los Perros* out of the top of my rucksack.

'It's a difficult book to understand,' said Hector, 'but he's a great writer.'

Our conversation, the most animated until that point, was interrupted by a small family group entering the compartment. There was a thin, willowy young man of about my age and what were clearly his middle-aged parents. His mother was fussing over him, brushing his collar and jacket with her hand, and his father was struggling with several suitcases.

'Make sure you call us as soon as you get there,' the mother instructed her son, 'and don't forget to take a tablet if you have any stomach problems.'

'Yes, Mama,' he dutifully nodded.

'Here's a bit more for you, as well,' said the father, passing the boy a one thousand peseta note as discreetly as the cramped compartment would allow.

We bumped against each other. Santiago winced and gave a small yelp as the mother trod on his foot, her high heel accidentally but firmly placed on his instep.

'Oh, pardon me,' she said with a nervous giggle. 'Did I tread on you?'

Santiago just smiled and then said,

'We'd better get off if we don't want to go with you.' He held out his hand and I shook it. Hector did the same.

'*Buen viaje*,' he said. 'Have a good journey.'

They, my two friends and the anxious parents, all got off.

'Are you going to England?' I asked the willowy boy.

'Yes,' he said. 'I'm going to stay with a family near Oxford for three months. They've got me a job in a hotel. I'm looking forward to it.'

He gave a nervous laugh, indicating a degree of excitement tempered by apprehension that I could identify with only too well. At least he was going to stay with a family and not have to live in a dingy bedsit. I decided to give him a confidence-boosting pep talk on the journey about what a good time he would have. After all, I was a seasoned traveller and an old hand at this sort of thing now and, whatever the outcome, that's what you had to believe at the beginning of life's adventures.

I looked out of the window. Santiago and Hector were talking to the anxious parents on the platform. Then they both turned and waved to me and, just for a moment as I stared through and beyond them, I caught a glimpse of everyone who had been a part of my life in Spain.

Tim and Milan were there to say goodbye, Milan still trying to decide whether to smile or scowl, along with Hilary and Chris and Sabin and Madeleine with her arm looped around Manolo's neck and Peter Garrett and his sister-in-law, the strangely named Mariuca and Elena beaming at me with the three nurses and the ever-stern Dolores and her disappointed artist lover. José Carlos was laughing as usual, his eyes twinkling behind the thick black-rimmed glasses, and Enrique was looking every inch the *macho*, a faint, indulgent smile playing at the corners of his mouth.

Doctor Gutierrez was there with Anton and Brian and Robin, and there were other, vaguer outlines, mere shapes of people, from the Instituto and the Tankstelle and *hostales* and bars and restaurants from Madrid to Cordoba to Gandia to the green heart of Galicia.

They hovered there for a second, this strange group of people who had formed the backbone to my life for the past six months, and then a whistle blew and they vanished from in front of me and flew deep into the recesses of some as yet unexplored part of my brain.

The anxious mother was making strange signs to her son from the platform. As I concentrated I realised that she was blowing kisses. For some unaccountable reason I blew a kiss back to her and she laughed, and Santiago and Hector waved again as the train gave a sudden lurch and pulled out of the station and my short reign in Spain came to an end.

My Reign in Spain

Michael Giddings

My Reign in Spain

Michael Giddings

My Reign in Spain

Michael Giddings

www.ingramcontent.com/pod-product-compliance
Lightning Source LLC
Chambersburg PA
CBHW020857110526
R18273100001B/R182731PG44587CBX00002B/3